CAREER TRANSITIONS

The Best Resources To Help You Advance

David Goodenough, MA, CMHC

Editor

A Resource Pathways Guidebook

Seattle, Washington

Published by Resource Pathways, Inc.
22525 S.E. 64th Place, Suite 253
Issaquah, WA 98027

Editor: David Goodenough, MA, CMHC

Managing Editor:
        Jacquelline Cobb Fuller, MPP

Associate Editors:
        Dana Lynch, Pamela Robenolt, MA

Researchers:
        Lillias Bever, Lesa Haakenson

Book Design and Production:
        Sandra Harner and Kelly Rush,
        Laing Communications Inc., Redmond, WA

Printing: Hignell Book Printing, Winnipeg, Manitoba, Canada

Publisher's Cataloging-in-Publication

Career transitions : the best resources to help you
        advance / David Goodenough, editor. -- 1st ed.
        p. cm.
        Includes bibliographical references and index.
        LCCN: 99-60548
        ISBN: 1-892148-08-0

    1. Career changes--Bibliography.   2. Career
development--Bibliography.   I. Goodenough,
David. II. Resource Pathways (Firm)

    Z7164.V6C37 1999   016.65014
                QBI99-409

Printed in Canada.

CONTENTS

INTRODUCTION

LET US HELP YOU!

We've designed *Career Transitions* to help you in four crucial ways:

- By describing the broad issues you need to consider as you experience various career transitions—what you need to do, how to do it, and when it needs to get done.

- By creating clear "pathways" to the most useful resources at each stage and for each aspect of the transition—a unique feature of this guide. We tell you who has worthwhile information, and where to find it.

- By providing detailed and candid full-page reviews of all the resources we cover—195 of them—so you'll know what's available for free on the Internet, and what's worth buying.

- By building "search engines" and making it easy to find and sort reviews—that's why we include multiple indices and appendices.

CAREER TRANSITIONS IN 2000 AND BEYOND

At the turn of the new millennium, the adage that there is nothing constant but change rings ever true, especially in the job market.

Professionals can expect to change careers four to six times in a lifetime, and hold up to fifteen or twenty jobs. Whatever name you give it—downsizing, rightsizing, layoffs, corporate anorexia—the probability of working for one company for most of one's professional life is dwindling.

Industries shrink or disappear. Others appear, seemingly overnight. Technology replaces some jobs and creates others. Seasoned workers decide to strike out on their own. Mothers sequence from a time at home with young children back to their careers, either full or part-time. Switching jobs, or even careers, to find a work that is personally enriching, is more common. Job sharing and self-employment are on the rise. Whatever the source, an economic shiver or midlife reevaluation, career transitions are dynamic, dramatic and unavoidable.

A Pivotal Event

A career transition, even if it's self-initiated, can be a stressful, volatile, gut-wrenching experience. For many professionals, a career is much more than a source of income. It may provide a venue for self-expression and self-actualization. Some professionals are so intertwined with their work that who they are becomes synonymous with what they do. For many, the worksite represents a positive social outlet, perhaps the source of many close relationships. In sum, a career touches upon many elements of life.

It is understandable that we often approach a transition in our career, whether it's precipitated by a layoff or our desire to become an entrepreneur, with a measure of anxiety. As with other major life decisions and events, a career transition can be eased by being informed, prepared and well-advised. This guide can help you actively manage your career by pointing the way to the best resources available to help you with each aspect of your career transition.

Taking Charge In An Environment Of Frequent Change

There are some basics you'll want to keep in mind as you use this text and the resources we recommend. Choose with your heart and implement with your head. In other words, always focus on choosing things you enjoy and that you are naturally suited to doing. It is a safe bet that you will be skilled at things you find interesting.

I see many discouraged professionals in my career consulting practice who don't understand why they are not motivated to perform at their best on the job. Often these are the ones who made a career choice based on salary. They have stifled interests and are pursuing a career path that does not resonate with their values or life priorities. You are more likely to motivated to go to work every morning if your daily work reflects your values and interests. Motivated employees are highly favored, and for good reason. Their positive energy has an uplifting effect on the whole work environment and they are more productive.

In a rapidly changing environment, those people who are life long learners will have an edge over colleagues who do not continually evolve. Once you begin a career path, make sure that you keep upgrading your technical, professional and managerial skills. Life long learners are readers; they seek out stimulating workshops or seminars; they embrace technical changes rather than fight them. Finding a mentor who has succeeded in your chosen career field can be a source of learning and inspiration. Being a life-long learner is a selling point when you are seeking a new job.

As you will see, this book is not just focused on one type of career transition issue or one type of person. The materials we've selected for review range from legal advice after a brutal firing, to job search advice for professionals interested in working for a non-profit, to reflective guides for midlife reevaluation. By consulting our guide, you have already taken the first step toward successfully managing the career transitions ahead.

In conclusion, I'd like to make an observation from my two decades as a career counselor. I am confident that most of our readers will find in this guide the resources they need to inform, advise and encourage through their career transition. However, others will get "stuck" because of some long-term personal issue like a lack of confidence, or a poor self-image, a depression due to job loss, or a bad work experience that you cannot put behind you.

Please remember that we recognize that although these books, websites and other materials are excellent resources, you may still find that you cannot pull yourself out of a career or personal crisis without help from another human being. We recognize the need many professionals in transition have for good counseling in either a career development or mental health setting. If you find yourself repeatedly or continually stalled or frustrated with your progress in your career transition, we strongly encourage you to consider consulting with a professional counselor in addition to using the resources found here.

HOW THIS BOOK IS ORGANIZED

As part of our ongoing research and analysis, we've identified books, web sites, audiotapes, CD-ROMs and other software that are widely available to professionals on the topic of career transitions.

We've organized these resources into five broad categories with related sub-topics, found in chapters II through VI:

Career Exploration & Research

- Exploring Career Options To Discover What's Right For You
- Aptitude And Interest Analysis
- Career And Job Descriptions
- Employer Research

Career Transitions

- Career-Transitions
- Moving Ahead
- Job Loss Or Termination

Using The Internet To Find The Right Job And Career

- Guides To Using The Internet
- Internet Job And Resume Databases

How To Land The Job You Want

- Overviews Of The Job Search Process
- Resumes
- Cover Letters
- Networking
- Interviewing
- Salary Negotiations

Going Solo

- General Self-Employment
- Freelance and Consulting
- Entrepreneurship

Some resources comprehensively cover more than one aspect of career transitions, and in these cases we note in the side-bar a secondary subject addressed.

Each chapter provides background information and time-saving advice. Reviews of resources covering each topic form the heart of each chapter. These full-page, fact-filled, candid reviews offer an appraisal that's rich in specifics. And each follows the same format.

We separate evaluations from descriptions, so you can focus either on what a resource contains or what we think of it—and why. Facts of publication appear in a sidebar. A phrase sums up ease of use and our overall rating, and we give each 1–4 stars. We always list the highest-rated resources first. If there are more than one resource with the same Star Rating, we list them alphabetically by title. Abbreviated "non-rated" reviews are used for resources that warrant your attention but not a full review.

Four Star Rating System	
★★★★	Highly recommended! It offers top quality at a fair price.
★★★	Well done; a good resource but not outstanding.
★★	Worth considering; check the description for strong chapters.
★	Your time and money could be better spent elsewhere.

Chapter VII gathers all resources that are either written expressly for, or which contain significant content targeted to, specific groups. We provide a short description of the resources and note the page number for its full-length review. Resources are identified for:

- Racial and ethnic minorities
- Women
- The disabled
- Academics and PhDs
- Those seeking to work in the non-profit sector
- Those returning to the workplace after an absence

At the end of the book, we've provided several useful indices which list all the resources reviewed, alphabetically by Title, Author, Publisher, Media and Subject.

MEET RESOURCE PATHWAYS

As consumers in the Information Age, we all want to take advantage of the many sources of information available to help us make important decisions or deal with major events we experience. Unfortunately, we don't always know where to find these sources of information. Often, we don't know very much about their quality, value, or relevance. In addition, we often don't know much about the issue we've encountered, and as a result don't really know where to begin our learning process.

Resource Pathways' guidebooks solve the problem of "information overload" faced by those who want to learn about a topic of critical importance in their life (like managing career transitions, financing a college education, or weathering a divorce). Those interested in doing such research typically:

- Don't know what resources are available, particularly those outside traditional print media.

- Don't know where to find most of those resources, particularly since most bookstores stock only a limited selection.

- Can't assess the quality or focus of those resources **before** spending time and money first finding, then evaluating, and perhaps buying them.

- Don't understand which resources will be particularly useful for each dimension of a multi-dimensional issue. For **each** aspect of the challenge we're trying to deal with, certain resources will be very helpful, while others may be completely worthless.

This guidebook, focused on the best resources for helping professionals facing career transitions, will help you overcome these hurdles. In this guidebook, you will find that:

- Virtually all available quality resources are reviewed, including those from "high-technology" media like the Internet or CD-ROMs.

- We make a reasoned judgment about the quality of each resource, and decide whether or not a resource should be recommended (only 25% are recommended).

- We define and explain the different steps typically encountered while choosing a career and finding a job, and classify each resource we review according to its primary focus. This helps ensure that you buy or access only the **best** resource for each step.

- Where to buy or how to access each resource is provided in each review, including ISBN numbers for print media, direct order numbers for publishers, and URL "addresses" for sites on the Internet's World Wide Web.

After you have used this guidebook to learn which sources of information are best suited to you, you can then acquire or access those resources knowing that your time and money will be well spent.

How We Develop Our Reviews & Recommendations

This guidebook includes our reviews of 195 resources that can help you successfully manage career transitions.

Our Editors and Researchers have found virtually all available sources of information focused on career transitions, including books, the Internet, software, CD-ROMs, audiotapes, etc. We've created a concise, one-page review of each resource. Each review contains information about the resource (author, publisher, edition, etc.), describes the resource's content and focus, evaluates the quality, style, comprehensiveness, and effectiveness of the resource, and summarizes its findings in one rating for overall quality and one for design (a "1–4 Star" rating system is used). We expand these ratings with written evaluations explaining the rationale behind our ratings and providing guidance on how each source can be best applied. We also provide prices and "where to buy" information for each product.

We put a great deal of time and effort into reviewing and evaluating each resource carefully. Here's what that process includes:

- **Printed Guidebooks**: For these resources, we read the book from cover to cover, identify the particular focus taken by each author, and make a judgment about how the book's contents could be best applied. Our judgment about the relative quality of each source is based upon readability, organization, depth, and style. We make every effort to ensure that the latest editions of books are reviewed, and that no out-of-print resources are included.

- **Internet Websites & Online Services**: We review all web sites and online services that have any significant amount of original material related to the subject of starting your career. Our reviews include judgments about the site's graphic and navigation design, as well as the usefulness of material provided relative to that available in other media. We revisit sites frequently to stay abreast of changes and improvements.

- **CD-ROM & Software**: We carefully review each facet of each CD, including all branches and multimedia options, and thoroughly test software applications available on disk. Our reviews include judgments about the "cost/benefit" of multimedia additions, as well as the usefulness of the content provided relevant to the same offering in other media by the same publisher. We note technical problems in loading or using programs provided.

CAREER
EXPLORATION
AND RESEARCH

CAREER EXPLORATION

How did you choose your first job out of college? By scanning the want ads. A serendipitous combination of being in a given place at a given time. Or perhaps an uncle thought "you'd be a good lawyer." Whatever the circumstances, many of us stumbled into a first job only to change jobs, if not careers, frequently in the following years.

It's only been in the last decade or so that we have begun to systematically provide career exploration for college graduates and other young people beginning their careers. When today's professionals were in school, a resume workshop was usually the extent of any career counseling. Today many college campuses have well staffed career service offices which assist students in the reflective process of thinking through the question, "What do I want to do when I grow up?"

If you plunged headfirst into a career without doing much career exploration, or if a midlife reevaluation has presented a timely opportunity to rethink your career options, there are some wonderful resources to help guide you through the process. Some of the resources reviewed in this chapter provide questions, exercises and thought-provoking essays to help raise the issues for you to consider. Many are geared toward finding not just a job, but a calling.

Career exploration for someone in mid-career looks different than for a recent college graduate. Internships, a wonderful way to get a realistic feel for a specific job or field of interest, are not common for positions above entry level. I always counsel professionals considering a career change to become intimate with the new field before they make and emotional or economic commitment to it. I encourage them to read about the area and interview people in the field. It's sort of like dating; you wouldn't want to choose a spouse without first getting to know that person.

Career Exploration

FIND YOUR CALLING, LOVE YOUR LIFE

★★★

 Recommended For:
Career Exploration

Description:

Ms. Finney and Ms. Dasch believe that everyone has a "true calling." The question is: are you listening for it and are you ready to heed it? Since nothing could be more personal than an individual's "calling," these authors offer no "road maps" to the "right path." Rather, their purpose is inspirational, to give you courage, hope, and ideas for finding your own "life's work." To do this, they have assembled 20 profiles of individuals who are engaged in that most rare activity: doing work that they love. These individuals range in a age from 28 to 86 and represent such diverse occupations as "Mystery Writer," "Airport Director," and "Television Executive." Their stories are told in a combination of styles: prose, interviews, and first-person narratives. Each profile occupies its own chapter and is used to highlight an aspect of "finding your calling." For example, profiles reflect "Following Those Twists of Fate," "Engaging Both Your Head and Your Heart," and "Turning Handicaps into Assets."

Evaluation:

This book is a joy to read! The stories are warm, engaging, and triumphant. They also possess the admirable quality of being both highly personalized and universal. You'll find yourself identifying with aspects of each profile, no matter how divergent the individual's work is from your own. If you dream of adventure, there's the "Mystery Writer's" story of "Rejecting Fear" to travel solo around the world, working odd jobs to support/supplement her writing. Or perhaps you have a hobby/activity you love, like the "Dive Store Manager," whose love of scuba diving led her to her "life's work" on the island of Bonaire. These are the people whose happiness and fulfillment shine like neon signs, announcing, "I love what I do!" As an "inspirational" read, this a wonderful choice. If you're depressed in your current job, stymied in your career, or "down in the dumps" about work in general, this book may give you the hope you need to keep going, make a change, or follow your own "true calling."

Where To Find/Buy:

Bookstores and libraries.

Overall Rating
★★★
Triumphant, touching profiles of 20 people who love what they do; inspirational

Design, Ease Of Use
★★★★
Engaging, very well written; combines interviews and first-person narratives

1–4 Stars

Author:
Martha Finney and Deborah Dasch

Ms. Finney has been writing about work in America for over 10 years. Ms. Dasch is a writer, producer, and aspiring novelist.

Publisher:
Simon & Schuster

Edition:
1998

Price:
$22.00

Pages:
286

ISBN:
0684831694

Media:
Book

Principal Subject:
Career Exploration

Career Exploration

★★★

Overall Rating
★★★
Informative and insightful;
a good choice for self-
assessment and "future trends"

Design, Ease Of Use
★★★
Well written; includes
interactive exercises, lists
and charts

1–4 Stars

Author:
Ron and Caryl Krannich, PhDs

Ron Krannich, Ph.D., and Caryl Rae
Krannich, Ph.D., are former
university professors who now
operate Development Concepts
Incorporated, a training, consulting,
and publishing firm. They are also
the authors of several career-
related guides.

Publisher:
Impact Publications

Edition:
3rd (1998)

Price:
$14.95

Pages:
198

ISBN:
1570230870

Media:
Book

Principal Subject:
Career Exploration

Secondary Subject:
Aptitude/Interest Analysis

DISCOVER THE BEST JOBS FOR YOU

Description:
According to the authors, the key to job search, whether you're currently out of work or contemplating a career change, is to set a job objective. To set such an objective, you must "know yourself." Thus, this guide's primary focus is on self-evaluation and goal setting. (Interactive exercise, charts, and checklists are used throughout.) The first step is to "Test Your Career Competencies." Next, the authors explore the "career development process," options for "professional assistance," and how to choose the "right" self-assessment approach for you. Subsequent chapters evaluate your skills and abilities, interests and values, and "MAS" (Motivated Abilities & Skills). Setting goals and specifying objectives is discussed, as are developing "strategies for success" and discovering "the right resources for you." There are also chapters on using career resources, i.e. other guidebooks, and on the "Best Jobs for Tomorrow." The "Best Jobs" chapter includes 100 "best jobs," 30 "fastest growing occupations" and "job trends for the 21st century."

Evaluation:
There are a lot of nice touches in this earnest, thorough self-assessment guide. Among the laudable inclusions are the chapters "Discover the Right Resources" and "Identify the Best Jobs for Tomorrow." These chapters, like the rest of the text, typify the authors' desire to provoke thought. In this guide, the onus is always on the reader. While other authors tell you what to think, the Kranniches (who are former teachers) consistently encourage you to think for yourself. For example, the "Resources" chapter doesn't present a mere list; it examines the types of books available, explains their agendas, etc. Similarly, the "Best Jobs" chapter offers advice for evaluating "top job" lists, etc.; it's a mini "buyer's guide" to career predictions. The self-assessment strategies are sensible and practical; they're fairly "traditional" with few surprises, but highly effective. With its smart insights, informative air, and clear, concise style, this book could convert the most hardened anti-self-assessment nay sayer; fans of the genre will love it.

Where To Find/Buy:
Bookstores and libraries.

Career Exploration

STARTING OUT, STARTING OVER
Finding The Work That's Waiting For You

★★★

Description:
According to Ms. Peterson, finding the "right" job requires two prepatory acts: self-evaluation and job research. Her guide focuses on these two areas, beginning with self-evaluation. Using a variety of interactive exercises and quizzes, Chapters 1–4 explore "Making a Career Choice," "Career Matchmaking," "Personality Type," and completing "Your Career Profile." (Exercises include derivatives of the "Strong Interest Survey" and the "Myers-Briggs Type Indicator.") Chapters 5–7 discuss options for conducting career research, such as "Getting Out Your Library Card," using the Internet, networking and informational interviews. In Chapter 8, "Making Sense of Your Research," fill-in-the-blank "matchmaker charts" are used to assess research results. Methods for "test driving" your job choice, i.e. internships, temping, etc., are discussed in Chapter 9, while the final chapter, Chapter 10, explains how to "find the right program" for furthering your education. An index of topics is also provided.

Evaluation:
It's hard to find fault with the theory behind Ms. Peterson's approach. Certainly, knowing where you want to end up is a necessary precursor to a successful job search. And knowing how to conduct job research efficiently can save hours and hassle. Both topics are well treated here, particularly conducting research. Since her guide was written both for first-time job seekers and career changers, more experienced readers may find her advice a remedial, but, though basic, her tips are time-tested and apt. She's on target, insightful, and timely, especially in the chapter on using the Internet, which includes descriptions of servers and online services (there aren't any URLs, though). For a quality refresher course in researching, this is a fine resource. The self-evaluative chapters are also above-average. They're smartly constructed and resist the patronizing tendencies common to many such guides; the exercises won't make you feel as if you're completing a 10th grade interest survey. There are lots of valuable book reviews, too.

Where To Find/Buy:
Bookstores and libraries.

Overall Rating
★★★
Smart self-assessment exercises and good tips on conducting job research

Design, Ease Of Use
★★★
Includes interactive exercises and resource reviews

1–4 Stars

Author:
Linda Peterson
Ms. Peterson is the author of two books in Davies-Black's "Careers Without College" series. She is also a columnist and contributing editor to "Arts & Entertainment Monthly."

Publisher:
Davies-Black Publishing

Edition:
1995

Price:
$14.95

Pages:
190

ISBN:
0891060731

Media:
Book

Principal Subject:
Career Exploration

Secondary Subject:
Aptitude/Interest Analysis

★★★

Overall Rating
★★★
A guide to discovering your life's calling

Design, Ease Of Use
★
New Age platitudes are liberally sprinkled throughout

1–4 Stars

Author:
Richard Leider

Mr. Leider is the founder of The Inventure Group, a training firm in Minneapolis, devoted to helping people to "discover the power of purpose." He is a respected author, career coach and speaker.

Edition:
1997

Price:
$20.00

Pages:
162

ISBN:
1576750213

Media:
Book

Principal Subject:
Career Exploration

Career Exploration

THE POWER OF PURPOSE
Creating Meaning In Your Life And Work

Description:

Do you see your work as a way to earn a living, or as a calling? According to the author, a job can be more than a way to pay for our existence, it can enhance and lend meaning to that existence. Leider presents a compelling case for seeking to marry our talents, gifts and passions to our vocation. After a series of narratives that drive home his premise, Leider spends the rest of his pages guiding readers in a self-discovery process for finding their true calling. He uses stories of people living according to purpose to inspire and awaken a hunger for purpose. He shares stories of "successful" people whose careers are fatally mismatched to their personhood to illustrate the source of much modern day stress, anxiety and malaise. Poetry, prose, narratives and self-discovery questionnaires comprise the pages of this weekend-long book. Though brief, most every paragraph is written with a built-in pause implied for the reader to reflect and chew on the offering. While the emphasis is on self-discovery, Leider's view that self-fulfillment is often attained through serving others seasons the book and may influence your conclusions as well.

Evaluation:

To enjoy his book, you must buy into Leider's foundational premise, that humans crave having a sense of purpose, and blossom when that purpose is explored and fulfilled by their daily work. If this premise resonates with you, reading this guide may help to clarify your "purpose" or "calling" in life. Leider's guide is a deeper, more spiritual (though not necessarily theistic) complement to well-known personality tests. Rather than trying to pinpoint your analytical strengths, for example, the guide prompts you to consider "what moves you." The list he offers to prod you toward discovery of your passion is heavy on "challenged populations" and issues such as recycling and youth outreach. Missing from the list are many of things driving career decisions in real life, such as financial security or job image. These are no accidental omissions, as Leider strongly believes that it is through serving others or working toward worthy goals (such as civil rights) that most people find their raison d'etre. Be warned that some of the chapters are long on New Age platitudes and what Dilbert would call jobbish pyschobabble. Sample prose: "Life is a continuous spiral of lessons to be learned as we grow back toward our birth source." If the guru style doesn't turn you off after the introduction, read on. This book may help unlock your life's purpose.

Where To Find/Buy:

Bookstores and libraries.

Career Exploration

IT'S NEVER TOO LATE
150 Men And Women Who Changed Their Careers

There are a million personal reasons to want to change your career, and an equal number of excuses not to—primary among them "it's too late." Mr. Otterbourg's book demonstrates, whether you're 35 or 60, "it's never too late." There are two parts to this guide: an explanatory, investigative section on "How and Why" people change careers, and a section which combines career descriptions with personal profiles. In the "How and Why" section, chapters address such issues as "Selecting a New Career," recovering from a "pink slip," "Overcoming Inertia," "Career Assessment," and entrepreneurism. As is the case in the second section, personal stories are used to illustrate and explore each issue. The second section presents a wide range of careers fields, i.e. "Education," "Health Care," "Retail and Service Businesses," etc. Each chapter contains an overview of opportunities in the highlighted field, followed by a series of profiles of people who have successfully "switched." Summarized "Points to Remember" appear at the end of each chapter; a list of resources is included.

Evaluation:

Unlike "Find Your Calling, Love Your Life" (see review), a book which also uses personal profiles to demonstrate career changes/paths, this guide wastes the 150 personal examples it contains. While the stories in "Find Your Calling" allow readers a window into the experience and lives of others, the stories found here are too short to offer more than a brief glimpse. Reading these stories is like judging the quality of a pie by licking the crust: pointless. For example, in the case of the "dancer turned translator," the story is: she danced, she "questioned her future," and then a "career counseling course stimulated her to use her language skills as a court translator and to form Inter-National Interpreters and Translators." (Surely the transition from dancer to business owner was a little harder than that!) This work is plagued by over-simplification, both in its illustrative stories and in its advice. There is some insight into leaving, i.e. firing, downsizing, but it can't compensate for the general lack of particulars.

Where To Find/Buy:

Bookstores and libraries.

Overall Rating

★

Lots of personal examples from career changers, but few practical suggestions

Design, Ease Of Use

★★

Easy to read; includes bulleted "Points to Remember"

1–4 Stars

Author:
Robert K. Otterbourg

Mr. Otterbourg is a freelance business writer whose articles have appeared in such publications as "National Business Employment Weekly."

Publisher:
Barron's

Edition:
1993

Price:
$9.95

Pages:
214

ISBN:
0812014642

Media:
Book

Principal Subject:
Career Exploration

Secondary Subject:
Career Transitions

Of Interest To:
Returning To The Workplace

II. Career Exploration And Research

APTITUDE AND INTEREST ANALYSIS

Readers should keep in mind the fact that natural interests are supported by natural skills. This being the case, you should look at career options that you have an affinity for versus ones that just sound prestigious or economically rewarding.

In this chapter we review several resources designed to help you discover your interests, aptitudes and priorities. The role of self-assessment, particularly personality testing, in career decision making has been popularized by the best-selling success of books like *What Color Is Your Parachute?* Many resources take the additional step of helping the user to tie results from the analysis to specific career fields of interest.

The rule of thumb here is simple—don't take the data literally. If a test or process suggest that you would be good at being a "forest ranger," then you should not conclude that this is the only position for which you are well-suited. Look at these tests as a means of creating baseline metaphors for what would work well for you. For example, the interest inventories that might say someone should be a "forest ranger" are keying on a person's desire to:

- Move physically at work.

- Do tangible things that either make something or work with nature.

- Work with living things.

- Use science and research in their daily worklife.

In this case it might be better to think of all the jobs where you could have the list of characteristics I just mentioned instead of taking the survey literally and becoming a "forest ranger." It is not that "forest ranger" is not right for someone with these interests, but they also might prefer fish biology or farming.

Aptitude And Interest Analysis

I COULD DO ANYTHING IF ONLY I KNEW WHAT IT WAS

 Recommended For:
Aptitude/Interest Analysis

Description:

As the introduction explains, there are two primary reasons people "don't know what they want to do." First, there are an overwhelming range of options. Second, "something inside you is stopping you from knowing." Ms. Sher calls this "something inside" an "inner conflict" or "resistance." The first step toward discovering what you want is to identify your particular inner conflict. In Chapters 1–3, Sher explores causes of conflict and provides a series of self-assessment exercises designed to help readers hear the "voice" of their conflict. Then, in Chapters 1–14, she offers advice and strategies for overcoming specific types of conflict. For example, if your "voice" says, "I'd have to quit my job to get what I really want and I can't do that—I'd starve," turn to Chapter 4; if your "voice" says, "Every time I go after what I want, I drop the ball and I don't know why," head to Chapter 5. Other chapters address "walking away from success," "trying hard to love something you don't really want," and "disabled desire."

Evaluation:

This is hands-down one of the best self-help guides for changing your outlook on work (and life). It's smart, straightforward, inspirational, and sympathetic, all attributes which contribute to its persuasiveness. If you buy her premise, that you know what you want to do, deep down, but that something—expectations, fears, fantasies, whatever—is keeping you from figuring it out, then this book may help you resolve your conflict. The authors help you pinpoint your conflict and provide realistic, practical tips for overcoming it. After that, acting on your new knowledge, i.e. changing careers, getting a job, etc., is up to you. It makes sense to resolve the big picture question, what do I really want to do, before pouring time and energy into a job search. Even if she can't help you get over the conflict(s), facing an enemy with a name is infinitely better than facing shadows. If you feel "blocked," unable to make a decision, or envious of people who do know what they want, this is the book for you.

Where To Find/Buy:

Bookstores and libraries.

★★★★

Overall Rating
★★★★
Persuasive, practical, insightful

Design, Ease Of Use
★★★★
Well written and engaging; combines personal stories with interactive exercises

1–4 Stars

Author:
Barbara Sher with Barbara Smith
Ms. Sher is a therapist and career counselor who conducts workshops all over the U.S. Ms. Smith writes a column for "New York Woman" and teaches fiction writing at Yale.

Publisher:
Dell

Edition:
1994

Price:
$12.95

Pages:
322

ISBN:
0440505003

Media:
Book

Principal Subject:
Aptitude/Interest Analysis

★★★★

Overall Rating
★★★★
An intelligent and insightful guide to creating a fulfilling career

Design, Ease Of Use
★★★★
Entertaining, imaginative writing throughout; thoughtful "inquiries" for reflection

1–4 Stars

Author:
Nicholas Lore
The author is the founder of Rockport Institute, "an international career-counseling network" based in Rockport, Maine. He acts as a mentor to many other coaches and counselors all over the world.

Publisher:
Simon & Schuster

Edition:
1998

Price:
$14.00

Pages:
385

ISBN:
0684823993

Media:
Book

Principal Subject:
Aptitude/Interest Analysis

Aptitude And Interest Analysis

THE PATHFINDER
How To Choose Or Change Your Career For A Lifetime Of Satisfaction And Success

 Recommended For:
Aptitude/Interest Analysis

Description:
The author founded Rockport Institute, a career counseling network that coaches people of all ages and backgrounds who are choosing a new career. Many of the techniques and ideas in "The Pathfinder" were born and developed in this organization, which was created to confront the question, "How can an intelligent person, committed to choosing a new career path, decide exactly which direction to pursue?" This book plots a path towards self-discovery and "career-discovery" through a combination of exercises, reflective "inquiries," and discussion. Part 1 discusses how to figure out whether or not your present career is a good fit, and explore the components of your ideal career. Part 2 is a compilation of chapters teaching concepts about human psychology and behavior, commitment, doubt, and goal-setting. Part 3 is concerned primarily with creating and designing your new career, with exercises to help you discover your temperament, natural talents, and abilities. This last section also contains job-hunting tips.

Evaluation:
This guide begins with a winning premise: that you must know yourself before you can know what career would fit you best. The author, in an uplifting manner, prompts and pushes the reader to explore and evaluate himself/herself, and finally make decisions about an ideal career. It is his belief that you must design a career out of yourself, your own unique nature and abilities, and that you must (as Leonardo Da Vinci said) "Make your work in keeping with your purpose." This is a highly creative, somewhat unorthodox, and demanding career guide that inspires thoughtful self-analysis. Readers looking for a guide to help them make safe, comfortable choices will not find a lot of help here. It is also not a good buy for those hoping to make a quick choice, or looking for practical job-hunting tips. This book demands time, self-reflection, and boldness—but will, if given these, help you chart your path towards an ideal career with imagination and spirit.

Where To Find/Buy:
Bookstores and libraries.

Aptitude And Interest Analysis

WHAT COLOR IS YOUR PARACHUTE?
A Practical Manual For Job-Hunters And Career-Changers

 Recommended For:
Aptitude/Interest Analysis

Description:
Richard Bolles, a pioneering expert in the field of career counseling, is the author of this best-selling career guide, almost equally divided between "Parachute" proper, and the "Parachute Workbook and Resource Guide." This book teaches readers how to go about a successful job hunt or career change, with an understanding of the whole process that will last you "the rest of your life." The first half of the book opens with a section for "The Impatient Job-Hunter," with techniques to help you evaluate yourself and a career, and practical job-hunting tips. The next more extensive and detailed section is for "The Determined Job-Hunter and Career-Changer," discussing the "what," "where," and "how" of the job-hunting process. The second half of the book, consisting of the workbook and resource guide, opens with a series of exercises culminating in the "Flower" picture, a complete diagram of your skills, interests, and talents. Research techniques and job-hunting tips for special populations are also detailed.

Evaluation:
First published in 1970 and revised nearly every year following, "Parachute" began as a pioneering work in the then little-known "careers" field. Today, it's a well-loved classic. It's a quirky, down-to-earth, and inspirational read, chock-full of cartoons and anecdotes a s well as sensible advice about how to find a job you'll love. Richard Bolles, the "inventor" of this unusual work, maintains a jovial presence throughout these pages, helping to ground the advice in an atmosphere of caring from start to finish. Empowering advice for those in the throes of a job-hunt or looking to find/change careers is spliced in along with in-depth, self-exploratory exercises. These culminate in the famous "Flower Diagram," a holistic representation of your personality, skills, and interests. Bolles' book, however, is not for everyone. It requires a serious investment of time and attention—this is not (overall) a guide for the distractible or impatient. For readers willing to make the commitment, the experience will be revelatory.

Where To Find/Buy:
Bookstores and libraries.

★★★★

Overall Rating
★★★★
An inspirational and practical guide to choosing a career and landing a job

Design, Ease Of Use
★★★★
Nearly every page is enlivened with colorful cartoons and graphics

1–4 Stars

Author:
Richard Nelson Bolles

Richard Nelson Bolles is the author of this classic guide to job-hunting and careers, now in its 28th edition. He is widely acknowledged as a pioneer and leader in the field of career counseling, and has been featured in many media forums, including magazines and T.V.

Publisher:
Ten Speed Press

Edition:
28th (1997)

Price:
$16.95

Pages:
521

ISBN:
0898159318

Media:
Book

Principal Subject:
Aptitude/Interest Analysis

★ ★ ★

Overall Rating
★★★
Lots of helpful forms and worksheets; one of the best online career development manuals

Design, Ease Of Use
★★★★
User-friendly, easy to move around; great for users who generally prefer books

1–4 Stars

Author:
Marlene Bryan

Publisher:
University of Waterloo

Edition:
2nd (1997)

Media:
Internet

Principal Subject:
Aptitude/Interest Analysis

Aptitude And Interest Analysis

CAREER DEVELOPMENT MANUAL
Steps To Career/Life Planning Success

Description:

This is an online version of Ms. Bryan's Career Development Manual and it is formatted accordingly: the home page is an introduction and the "main menu" (always located in a separate frame on the left) functions as a "table of contents." The site is designed to take users through the entire career planning/job hunting process in 6 "steps," from choosing a career to accepting an offer. First, users create a "personal career profile" based on the completion of a series of self-assessment exercises. The next "step" is to conduct "occupational research." Techniques explored include internships and "informational interviews;" forms for record-keeping are provided. "Step 3" involves such "decision making" tasks as defining personal and career objectives and "setting up your action plan." Developing job search skills is "Step 4." There are worksheets and tips for creating resumes, writing letters, interviewing, etc. Job offers and "success at work," are addressed in "Step 5;" "Step 6" offers summary advice on career/life planning.

Evaluation:

For users more familiar with print resources than online ones, this is the perfect hybrid. It's formatted like a book, but with the added technological advantages of quick access and worksheets users can complete online. (If you really hate computers, print out the worksheets for the traditional, "pen and pencil" approach.) Aside from its user-friendly layout, this is a great workbook for career planning needs. The self-assessment exercises and decision making tasks are designed to help you evaluate and define your interests and goals (they are not "personality tests"), but that's not the best part of this guide. There are forms you can print out to take to informational interviews, to keep track of research, and to develop schedules. For organizing and developing a resume (and for interview preparation), there is a truly valuable, thought-provoking "form" wherein users complete sections such as "give a good a example of your teamwork." Some print resources are more in depth, but heck, this one's "free."

Where To Find/Buy:

On the Internet at http://www.adm.uwaterloo.ca/infocecs/CRC/manual-home.html

Aptitude And Interest Analysis

DISCOVER WHAT YOU'RE BEST AT
The National Career Aptitude System And Career Directory

★★★

Description:
The National Career Aptitude System (NCAS) measures aptitudes in six skill areas: business, clerical, logic, mechanical, numerical, and social. Readers take timed (25–30 minutes), multiple-choice tests on each subject; "answer sheets" are provided. Higher scores in certain areas indicate "comparative strengths." To find out which careers cater to their "strengths," readers refer to the "career clusters." Each "cluster" is a list of careers which share the same combination of aptitudes. Aptitude combinations are identified by the first letter of each skill area, i.e. "LM" (logic/mechanical) or "CL" (clerical/logic). For example, the "BCS" "cluster" contains jobs that involve business (B), clerical (C), and social (S) aptitude. The 41 "career clusters" are subdivided by level of education: high school, two-year college, four-year college, etc. Finally, readers can learn more about the job titles listed in their "clusters" by using the career directory. The directory includes brief descriptions of over 1,100 careers.

Evaluation:
This book works because it fulfills its stated objective: to help readers assess their abilities and to provide career suggestions based on that assessment. The tests are straightforward multiple-choice with succinct directions and scoring is simple. The idea is to measure "overall" aptitude (in so far as that is possible), so the skills tested are general, rather than specific. For example, the business test includes marketing, sales, managerial skills, etc. The tests aren't "easy," but they are designed for all ages (16+). The "career clusters" section, where career suggestions appear, is also very well organized. Readers can find careers which utilize one skill, two-skill combinations, and three-skill combinations. For a "test your aptitude, find a career" guide, this is a fine choice. Readers should keep in mind, however, that education and determination can develop any skill; use this book to build confidence in your "strengths," not as a "final verdict."

Where To Find/Buy:
Bookstores and libraries.

Overall Rating
★★★
A good choice for career suggestions based on aptitude testing

Design, Ease Of Use
★★★★
Easy-to-use, explicit directions, well organized

1–4 Stars

Author:
Barry and Linda Gale
Barry and Linda Gale are President and Executive Director of Career Aptitude Testing, Ltd. Mr. Gale holds degrees in education, counseling, and psychological testing; he is a noted lecturer and career counselor. Ms. Gale is the co-author of four career books.

Publisher:
Fireside

Edition:
2nd (1990)

Price:
$12.00

Pages:
170

ISBN:
0671695894

Media:
Book

Principal Subject:
Aptitude/Interest Analysis

II. Career Exploration And Research

★★★

Aptitude And Interest Analysis

FINDING THE CAREER THAT FITS YOU

Overall Rating
★★★
A useful workbook with several interesting self-surveys to work through

Design, Ease Of Use
★★★
Well-designed exercises; straightforward and humane

1–4 Stars

Author:
Lee Ellis and Larry Burkett

Lee Ellis is the director of Career Pathways, "the career guidance branch of Christian Financial Concepts (CFC)." Larry Burkett is founder and president of CFC, Inc., "a ministry devoted to teaching God's principles for financial management."

Publisher:
Moody Press

Edition:
1994

Price:
$21.99

ISBN:
0802416683

Media:
Book

Principal Subject:
Aptitude/Interest Analysis

Description:
"Finding The Career That Fits You" is the companion workbook to "Your Career In Changing Times," also written by Lee Ellis and Larry Burkett. The workbook's purpose, in the authors' words, is to "help you discover your talents and interests . . . The keys to finding your calling and the career that fits you." The first two chapters introduce the workplace in the '90s, and discuss the process of choosing a career. Chapter 3 includes two extensive, in-depth assessments that help you identify the basic elements of your personality and work behavior. Chapter 4 contains a "skills survey" to help you assess your strongest skills. Chapters 5–6 contain a "work priorities evaluation" and a "vocational interests survey." The next chapter summarizes the information gleaned from the surveys and self-assessments, and the final chapters help you apply what you've learned to choosing a career. Interspersed throughout are Biblical references for further reflections on topics raised.

Evaluation:
The authors have put together a useful and reflective workbook on choosing a career. The self-assessment surveys are particularly valuable and fun to work through, leaving you with a clear list of your personality traits, skills, and priorities, all of which can be usefully applied in the job hunt. The authors take the view that, as everyone is unique, it is important to be aware of one's differences in order to function harmoniously in our lives and in the workplace. The Christian touch, while light, is still significant, but this focus is never limiting. The book is also very interactive with lots of questions, exercises, and surveys. However, the book is based very heavily on its surveys, which, like all surveys of this type, are trying to capture the ineffable: qualities of one's personality and values. Some readers may also find its division of personalities into 4 major types rather narrow, but all in all one walks away from this workbook with some useful self-knowledge in hand.

Where To Find/Buy:
Christian bookstores or libraries, or order directly from publisher: (800) 722-1976.

Aptitude And Interest Analysis

GUIDE TO YOUR CAREER
How To Turn Your Interests Into A Career You Love

★★★

Description:

There are two parts to this guide: "Career Creation" and "Career Options." In "Career Creation," the first step is to define personal interests ("what you want/like to do") and personal style ("how you like to do things") via "The Birkman Career Style Summary." (This is an assessment "quiz" based on the "Birkman Method"). Interest and style are divided into four categories, each labeled by a color. For example, one can have "blue" interests and a "yellow" style. Both this exercise and the techniques learned in "Applying Your Memories" are used to discover which type of career will be most satisfying. Readers can then search the 150+ "Career Options" by color group or by job title. Each career profile includes information about "a day in the life," "paying your dues" (education/experience), and "quality of life" in two, five, and ten year increments. Icons and charts present a "professional profile," i.e. demographics, average hours, salary ranges, and major employers. "Interviewing As An Art Form" is also discussed.

Evaluation:

As far as career directories go, this is a fine preliminary resource. The career profiles paint a relatively vivid picture by including segments like "quality of life" at two, five, and ten years, along with the "basics" (i.e. salary ranges). Since most directories provide no search mechanisms (other than the "contents"), the "Birkman" color index is another distinguishing feature. It enables readers to narrow or begin their search by color/interest group, rather than browsing through listings. However, it is the non-directory portion, "Career Creation," which is the true selling point. Mr. Bernstein's background in psychotherapy is evident in the intelligent, thought-provoking exercises. For instance, readers learn to link "happy" activities to an experience of "timelessness." "Timelessness" is a state of mind considered by many (psychologists, philosophers) to have great psychological significance and to be one of the "keys" to happiness. It is rare to find such an educated approach to self-assessment.

Where To Find/Buy:

Bookstores and libraries, or through 800-793-2665.

Overall Rating
★★★
Intelligent self-assessment tools; includes "the basics" on a wide variety of careers

Design, Ease Of Use
★★★
Easy-to-use, simple, straightforward format; uses "quick reference" icons

1–4 Stars

Author:
Alan B. Bernstein, C.S.W., P.C., and Nicholas R. Schaffzin

Mr. Bernstein is a psychotherapist, author and career counselor. Currently in private practice, he has held faculty positions at NYU and Rutgers University. Mr. Schaffzin is the author of *The Princeton Review*'s "Reading Smart" and "Negotiate Smart."

Publisher:
The Princeton Review

Edition:
1997

Price:
$21.00

Pages:
414

ISBN:
0679778691

Media:
Book

Principal Subject:
Aptitude/Interest Analysis

II. Career Exploration And Research

II. Career Exploration And Research

★★★

Overall Rating
★★★

A sophisticated self-assessment tool, but lacks definitive, practical applications

Design, Ease Of Use
★★

The disk is fun and easy to use; the guide is dense and often difficult to read

1–4 Stars

Author:
Timothy Butler, Ph.D., and James Waldroop, Ph.D.

Dr. Butler and Dr. Waldroop are Directors of MBA Career Development Programs at the Harvard Business School; they are also principles in Waldroop Butler Associates, a firm which specializes in career assessment, counseling, and executive coaching.

Publisher:
Perseus Books

Edition:
1997

Price:
$22.00

Pages:
252

ISBN:
0201461358

Media:
Book + Software

Principal Subject:
Aptitude/Interest Analysis

Aptitude And Interest Analysis

DISCOVERING YOUR CAREER IN BUSINESS

Description:
Butler and Waldroop created the "Business Career Interest Inventory" (BCII) as a career counseling tool. Based on 10 years of research, the BCII is designed to asses your "patterns of interest" and "direct" you toward appropriate work environments and activities. To bring the BCII into your home, Butler and Waldroop created this dual resource (book and disk). To begin, the authors ask you to read the first 3 chapters of the print guide. Chapter 1 explains the premise behind the BCII, Chapter 2 explores the reasons people are "pulled off" their career tracks, and Chapter 3 provides a series of preliminary self-assessment exercises. Chapter 4 introduces the BCII and readers set aside the guide to use the disk. The BCII comprises 4 sections: "occupations," "personal attributes," "subjects for study," and "activities." In each section, you rate you're preferences; "scores" appear at the end. After completing the BCII, Chapters 5–7 help you analyze the results, form a "business career profile," and understand how that profile relates to business activities. Chapters 8 and 9 explore the career-decision making process and present case studies. Chapter 10 teaches you to evaluate work opportunities based on your new self-knowledge.

Evaluation:
As both Directors of the MBA career development program at Harvard Business School and career counselors, Butler, Waldroop, and their creation, the BCII, do inspire confidence. In comparison to other, similarly targeted self-assessment tools, the BCII is the most sophisticated and nuanced. It's easy to use, takes about 30 minutes to complete, and has a simple, clear format. Yet, while the BCII does produce enlightening, intriguing results (you may learn something new about yourself!), it's difficult to gauge how practical this system really is. Taken in the offices of Butler and Waldroop and supplemented by their advice, the BCII is probably highly effective. Without their interpretation and guidance, however, the BCII can't do much more than aim you in a general, and rather broad, direction. The chapters dedicated to interpreting the BCII results are replete with awkward language (i.e. "the LLH profile type with the Enterprise Control business function elevated . . .") and generalities (i.e. "[LHL] types are drawn to industries where the mission is doing good, such as health care"), which makes forming conclusions difficult. The chapter on using the results to evaluate work opportunities is similarly impaired. The BCII is a terrific tool, but you'll have to apply the results to specific jobs on your own. (Software is for PCs only).

Where To Find/Buy:
Bookstores and libraries.

Aptitude And Interest Analysis

THE CAREER DISCOVERY PROJECT
Find The Perfect Fit Between Your Work And Your Life

Description:
To promote better career choices, Dr. Sturman has designed a "Personal Career Profile," a self-assessment tool for anyone seeking career satisfaction. The Profile is based on personal characteristics: motivation/work preferences, work style, career type, skills, "internal barriers," and personal values and needs. Each characteristic is discussed and analyzed separately. Motivation is examined via checklists for people, place, job, and culture preferences. A "work-related" test based on the MBTI reveals work style. There are 16 possible work styles based on four-trait combinations: extrovert vs. introvert, sensing vs. intuition, thinking vs. feeling, and judging vs. perceiving. Readers determine their own career types (i.e. "realistic," "artistic") by reading each of the 6 career type profiles. There are 4 inventories for evaluating "functional skills" and "adaptive skills;" "internal barriers," values and needs are rated by checklist. A fill-in-the-blank Profile is included, along with suggestions and advice on application.

Evaluation:
With the exception of the "test" for work style (a work-related derivative of the Myers-Briggs Type Indicator), the self-assessment exercises are primarily checklists and inventories designed to display "what you already know." Self-discovery is a result of the endeavor, the actual process of completing the inventories, etc. The Personal Career Profile is, therefore, a way to bring career related personality issues to the forefront, to see those issues laid out "before your very eyes." Readers who find it difficult to organize thoughts, articulate feelings, etc., but who are interested in self-evaluation will benefit the most from this guide. However, there is little discussion of concrete applications for the Profile. Dr. Sturman makes the vague promise that it will increase self-awareness, self-esteem, and "support you in making decisions." No specifics are given, only general advice, i.e. "patterns may suggest . . . work environments . . . to explore." The Profile's impact upon career choice depends on how greatly it impacts reader.

Where To Find/Buy:
Bookstores and libraries.

Overall Rating
★★
Tells readers how to create a Personal Career Profile, but not how to use it

Design, Ease Of Use
★★★
Easy to use, explicit instructions; takes time to complete the process

1–4 Stars

Author:
Gerald M. Sturman, Ph.D.

Publisher:
Doubleday

Edition:
1993

Price:
$14.00

Pages:
116

ISBN:
0385423403

Media:
Book

Principal Subject:
Aptitude/Interest Analysis

II. Career Exploration And Research

★★

Overall Rating
★★

Best for people who believe in/have experience with "Personality Typing"

Design, Ease Of Use
★★

No "tests" are included; finding the right "Type" can be difficult

1–4 Stars

Author:
Paul Tieger and Barbara Barron-Tieger

Paul Tieger and Barbara Barron-Tieger are the principals of Communication Consultants where they teach individuals and groups how to improve effectiveness. They have been training professionals in the use of Personality Type for over ten years.

Publisher:
Little, Brown and Company

Edition:
2nd (1995)

Price:
$17.95

Pages:
350

ISBN:
0316845221

Media:
Book

Principal Subject:
Aptitude/Interest Analysis

DO WHAT YOU ARE
Discover The Perfect Career For You Through The Secrets Of Personality Type

Description:

The Myers-Briggs Type Indicator (the basis for Personality Type) examines four "dimensions" of personal preference: extroversion (E) vs. introversion (I), sensing (S) vs. intuition (N), thinking (T) vs. feeling (F), and judging (J) vs. perceiving (P). These preferences relate to "how we interact," "the kind of information we naturally notice," "how we make decisions," and "how we live," respectfully. The 16 trait combinations, i.e. ISTJ or ENFP, represent the 16 different Types. Readers identify their Type based on descriptions of each pair of preferences and "Verifying Type Profiles." Temperament and "innate strengths" for each Type provide clues about career options, as do "Typograms," graphic representations of the various Types' public vs. private personas. The final segment of this guide combines case studies of successful people with Type-specific career advice. Advice includes specifics for career satisfaction, popular occupations, work-related strengths and weaknesses, and "pathways to success."

Evaluation:

This guide doesn't include a version of the MBTI, probably because the MBTI can only be interpreted by a trained professional. However, most guides which deal with MBTI Personality Type provide a layman's version, or a test created to produce the same four-trait combinations. Without any tests at all, readers face the alternative used here: read through the first four descriptions and see which one "feels" right, then read through the profiles and see which one "feels" right. . . . Readers who are lucky enough to find a profile that "fits" may gain a great deal of insightful, informative feedback; readers who are not as lucky will feel very, very frustrated. As is usually the case, in personality-assessment guides, one must be an active reader, constantly interpreting the text, analyzing patterns, etc., but here there is no "fun" factor (completing a test). For positive results, readers must have a strong faith in "Personality Typing." Skeptics will find this guide useless.

Where To Find/Buy:

Bookstores and libraries.

Aptitude And Interest Analysis

CHANGING COURSE

Description:

In this 10-chapter guide/workbook, the interactive, self-assessment exercises are the primary focus. (Though advice and information is provided, each chapter is built around a series of exercises.) These exercises are designed to help readers make career/life decisions by exploring their options, opportunities, and self-awareness. After an introductory chapter, Chapter 2 explores the financial ramifications of change and your feelings about the future. Chapter 3 analyses the "The Management of Change;" exercises include "My Transitions Lifeline" and "Transition Patterns." Chapter 4 looks at "The Middle Years," i.e. "stages of adulthood," "stocktaking," etc. The reader's personal life is examined in Chapter 5, i.e. "rethinking relationships," while Chapter 6 examines the reader's personality; exercises evaluate interests, priorities, values, etc. Chapters 7, 8, and 9 assess "Practical Options," the reader's health, and "Your Personal Philosophy," respectively. Chapter 10 suggests resources for further research.

Evaluation:

There can be no doubt that career transitions, i.e. reentering the work force, early retirement, job loss, etc., inspire a lot of questions about yourself and your future, including "What do I want to do?" If you're waffling between ideas, or unsure how to evaluate your wants/need, a good self-assessment guide is a great tool. Unfortunately, this one is very rudimentary. Smith's book comes across as simplistic, immature and even patronizing. For example, the first exercise determines whether your "face of decision" matches the face of "Clever Chris," "Hopeful Helen," or the woe begotten "Despairing Dennis." Exercises demand such tasks as writing 10 sentences that begin with "I am a woman/man who. . . ." and ask such questions as "When did you realize you needed to make a decision?" They all ask "How did you feel . . . ?" Every self-assessment cliché can be found in this book, in one form or another. Pass on this one, there are better resources available.

Where To Find/Buy:

Bookstores and libraries.

Overall Rating
★
Simplistic

Design, Ease Of Use
★★
Written at about an 8th grade reading level

1–4 Stars

Author:
Maggie Smith

Ms. Smith is the director of Branching Out. She designs programs in Career Transitions, Counseling Skills, and Mid-Life Planning.

Publisher:
Pfeiffer & Company

Edition:
3rd (1993)

Price:
$12.99

Pages:
258

ISBN:
0893842095

Media:
Book

Principal Subject:
Aptitude/Interest Analysis

Aptitude And Interest Analysis

HOW TO FIND THE WORK YOU LOVE

Overall Rating

★

A heartfelt but nebulous exploration of finding your "unique life's work"

Design, Ease Of Use

★★

Some writing is truly inspirational, but other passages are vague and hackneyed

1–4 Stars

Author:

Laurence G. Boldt

Laurence G. Boldt is a career consultant, and the author of "Zen and the Art of Making a Living" and "Zen Soup."

Publisher:

Arkana (Penguin)

Edition:

1996

Price:

$10.95

Pages:

154

ISBN:

0140195246

Media:

Book

Principal Subject:

Aptitude/Interest Analysis

Description:

Seven chapters, including an introduction and an epilogue, make up the whole of this "discussion" about modern life and work. The author believes that, with the redefinition of work in the 21st century, we must "empower" a whole new work force, a process which begins "with each individual finding the work he or she loves." This slim tome is intended as a guide along the path of finding your own "unique life's work." Chapters 1–3 discuss how the work you love may be "calling," and how to learn how to heed that call by becoming aware of the voices of self-doubt, and asking yourself "focusing questions." Chapters 4, 5, 6, and 7 explore the different "calls" of work: the call of conscience, the call of compassion, the call of talent, and the call to greatness. Each of these "calls" embody a particular principle: integrity, service, enjoyment, and excellence. These chapters finish with several focus questions for contemplation. The epilogue briefly describes how to make the "ideal" into the "real."

Evaluation:

Mr. Boldt's guide is chock-full of "new age" philosophy, nuggets of authorial wisdom, and good intentions. It truly wants to help you discover your "unique life's work" through its heartfelt discussion and exploration of your "inner self." The question is, will it? The "feel-good" attitude here might very well be what some people are looking for—in particular, those stuck in dead-end jobs or careers without the mental/spiritual energy necessary to launch them on their way. However, others may not be so taken with such ethereal advice as, "Determine to play your part in creating the kind of world you want to live in," and at times the writing verges on the pompous: "Ultimately the discovery of a life's work begins with the realization of what it means to be a human being. . . ." There are some valuable nuggets here, buried in a lot of fluff; but a book with pretensions towards becoming a spiritual advisor for the new work force is, after all, a tough feat to pull off.

Where To Find/Buy:

Bookstores and libraries.

CAREER AND JOB DESCRIPTIONS

What are the hottest jobs in today's job market? What fields are growing? What portable skills are most sought after by employers? What are the educational requirements to become a technical writer? And just what does a Webmaster do on a day to day basis?

These questions are representative of the inquiries answered by the resources in this chapter. On the whole, they offer career and industry descriptions, forecasts and trends for employment, regional "outlooks," and tips on "best bets" and "in demand" jobs. Career profiles usually include a job description, salary information, education and experience requirements, and employment opportunities. Some guides include related information on associations, professional organizations, publications, etc., for networking.

There are dozens of job descriptions written in many different forms. I counsel job seekers to get a handle on the daily functions of the job. In other words, what would you be doing on a typical day. Don't confuse a description of the overall job duties with daily activities.

Using the forest ranger example, a job candidate might read a generic job description and learn that rangers are often in charge of forest resource management. However on a daily basis this could mean being in the forest, measuring and researching which trees to harvest, or it could mean sitting in an office tracking logging spread sheets or trail planning documents. The lesson: do enough research to be certain that you really know what you would be doing, and for what percentage of your time, on a daily basis.

★★★★

Overall Rating
★★★★
A great beginning for job research in certain areas; lots of idea-generating profiles

Design, Ease Of Use
★★★★
Explicit table of contents; easy to read and fun to use

1–4 Stars

Author:
Scott A. Meyer

Mr. Meyer is currently a senior editor at "Organic Gardening" magazine as well as an author. He has been a reporter and editor at weekly newspapers and trade magazines.

Publisher:
Macmillan

Edition:
1996

Price:
$14.95

Pages:
211

ISBN:
0028614321

Media:
Book

Principal Subject:
Career/Job Descriptions

Career And Job Descriptions

100 JOBS IN WORDS (SERIES)

 Recommended For:
Career/Job Descriptions

Description:
For readers who have certain areas of interest, i.e. working with "words," "technology," or for "social change," but aren't sure of the specifics (e.g. the exact job title), Macmillan's "100 Jobs In . . ." series offers profiles of 100 occupations. The types of careers profiled, though all related by general "category," represent a wide spectrum of possibilities. For example, for readers who like "words," "100 Jobs In Words" explores such options as "literary agent," "rare book finder," "press secretary," "tour guide," and "columnist." The profiles include a general job description, salary information, and sections on "prospects" for employment (i.e. how competitive the field is, etc.), qualifications, and personal characteristics necessary for success. Each profile is followed by an interview with a professional currently at work in the field. The professionals discuss how they got their job, what they "do all day," and where they "see this job leading." Job titles are arranged alphabetically in the table of contents.

Evaluation:
If you'd like to work in "technology," the "environment," with "words," or for "social change," this series offers a offers hundreds of career possibilities (100 per "category"). For a career changer, these books can help you generate ideas and consider new options. The wide variety of jobs detailed guarantees at least one "Hey, I can do that!" (In "100 Jobs In Words," the profiles are as divergent as "medical writer" and "typefont designer.") As a preliminary resource for researching a "field" of interest, these books are fun, encouraging places to start. They answer the question "what's out there" in a dynamic way. They do not, however, include any practical, "how to" information for actually finding or acquiring positions. Though the importance of well-honed job searching skills is illustrated in the professional interviews, there are no tips or techniques for writing resumes, networking, etc., either. These guides are designed to inspire a more creative, dynamic job hunt, not to get you the job.

Where To Find/Buy:
Bookstores and libraries.

Career And Job Descriptions

OCCUPATIONAL OUTLOOK HANDBOOK

 Recommended For:
Career/Job Descriptions

Description:

The chief goal of the BLS "Handbook" is to provide a tool for individuals conducting career-related research. Although there are segments on "sources of career information" (i.e. networking), "finding a job" (i.e. resume tips), and "evaluating a job offer," the 250 occupational profiles are the guide's primary focus and account for the bulk of its content. Each profile describes the "nature of work," working conditions, employment, training and education needs, job outlook, earnings, related occupations (linked to other profiles), and sources for additional research. To search for a career profile, users can use the keyword search mechanism, i.e. "actuary," expand their query, i.e. "bank AND teller," or scan the alphabetized index and click on a job title. Careers are also arranged into "categories," i.e. "marketing and sales occupations" (under "Outlook for Specific Occupations"); click on a "category" for a list of related jobs. Highlights of BLS labor force and employment projections are also included ("Tomorrow's Jobs").

Evaluation:

For 50 years, the Bureau of Labor Statistics' "Occupational Outlook Handbook" has been a nationally recognized (and commonly used) source of descriptive occupational information. Its content has been appropriated time and again, by print resources as well as online services. What it's known for, and what it does best, are occupational profiles. There are some rudimentary tips on resumes and job searching, but they're so basic they're not even worth browsing. (The "chapter" on "Tomorrow's Jobs," however, is definitely worth a read-through.) For an introductory overview of careers, this is the place to go. The site contains the same material found in the print version, it's "free," and the technology allows for ridiculously easy searches. The BLS employs the "Microsoft Index Server" for fast, effective searching: keywords, complex queries, all forms of a word, etc.; plus users can access "related occupations" directly from the profile they're browsing. Take advantage!

Where To Find/Buy:

On the Internet at http://www.bls.gov/ocohome.htm or order by mail from Bureau of Labor Statistics, Publications Sales Center, P.O. Box 2145, Chicago, IL 60690

★★★★

Overall Rating
★★★★
The primary source for basic career descriptions

Design, Ease Of Use
★★★★
Simple, "no frills" site, text-based, user-friendly; great search mechanism

---

1–4 Stars

Author:
The Handbook was produced in the Bureau of Labor Statistics under the direction of Neal H. Rosenthal, Associate Commissioner for Employment Projections. Mike Pilot and Alan Eck were responsible for planning and day-to-day direction.

Publisher:
Bureau of Labor Statistics

Edition:
1998

Media:
Internet

Principal Subject:
Career/Job Descriptions

II. Career Exploration And Research

Career And Job Descriptions

★★★★

Overall Rating
★★★★
Smart and informative; relevant advice for future-oriented career planners

Design, Ease Of Use
★★★
Well written and well formatted; occasionally uses sophisticated language

1–4 Stars

Author:
Ronald and Caryl Rae Krannich, Ph.Ds

Dr. Ronald Krannich and Dr. Caryl Rae Krannich operate Development Concepts Inc., a training, consulting, and publishing firm. They are the authors of 28 career books, one of today's most extensive collections of career writing.

Publisher:
Impact Publications

Edition:
3rd (1998)

Price:
$19.95

Pages:
294

ISBN:
1570230919

Media:
Book

Principal Subject:
Career/Job Descriptions

THE BEST JOBS FOR THE 21ST CENTURY

 **Recommended For:**
Career/Job Descriptions

Description:
There are two parts to this guide: Part 1 "Consider Your Future" and Part 2 "The Best Jobs." Part 1 analyzes current and future socioeconomic trends, such as "employment dynamics in a dual society" (i.e. the paradox of unemployment and labor shortage), and "structural unemployment." Predictions for an "uncertain future" and their implications are presented and discussed, as are "33 coming changes." Salary ranges and the "best places to live and work" are also explored. The criteria used to evaluate "best jobs for the future," both in this guide and in other, similar books, is examined; job lists from three books are provided and critiqued. Charts and tables of statistics, "Top 50" lists, etc., are scattered throughout. Part 2 comprises nearly 100 profiles of "fast growing" careers. Individual careers are organized into field/industry chapters, i.e. Chapter 7 "Medical and Health Care Careers." Each career profile includes an "employment outlook" and descriptions of qualifications, working conditions, and earnings.

Evaluation:
Although the career profiles offer only a rudimentary overview, the explanation of socioeconomic trends and the analysis of the "best jobs" selection process is so superior to the average career guide that any shortcomings can be forgiven. Actually, the brevity of the profiles is the only shortcoming; but since most "best jobs" books are really providing a list of "starting points" (all require further research), the authors have done their duty. In all other ways they excel. Relevant economic issues and "futurist" concerns are clearly presented and examined, and statistics are included for current employment, job growth and decline, and state/city unemployment/growth. Another valuable attribute is the distinction made between "growing" fields with high-salary or lifestyle benefits and those which, while in demand, are low-paying "dead ends," i.e. home health aide. In this guide, the reader is treated as a player, not a pawn, capable of understanding economic forecasts and using that knowledge advantageously.

Where To Find/Buy:
Bookstores and libraries, or directly from the publisher at 800-361-1055.

Career And Job Descriptions

THE ENHANCED OCCUPATIONAL OUTLOOK HANDBOOK

★★★★

 Recommended For:
Career/Job Descriptions

Description:

The BLS's "Occupational Outlook Handbook" (OOH) and "Dictionary of Occupational Titles" (DOT) are two of the most frequently used references for career data. The OOH profiles 250 "major occupations," offering details on "nature of work," "working conditions," employment outlook, earnings, qualifications, etc. The DOT functions as a companion guide, providing 2,600 paragraph-length descriptions (synopses of the "nature of work") and 4,700 titles of more specific jobs. O*Net, another "informational system" from the U.S. Department of Labor, includes similar descriptions for an additional (approx.) 1,000 jobs. In their version, Jist has "enhanced" the OOH profiles by incorporating the DOT and O*Net data; in effect, they have combined all three resources. Each of the 250 OOH profiles are presented intact, with added descriptions of "associated occupations" (from O*Net and the DOT). This guide also contains a "how to use this book" introduction and search indexes for OOH, DOT and O*Net titles/codes.

Evaluation:

By combining the data from these three U.S. Department of Labor resources (the OOH, DOT, and O*Net), Jist has created one of the most comprehensive career description guides available. The 250 OOH profiles of "major occupations" offer the necessary, general information on employment outlook, earnings, type of employers, etc., while the DOT and O*Net short descriptions illustrate the variety of jobs found in each field. For example, under "Science Technicians," readers will find the OOH profile as well as "nature of work" summaries for such jobs as "Biology Specimen Technician," "Meteorological Technician," and "Artificial Inseminator." Since few job seekers are satisfied with the OOH's "overview" profiles (due to the limited specifics), the incorporation of additional data is highly beneficial: it gives readers lots of options to explore in their field(s) of interest. The DOT uses 9 digit identifier codes, so locating entries can be frustrating. Still, for investigating careers, this is a fantastic resource!

Where To Find/Buy:

Bookstores and libraries.

Overall Rating
★★★★
One of the most thorough and comprehensive "career description" guides

Design, Ease Of Use
★★★
Well formatted; takes time to locate specific entries

1–4 Stars

Author:
J. Michael Farr, LaVerne Ludden, Paul Mangin

This book was developed under the direction of Mr. Farr and Ms. Ludden, with database work by Paul Mangin. The data was provided by the U.S. Department of Labor's Bureau of Labor Statistics (the producers of the OOH and DOT).

Publisher:
JIST

Edition:
2nd (1998)

Price:
$34.95

Pages:
850

ISBN:
1563705230

Media:
Book

Principal Subject:
Career/Job Descriptions

★★★

Overall Rating
★★★
OOH career profiles, plus appendices and job search tips

Design, Ease Of Use
★★★
Very well organized, extensive index

1–4 Stars

Author:
The Occupational Outlook Handbook was produced in the Bureau of Labor Statistics under the general guidance and direction of Ronald E. Kutscher, Associated commissioner for Employment Projections and Neal H. Rosenthal, Chief, division of Occupation Outlook.

Publisher:
JIST

Edition:
6th (1998)

Price:
$18.95

Pages:
570

ISBN:
1563704668

Media:
Book

Principal Subject:
Career/Job Descriptions

Career And Job Descriptions

AMERICA'S TOP 300 JOBS
A Complete Career Handbook

Description:

Based on the Bureau of Labor Statistics' "Occupational Outlook Handbook" (OOH), this guide combines the OOH's 250 occupational profiles and summary descriptions of 73 job titles with job searching tips and an annotated bibliography of "useful resources." The OOH career profiles include the following information: "significant points," nature of work, working conditions, training and qualifications, employment outlook, earnings, and "related occupations." The "significant points" section contains two to three highlighted details about each career. For example, under "Architect," one "significant point" is that, "Nearly 30 percent are self-employed, practicing as partners in architecture firms or on their own." Besides the profiles, this guide also contains the OOH's "Data for Occupations Not Studied in Detail" (73 short descriptions) and "Tomorrow's Jobs" (market trends). Jist's original contribution, "The Quick Job Search," offers interactive exercises to help readers identify skills and objectives.

Evaluation:

Basically, this guide is a repackaged and slightly fattened version of the OOH. The only difference between Jist's version and the original is that this book includes the brief "Quick Job Search" section and a series of helpful appendices, i.e. an annotated bibliography of "useful resources for career planning and job seeking. "For readers who can live without the "fat" (job search tips, appendices) and who have Internet access, the OOH web site is a better bet: it's leaner, but it's free. The site contains the same 250 profiles and 73 short descriptions, and no search index can match the ease of an online search engine. (See the OOH review for details.) For those without Net access, Jist makes a superior print product: "The Enhanced Occupational Outlook Handbook" (see review). Jist's "Enhanced" guide is a thorough, more comprehensive "career description" guide; it combines the OOH profiles with material from the BLS' "Dictionary of Occupational Titles" and O*Net and outshines the competition.

Where To Find/Buy:

Bookstores and libraries.

Career And Job Descriptions

THE BIG BOOK OF JOBS

Description:

The editors at VGM have combined the Bureau of Labor Statistics' famous career resource, the Occupational Outlook Handbook (OOH), with job searching tips and advice to form a 2-part guide. Section 1, "The Job Seeker's Guide," consists of seven short chapters which explore such topics as "building career management skills," "researching careers in the information age," and "finding job leads" via networking. There are also chapters on writing cover letters and resumes (samples included) and interview techniques. Section 2 reproduces the complete OOH: 250 occupational profiles and additional data, i.e. "Data for Occupations Not Studied in Detail" and "Tomorrow's Jobs" (labor trends). Each profile contains descriptions of the nature of work, working conditions, employment, training needed, job outlook, earnings, "related occupations" and sources of additional information. The OOH's table of contents groups occupations by "category;" a search index provides alphabetically listings of career titles.

Evaluation:

VGM's objective in creating this resource is clear: take the career-related information found in the OOH and combine it with a "Job Seeker's Guide." In theory, the concept should work well. The OOH provides up-to-date information on national trends and earnings in 250 occupational fields and good overviews of the nature of work, etc., but it offers no tips on job searching. In practice, however, the concept suffers in comparison to the available alternatives. While this guide's job searching section does cover the necessary basics, it doesn't measure up to the advice and coaching of a more in-depth resource solely dedicated to the subject. So, "The Job Seeker's Guide" cannot be considered a "selling point." As for the OOH portion, the same material can be viewed online at the OOH's website, which is "free" and far easier to use (better search engines). (See review.) Job seekers without Internet access can find the same material plus lots more in Jist's book, "The Enhanced Occupational Outlook Handbook," a superior choice. (See review.)

Where To Find/Buy:

Bookstores and libraries.

Overall Rating
★★★
OOH career descriptions plus tips and advice on job search basics

Design, Ease Of Use
★★★
Very well organized, includes graphics, bulleted points and tables

1–4 Stars

Publisher:
VGM Career Horizons

Edition:
1997

Price:
$18.95

Pages:
507

ISBN:
0844245283

Media:
Book

Principal Subject:
Career/Job Descriptions

★★★

Overall Rating
★★★
Profiles of industries, not occupations; statistics, facts and charts galore

Design, Ease Of Use
★★★
Tables and bullet points convey data quickly

1–4 Stars

Author:
The Occupational Outlook Handbook was produced in the Bureau of Labor Statistics under the general guidance and direction of Ronald E. Kutscher, Associated commissioner for Employment Projections and Neal H. Rosenthal, Chief, division of Occupation Outlook.

Publisher:
JIST

Edition:
1998

Price:
$16.95

Pages:
207

ISBN:
156370465X

Media:
Book

Principal Subject:
Career/Job Descriptions

Career And Job Descriptions

CAREER GUIDE TO AMERICA'S TOP INDUSTRIES
An Essential Guide To Industry Trends And Opportunities

Description:
This resource book reviews the top 40 industries in the United States. The work is divided into two major sections: Goods-producing industries and Service-producing industries. The first section covers fields such as Agricultural Services, Construction, Steel Manufacturing, Food Processing and Aerospace careers. The Service-producing industries section contains fields like Advertising, Banking, Air Transportation and Educational Services. Each industry "profile" includes information on working conditions, the nature of the industry, employment, different occupations in the industry, training necessary, advancement potential, earnings, and future outlook. A number of tables are used throughout the work to display research and statistical figures relating to the specific industry. Also included in this text is a section titled "Sources of State and Local Job Outlook Information," which can be used to find job market and career information pertaining to specific states.

Evaluation:
Although the information included in this book is based on analysis from the United States Department of Labor, this is not a reproduction or revised version of the famous Occupational Outlook Handbook (OOH). Instead, Jist has designed this guide to function as a companion resource to the OOH; it offers profiles of industries in contrast to the OOH's profiles of occupational fields. That means that while readers will find brief descriptions of specific jobs in each industry, the vast majority of these profiles are dedicated to industry-wide data: i.e. employment outlook, salaries, etc. As the editors state in their introduction, this is a guide for people who "think in terms of industries, rather than occupations." For readers who fall into that category, this is a fine tool for researching market and labor trends within individual industries. For job hunters who seek information on particular careers or job titles, Jist's print resource "The Enhanced Occupational Outlook Handbook" is a better choice. (See review).

Where To Find/Buy:
Bookstores and libraries.

Career And Job Descriptions

CAREERS FOR CYBERSURFERS & OTHER ONLINE TYPES (SERIES)

★★★

Description:

Though there is a brief introduction to the Internet, the authors' approach assumes (at least) a familiarity with the medium. "Background" information is provided, however, for each of the Internet-related jobs presented. For instance, in Chapter 2 "Providing Access to the Internet," a diagram illustrates the Internet's "traffic pattern," and network access points and "major backbone operators" are detailed. To give readers an idea of the types of jobs available, online providers such as America Online are referenced, and a few specific jobs, i.e. "junior programmer," are described. There are also personal success stories and addresses to pertinent websites. Subsequent chapters are formatted in a similar manner: general overview of the job area, company-as-illustration, examples, etc. Job areas explored include outfitting companies/individuals with the proper hardware, software development, and Webmaster. "Becoming an Internet Entrepreneur" offers additional "start-up" advice.

Evaluation:

This isn't the "final destination" for job searchers interested in the Internet, but it is a great "first step." The authors cover a variety of careers, from the well-known, i.e. access providers and Webmasters, to the lesser known, such as webcasting, online banking, and "information brokers." Although the guide's wide scope precludes an in-depth analysis of any one field, it has definite advantages. Not only can readers get an idea of "what's out there" in cyberspace, they'll also be enthused about the myriad job/career possibilities. The chapter on "Becoming an Internet Entrepreneur" is guaranteed to start the mind's wheels spinning. If there is one thing the authors (implicitly) emphasize, it's that everyone, in some capacity, can find worthwhile opportunities on the Net. This a valuable resource for any job searcher, cybersurfer or not, and may be especially pertinent to potential entrepreneurs and readers who'd love to work at home.

Where To Find/Buy:

Bookstores and libraries.

Overall Rating
★★★
Introduces readers to the myriad possibilities of the Net; valuable website addresses

Design, Ease Of Use
★★★
Well written, explicit language; uses diagrams to illustrate difficult concepts

1–4 Stars

Author:
Marjorie Eberts and Rachel Kelsey

Ms. Eberts is the author of more than 60 books; she also has a nationally syndicated newspaper column, "Dear Teacher." Ms. Kelsey has extensive experience with computers and has written several software programs. Both are graduates of Stanford University.

Publisher:
VGM Career Horizons

Edition:
1998

Price:
$14.95

ISBN:
0844222968

Media:
Book

Principal Subject:
Career/Job Descriptions

Secondary Subject:
Entrepreneurship

II. Career Exploration And Research

★★★

Career And Job Descriptions

THE AMERICAN ALMANAC OF JOBS AND SALARIES

Overall Rating
★★★
A smart, comprehensive career/salary guide with a sociological bent; wide-ranging

Design, Ease Of Use
★★
Well-written but very dense; lots of material to wade through; searching can be tricky

1–4 Stars

Author:
John W. Wright

Publisher:
Avon Books

Edition:
(6th) 1996

Price:
$20.00

Pages:
644

ISBN:
0380783614

Media:
Book

Principal Subject:
Career/Job Descriptions

Description:

It is Mr. Wright's goal to present reliable data on a wide range of occupations and their salaries. The data is arranged by "type" into such chapters as "On the Public Payroll" (i.e. government jobs), "In the Public Eye and Behind the Scenes" (i.e. entertainers, producers), "Science and Technology," "The Five Standard Professions" (i.e. doctor, lawyer), and "Key White Collar Jobs" (i.e. public relations). There are also chapters on business professions, jobs in health care, and the "workaday world" (i.e. clerks, trade workers). The information provided for each job is primarily statistic-oriented, aimed at salaries and job growth. (Charts are frequently employed.) Descriptive segments are scattered throughout: introductory overviews of the jobs/industries, opportunities for employment, tips on finding work, etc. The final chapter offers advice for "special groups," i.e. women, minorities, temporary workers, new MBAs, etc., as well as strategies for job searching. An index of job titles is included for "searching."

Evaluation:

As the title suggests, this is a book with two missions: to describe a wide variety of "jobs" and to provide salary information on said "jobs." It can be used, then, for myriad purposes: introductory information and research for job seekers, guidelines for career changers, women seeking equal pay for equal work, etc. Salary and job growth data is the primary focus, but the "job" descriptions do offer basic ideas about employment opportunities (type of work, where the work is done, etc.) The book is very dense, so searching for specific titles can be tedious: there are so many specific jobs under each general "area" that most readers will find themselves flipping back and forth between the index and the text. For example, look up "advertising" in the index, and you'll find 8 titles with varying page numbers, from "creative department personnel" to "actors in." Still, it's the guide's comprehensive nature which makes it a valuable resource. For a smart, informative catalog of careers/salaries, this is the book.

Where To Find/Buy:

Bookstores and libraries.

Career And Job Descriptions

★ ★

100 BEST CAREERS FOR THE 21ST CENTURY

Description:

Ms. Field has divided her guide into eleven sections: Medical Technology/Health Care, Geriatrics, Computers, Conservation/ Environment, Advertising/Communications/Public Relations, Sales/ Service, Fitness/Nutrition, Education, Hospitality/Travel, Science/ Engineering, and Home-Based Businesses. Each section begins with a brief introduction to the field(s) and a list of the individual careers profiled therein. Career profiles contain descriptions of the job and its responsibilities, employment and advancement opportunities, "expanding opportunities for the 21st century," earnings, and education/experience requirements. There are also "tips" for getting a job, resources for further information, and "summary boxes" for quick reference. For Home-Based Businesses, the summary boxes are expanded to include required equipment and supplies, "possible clients," and "details to consider" (i.e. zoning). Addresses and phone numbers for all trade associations and other organizations cited appear in the appendix.

Evaluation:

Ms. Field's list contains the typical fields/industries considered to be "growing," i.e. health care, technology, etc. The best inclusion is the section on Home-Based Businesses, not necessarily because of the business suggestions she makes, but because of the awareness of entrepreneurial possibilities she inspires. The career profiles are relatively in depth, in comparison to other such guides, and the "employment opportunities" give readers a clear idea of where to target their initial job search. The "tips" she provides for each career field can be overly simplistic, i.e. "try to . . . get hands-on experience." For a "starting point" in career choice, this is an adequate resource. However, readers should be aware that all job-trend forecasters use their own criteria for selecting the "best jobs." In this case, "best" means soon-to-be-in-demand, e.g. "fastest growing." But just because a job will be in-demand doesn't mean it will be high-paying, satisfying, or have advancement possibilities.

Where To Find/Buy:

Bookstores and libraries.

Overall Rating
★★
General overview of "growing" careers; some helpful "tips"

Design, Ease Of Use
★★★
Simple, straightforward format; detailed "contents," "summary boxes"

1–4 Stars

Author:
Shelly Field

Publisher:
Macmillan

Edition:
1996

Price:
$15.95

Pages:
304

ISBN:
0028605950

Media:
Book

Principal Subject:
Career/Job Descriptions

II. Career Exploration And Research

★★

Career And Job Descriptions

CAREER SMARTS
Jobs With A Future

Overall Rating
★★
Solid overview of 175 "high growth" jobs; good self-assessment tools

Design, Ease Of Use
★★★
Well written and organized

1–4 Stars

Author:
Martin Yate

Martin Yate's books include: *Knock 'Em Dead, Cover Letters That knock 'Em Dead*, and *Beat the Odds*. His previous positions include National Director of Training for Dunhill Personal System, Inc. and Director of Personal for Bell Industries' Computer Memory Division.

Publisher:
Ballantine (Random House)

Edition:
1997

Price:
$14.95

Pages:
484

ISBN:
0345395956

Media:
Book

Principal Subject:
Career/Job Descriptions

Description:

In this guide, the emphasis is on "healthy" jobs—jobs that will have the "greatest stability and opportunity for professional advancement over the coming years." According to the author, this book is about: "building a profession in the jobs that are going to be in demand tomorrow." Part One: "About the Jobs and Your Career Future," walks readers through a process of finding a job that fits their "unique personal preferences" and "professional competencies." Among the self-appraisal exercises are worksheets for creating "Mobility" and "Affinity" profiles. Part Two: "The Job Descriptions and Industry Analysis" presents the 175 jobs. Each job profile includes information on daily responsibilities, salary range, and future growth, as well as a "Professional Competency" table. The table rates different aspects of the job, i.e. leadership, experimentation, creativity, variety, etc., as "low," "average," or "high." Readers can thereby "match" career possibilities with the results of their self-assessment exercises.

Evaluation:

For a dual-purpose career guide—one that combines self-assessment with career choice—this isn't a bad one. The author is ambiguous about the source of his "high growth" job picks; he alludes to "federal statistics" and "interviews." Still, with jobs like electrical engineer and physical therapist, he's hedging his bets; of course there will be a need for home health care workers, the baby boomers are aging. Actually, like many guides on "secure" jobs, the 175 careers detailed here will come as little surprise to anyone who hasn't been hiding in a cave for 20 years. (This isn't the best choice for "creative" types!) However, the first section, dedicated to commentary and self-assessment, is nicely done. Mr. Yate is smart, easy to read, and, occasionally, quite insightful. For a decent introduction to "high growth" careers and some valuable self-assessment tasks, this is a good bet. (If you're looking for an in depth analysis of labor market trends, try "The Best Jobs for the 21st Century." See review)

Where To Find/Buy:

Bookstores and libraries.

Career And Job Descriptions

JOBS '98
From Entry-Level To Executive Positions—Leads On More Than 40 Million Jobs

★ ★

Description:
To organize the enormous bulk of job market information provided here, the authors have divided the material into 3 sections: "Career Outlooks," "Industry Forecasts," and "Regional Roundup." "Career Outlooks" describes a variety of career fields: i.e. accountants, scientists, journalists, etc. Each career "profile" contains a "brief background" of the field and segments on "employment outlook," "what's next" (future trends, changes in employment patterns), and salaries. There are contact addresses for major employers and for professional associations, directories, and magazines. "Industry Forecasts" explores various industries (i.e. aviation, utilities) in a similar manner. The "profiles" include an "industry outlook," "what's next," jobs "in demand," and contact addresses for top employers, etc. "Regional Roundup" discusses employment trends/ major employers by region (U.S.). The authors also provide a "how to use this book" introduction and a "special report" on using the Internet for job searching.

Evaluation:
It is difficult to gauge the effectiveness of this guide. On the one hand, its promoters claim readers "can access over 40 million jobs" by writing to the companies listed or networking via the professional associations, directories, etc., whose addresses are provided. No doubt a dedicated job searcher and avid networker could reap some benefits from mass mailings, but not everyone feels comfortable with that method of job searching. Of course, this is not just a "directory" of contacts. The authors offer lots of job market information, i.e. employment trends in industries and regions. This information is certainly valuable, but how helpful is it? Would you relocate if your job was "in demand" in another state? Would you cease hunting for an editing job if you knew the competition was "high" and the prospects only "fair?" (Keep in mind, too, that the careers described here are "umbrella" fields, not specific job titles.) Overall, this resource is best suited for serious networkers for whom "employment outlook" is a priority.

Where To Find/Buy:
Bookstores and libraries.

Overall Rating
★★
Primarily concerned with employment trends; nationwide contact/employer addresses

Design, Ease Of Use
★★★
Fairly well formatted, dense; includes a "how to use this book" introduction

1–4 Stars

Author:
Kathryn Petras, Ross Petras, and George Petras

Publisher:
Fireside

Edition:
4th (1997)

Price:
$16.00

Pages:
688

ISBN:
0684818264

Media:
Book

Principal Subject:
Career/Job Descriptions

Secondary Subject:
Employer Research

★★

Overall Rating
★★
Limited useful information

Design, Ease Of Use
★★
Confusing; disorganized

1–4 Stars

Author:
Gail Kuenstler

Gail Kuenstler, a trained anthropologist who published her first book in 1988, has worked as a full-time career counselor since 1986.

Publisher:
Career Press

Edition:
1996

Price:
$12.99

Pages:
247

ISBN:
1564142256

Media:
Book

Principal Subject:
Career/Job Descriptions

Career And Job Descriptions

THE CAREER ATLAS
How To Find A Good Job When Good Jobs Are Hard To Find

Description:

Ms. Kuenstler begins her guide with 5 chapters on "general" job searching. There is advice on "choosing a career," "preparing" for the job hunt (i.e. networking,), and "career-changing." Interactive exercises are provided for "self-assessment." The bulk of Ms. Kuenstler's work, however, is dedicated to examining the "career paths" to 130 occupations. The occupations are divided into broad categories, "Selling and Managing," "Arts and Communications," "The Sciences," etc., which are then subdivided into "fields," i.e. "hospitality," and jobs within each field, i.e. "cook." (Readers can also search for job titles via the index.) Individual job descriptions comprise about a paragraph-long overview followed by a number of "paths" leading to the job. For example, under hotel manager the "paths" presented include: internship, on-the-job training, assisting a convention services manager, bachelor's degree in hotel management, and running your own restaurant. Stories and anecdotes are used for illustration throughout.

Evaluation:

What distinguishes this guide from its "career description" peers is the author's tactic: focus on the "paths" and "routes" to various jobs, rather than the jobs themselves. Although such a guide cannot hope to replace an extensive, in depth look at careers, i.e. "The Enhanced Occupational Outlook Handbook" (see review), it could be used in tandem with such a resource. If it was well done. Unfortunately, Ms. Kuenstler's guide isn't well done. It's poorly organized. For example, she uses the ambiguous category "Solving Practical Problems" to group such divergent fields as "law enforcement," "hospitality," and "horticulture." Why? The author's greatest failure, however, is the less-than-insightful nature of her "path" suggestions. To be a biologist, she suggests working as a lab tech, interning, getting a B.A. in biology, or getting a Ph.D. in biology. Um, OK. Is there really anyone out there who has to pay $13 for that advice? This "Atlas" will get you on the "road" to your career, but you'd have to be very "lost" to need it.

Where To Find/Buy:

Bookstores and libraries.

EMPLOYER RESEARCH

Researching Potential Employers

During the initial stages of job research, it may be helpful to use employer guides to learn who the players are in your field of interest. Guides may be based on a geographic area (the greater Seattle area, for example) or on a specific field, such as health care or technology. Separate guides for the non-profit sector have proliferated, offering job seekers access to a host of information about foundations, trusts, organizations, staff led support groups and other non-profit employers.

Prior To Interviews

Remember that employers are people and they are proud of what they do. A classic example is that employees at Microsoft when interviewing candidates often ask what they know about the company. Candidates who are up to speed on the latest accomplishments and ventures of the firm are more often successful at landing jobs.

You can learn more about companies or organizations through annual reports and news reports. In this chapter, we highlight both print and Internet-based sources of information. Knowing about the employer can give you a competitive edge over other job candidates and make you feel more confident heading into the interview. The important issue is that you can talk intelligently to them about what they are doing. There is nothing less appealing to an employer than a perspective employee who doesn't even know what the company does.

★★★★

Overall Rating
★★★★
A great list of regional employers; includes job searching strategies

Design, Ease Of Use
★★★
Easy to use, straightforward format

1–4 Stars

Author:
Adams Media Corporation is a publisher of career books and software products, including the online resource CareerCity.

Publisher:
Adams

Edition:
9th (1997)

Price:
$16.95

Pages:
325

ISBN:
1558507914

Media:
Book

Principal Subject:
Employer Research

Employer Research

1998 SEATTLE JOBBANK (SERIES)
The Job Hunter's Guide To Washington

Recommended For:
Employer Research

Description:
The premise for Adams' "The . . . JobBank" series is to help job seekers make "direct contact" with employers in specific regions of the U.S. Each book in the series is divided into 5 sections: an introduction ("how to use this book"), "The Job Search," "Primary Employers," "Employment Services," and an alphabetized employer index. "The Job Search" section offers strategies for "job winning," (i.e. interviewing, networking), writing resumes and cover letters, and using the Internet. Section 2 arranges thousands of "Primary Employers" into industry categories (i.e. health care). All of the employer listings provide contact information; many also include a description of the company and its products/services. There are also hundreds of "secondary" listings for small- and mid-sized employers. Under "Employment Services," readers will find contact information and descriptions of temporary and permanent employment agencies, executive search firms, and contract services firms.

Evaluation:
Although they offer no statistics, Adams' claim that the "direct contact" method of job hunting is more effective than answering or perusing want ads is probably true. Still, if networking is the "top" method of finding jobs, it's hard to gauge where on the "scale" "direct contact" resides. Certainly job seekers who are great at "cold calls" and terrific at "selling themselves" will benefit the most from this guide. And, if that's your cup of tea, "The . . . JobBank" series is definitely a "best bet." By focusing on specific regions, these books offer a wider variety and greater number of employer listings than their competitors. (Even though the titles imply only citywide coverage, the books often encompass "greater areas;" for example, "The Seattle JobBank" includes Bellevue, Tacoma, Spokane, etc.) The series also features the "bonus" of smart job search strategies for networking, interviewing, using the Net, etc. Readers will need to do additional company research on their own, but for a list of regional employers, this is the place to go.

Where To Find/Buy:
Bookstores and libraries.

Employer Research

JOBBANK GUIDE TO COMPUTER & HIGH-TECH COMPANIES (SERIES)

★★★

 Recommended For:
Employer Research

Description:

As a "branch" of Adams' "The . . . JobBank" series, these guides share the same general format. The material is divided into 6 sections, beginning with a "how to use this book" introduction. Section 2 encompasses "The Job Search," providing strategies for "job winning" (i.e. networking, interviewing), writing resumes and cover letters, and using the Internet effectively. "Primary Employers" are arranged by "category" in Section 3. (The "Computer & High-Tech Companies" book, for example, has such categories as "computer consultants," "software developers," and "Internet providers.") The employer listings contain contact addresses and may include a description of the company and its services/products and/or relevant hiring information. Listings for executive search firms and permanent employment agencies comprise Section 4; Section 5 lists addresses for professional associations. The sixth section is dedicated to search indexes: readers can search for employers by name or geographic region (U.S.).

Evaluation:

As an "outgrowth" of Adams' "The . . . JobBank" series (employer listings by region), these guides were also created as "direct contact" tools. That is, the premise is to enable job seekers to find job openings by pursuing the company via "direct contact," rather than by waiting for the company to pursue them via want ads. For job seekers interested in this method of job hunting and who want to work within the high-tech or health care industries, these guides are a more rewarding choice than their regional brethren. There are more listings to choose from, similar job search strategies, and readers can always use the geographical index to find entries in a given area. As is the case with other employer directories, the listings are mainly addresses, not in-depth company profiles; be prepared to conduct further research. Also, consumers should check out Adams' online resource "CareerCity" (see review), which offers special sections for high-tech and health care employment.

Where To Find/Buy:

Bookstores and libraries.

Overall Rating
★★★
Thousands of industry-specific employer listings, plus basic job search strategies

Design, Ease Of Use
★★★★
Well formatted, includes search indexes and a "how to use this book" introduction

1–4 Stars

Author:
Adams Media Corporation is a publisher of career books and software products, including the online resource CareerCity.

Publisher:
Adams

Edition:
1997

Price:
$16.95

Pages:
694

ISBN:
155850740X

Media:
Book

Principal Subject:
Employer Research

★★★

Overall Rating
★★★
Introductory information and addresses for 100 nonprofits; a good place to start

Design, Ease Of Use
★★★
Straightforward layout; includes one "category"-type search index

1–4 Stars

Author:
Leslie Hamilton and Robert Tragert

Ms. Hamilton and Mr. Tragert are a wife-and-husband writing and researching team. Ms. Hamilton is also the author of *The Cheapskate's Guide to Living Cheaper and Better* (Carol Publishing); Mr. Tragert has worked in a variety of environmental areas.

Publisher:
Arco

Edition:
1998

Price:
$16.95

Pages:
282

ISBN:
0028618408

Media:
Book

Principal Subject:
Employer Research

Secondary Subject:
Career/Job Descriptions

Of Interest To:
Interested In Non-Profit Sector

100 BEST NONPROFITS TO WORK FOR
Find Your Dream Job—And Launch A Rewarding Career Doing Good!

Description:

For many people, the ideal job combines "doing well" with "doing good." Many nonprofit organizations can meet that need; now, more than ever, successful nonprofits can offer career stability and competitive levels of compensation. Of the 700,000 nonprofits operating in America, this guide profiles those "most likely" to offer "excellent employment opportunities." The 100 organizations chosen meet at least 3 out of 4 criteria: a staff of at least 100 employees, an operating budget of at least $1,000,000, at least 3 years in operation, and a strong "internal mission orientation" (e.g. dedicated personnel). Each profile provides contact information (including URLs), a summary of the nonprofit's operations and its mission statement, budgeting and staff data, advice on finding work, a "potent quote" by or about the group, and a segment on "what to expect." Profiles are arranged by name, and by category, i.e. "art-related, health-related," in the index. Further resources are detailed in the appendices.

Evaluation:

Job seekers interested in nonprofit work, caution the authors, should be aware of certain factors. First, as a reflection of their success, many of the organizations detailed in this guide are very "popular" (i.e. Amnesty International, American Red Cross), and paying jobs with such nonprofits are highly competitive. In addition, many of the paying jobs available at nonprofits (including those mentioned or alluded to here) are "specialized," since the non-specialized work is usually done by volunteers. For example, many of the research-oriented organizations are looking for candidates with advanced degrees (PhDs, MAs, etc.), and many of the medical/health groups are looking for MDs, RNs, etc. Keep in mind, too, that most nonprofits hire "from within," e.g. their volunteers. That said, this guide offers a fine place to start researching nonprofit employment options. The profiles are fairly brief, but they do provide an introductory overview, and they always include the organization's URL, for further research.

Where To Find/Buy:

Bookstores and libraries.

Employer Research

HOOVER'S ONLINE

★★★

Description:

Since Hoover's Online is a product of Hoover's, Inc., the business, not all of the information found at this site is free. (The site map distinguishes between free material and "member-only" terrain; use it, rather than the home page, to navigate.) What can be accessed, free of charge, are the 13,000 "Company Capsules," the 2–3 page "Industry Snapshots," Hoover's list of "top employers," and links to other online resources ("Career Resources," "List of Lists"). Users can search for "Company Capsules" by company name, by ticker, or by keyword. Each "Capsule" includes contact information (direct links if possible), "key numbers" (i.e. number of employees, sales figures), "key names" (i.e. president), and links to related sites, resources, and the corresponding "Industry Snapshot." The "Industry Snapshots" provide a descriptive overview, revenue data, "insider" trivia, and links to "example" businesses and relevant organizations. The list of "top employers" is linked to employer sites and to the "Company Capsules."

Evaluation:

Despite the fact that a large portion of this site is inaccessible to visitors (e.g. much of the content is for "members only"), this is still a valuable place to begin employer research. The "Company Capsules" are not as expansive as (for example) JobWeb's employer profiles, but there are lots to choose from (13,000) and they do supply the necessary basics: "key numbers," contact information, links, etc. They also represent a wide variety of employers. The "Industry Snapshots," while general overviews, are informative and engaging; they're actually fun to read. The list of "top employers" is fine too, and users can browse the list alphabetically, rather than searching by name or keyword. For non-members, the site doesn't offer much else; the links to "Career Resources" are too few and the "List of Lists" is just links to such lists as "The Biggest Companies & Richest People" and "Top Brands." Still, for free company information, Hoover's Online is a good place to start.

Where To Find/Buy:

On the Internet at http://www.hoovers.com

Overall Rating
★★★
A good starting place for researching companies/ employers

Design, Ease Of Use
★★★
Straightforward format; use the site map to navigate

1–4 Stars

Author:
Hoover's, Inc. is an Austin-based publisher of company information. In addition to their web site, Hoover's also publishes business reference books and software products.

Publisher:
Hoover's, Inc.

Edition:
1998

Media:
Internet

Principal Subject:
Employer Research

★★★

Overall Rating
★★★
Not a job search site, but a great research/information gathering tool

Design, Ease Of Use
★★
Difficult language; arduous to navigate

1–4 Stars

Author:
EDGAR, the Electronic Data Gathering, Analysis, and Retrieval system, performs automated collection, validation, indexing, acceptance, and forwarding of submissions by companies and others who file forms with the U.S. Securities and Exchange Commission.

Publisher:
U.S. Securities and Exchange Commission

Edition:
1998

Media:
Internet

Principal Subject:
Employer Research

Employer Research

EDGAR DATABASE OF CORPORATE INFORMATION

Description:
The EDGAR Database of corporate information is the U.S. Securities and Exchange Commission's (SEC) system for automated collection, analysis, indexing, etc., of the various forms public companies (and others) are required to file with the SEC. Since these forms include the annual report on Form 10-K or 10-KSB, which provides much of the same information found in a company's "annual report to shareholders," a comprehensive overview of the company's business, and "contact information" (mailing and business addresses), job searchers can use this site to research a company, prepare for an interview, etc. (For an explanation of all the types of forms filed at EDGAR, there's a "Guide to Corporate Filings," accessible from the home page.) EDGAR offers 2 "general" mechanisms for searching the database: by company name and by keyword. A search results in a list of company filings, arranged by date. Users can then click on a specific submission, i.e. the latest Form 10-K, to access that file.

Evaluation:
Obviously, the EDGAR database is not a job search site, per se. Since its main function is to "increase the efficiency and fairness of the securities market for . . . investors, corporations, and the economy," it isn't glossy, attractive, simple, or particularly user-friendly. However, users interested in learning about specific public companies, whether for research purposes or to prepare for an interview, will find valuable information at EDGAR. Here's what you do: use the "quick forms lookup" search interface to find a company's filings, click on the latest Form 10-K, and (unless you're really dedicated and patient, or you really know what you're doing) ignore the rest. The Form 10-K or 10-KSB has a wealth of detailed company data: a comprehensive overview of the business, financial data, legal proceedings, etc. (There's a mini table of contents, but no internal links; you'll have to scroll through the pages.) Though it can be difficult to navigate, this is a "must visit" for serious researchers.

Where To Find/Buy:
On the Internet at http://www.sec.gov/edgarhp.htm

Employer Research

INTERNET NONPROFIT CENTER

★★★

Description:

The Internet Nonprofit Center provides several tools for researching nonprofits, each of which are introduced on the home page. There's a "Library" of resources, such as bibliographies, featured essays, and a list of "Top 40 Charities." (At this time, 23 of the "Top 40" are profiled; profiles contain a link to the charity's home page, descriptions of its "purpose" and "activities," and statistics on its staff size, annual income.) Other features include a "Gallery" of links to nonprofit home pages and a "Parlor" for live chat and browsing volunteer postings. The site also enable visitors to find the addresses/locations of over 1 million tax-exempt organizations by using the "Nonprofit Locator." The "Locator" uses a keyword (i.e. "arts") and a U.S. state to search a database of information supplied by the IRS. The results of a search are an alphabetized (by name) list of nonprofits; click on the nonprofit's name for the address and IRS field and code data, or use the "MapBlast" feature to pinpoint the exact location on a map.

Evaluation:

OK, the site needs an overhaul, but it still contains some valuable tools. There's the list of "Top 40 Charities" and accompanying 23 profiles, the bibliographies, and the "Gallery" of links to nonprofit home pages, all of which are good for generating ideas and conducting preliminary research. Even better, there's the "MapBlast" feature, which not only pinpoints an organization's exact location, but also offers "local" information on transportation, airports, accommodations, etc. In fact, "MapBlast" is so cool, it compensates for the site's deficient "Nonprofit Locator." The "Locator" searches by a keyword in the organization's name, rather than a keyword in "area of focus" (e.g. the keyword "human ADJ rights" won't include "Amnesty International" in its results). And forget trying to understand the IRS "codes;" they might be helpful, but they're too poorly explained to decipher. Still, how many other sites can boast the addresses of 1.4 million nonprofits? If it's tax-exempt, you can locate it here.

Where To Find/Buy:

On the Internet at http://www.nonprofits.org

Overall Rating
★★★
Provides valuable "first step" tools for researching nonprofits in the U.S.

Design, Ease Of Use
★★
Easy to navigate, but the search mechanism needs to be improved

1–4 Stars

Author:
Originally sponsored by The American Institute of Philanthropy (today there is no formal relationship), the Internet Nonprofit Center is dedicated to providing fast, free information on nonprofit organizations. It has no paid staff.

Publisher:
Internet Nonprofit Center, Inc.

Edition:
1997

Media:
Internet

Principal Subject:
Employer Research

★ ★

Overall Rating
★★
An easy-to-use directory to 1,000+ nonprofits; a little outdated but still viable

Design, Ease Of Use
★★★
Well formatted, simple search indexes

1–4 Stars

Author:
Donna Colvin

Publisher:
Barricade Books

Edition:
5th (1994)

Price:
$24.00

Pages:
682

ISBN:
0962303283

Media:
Book

Principal Subject:
Employer Research

Of Interest To:
Interested In Non-Profit Sector

Employer Research

GOOD WORKS
A Guide To Careers In Social Change

Description:

To help job seekers find public interest employment, the editors of this guide have compiled over 1,000 profiles of organizations dedicated to social change. The profiles, arranged alphabetically by name in the "Directory," contain information on each organization's "purpose," methods of operation, recent "issues and projects," major publications, budget and funding. Names and addresses for contact, the number of employees and interns, salaries, benefits, and average "work week" hours are also detailed. For searching the entries, there are two indexes: topical (i.e. "energy," "health") and geographical (by state). In addition to the directory, the guide also provides lists of additional resources and profiles of activists currently working in social change. The additional resources comprise publications, networks and associations, and training schools. The "people" profiles demonstrate the diversity of both the work and the backgrounds/motivations of the individuals involved. A "how to use this guide" introduction is included.

Evaluation:

On the one hand, for a (relatively) comprehensive "directory" of nonprofits, "Good Works" does a good job. Its format is simple and the search indexes work well, so it's easy to find entries. The types of organizations profiled are wide-ranging and diverse, although readers should keep in mind that some of these nonprofits are so small that they do not presently have room/money for many employees. (Remember too, when looking at the number of employees, that one of the best ways to get hired by a nonprofit is to volunteer first.) The "activist" profiles are entertaining and inspiring, the lists of additional resources valuable, and the profiles themselves are solid, informative introductions. However (here's the other hand), this directory hasn't been revised since 1994. Unfortunately, the companion website, "Good Works Online" (see review), doesn't offer any updates, just a small job bank and a place to order this book. For now, because there are few thorough directories of nonprofits, this one may still be your best bet. Just be sure to follow up with additional research on the organizations of interest.

Where To Find/Buy:

Bookstores and libraries.

Employer Research

JOBS ALMANAC
All-In-One Career Guide

★★

Description:
Designed to assist with all aspects of the job search, this guide is divided into 5 "parts." Part 1, "The Job Market," explores the current job outlook and the future of America's industries and "major occupations." Part 2 offers strategies for job hunting, writing resumes and cover letters, negotiating salaries, and using the Internet. For researching employment options, there are 7,000 employer profiles. The profiles are arranged by category, i.e. "banking," "communications," etc., in Part 3, and contain contact information and a description of the company. Many profiles also include a list of "common positions," educational requirements, and such statistics as "number of employees." Part 4 explores "Working for the Federal Government," i.e. types of employment, starting salaries, and completing the application, etc. Search indexes, such as a geographical index of employers, are provided in Part 5. The "introduction" is an annotated list of the main topics, to be used in tandem with the table of contents.

Evaluation:
Due to the nature of the material found here, one cannot help but make comparisons between this guide and other Adams products. For example, the 7,000 employer listings contain no more information than those found in Adams' "The . . . JobBank" series (see review), which provides thousands of regional listings as well as similar (if not the same) job search strategies. Readers who can narrow their scope by region, therefore, will gain more entries and greater variety from the "JobBank" books. Adams also produces better employer directories for high-tech and health care companies (i.e. "The JobBank Guide to Computer and High-Tech Companies," see review). This guide is especially outshone by Adams' online resource "CareerCity" (see review), which offers access to thousands of employer sites, job searching tips, etc. (Keep in mind that this book's employer listings are primarily addresses; additional research will be required.) In the pantheon of Adams career products, this is the poorest choice.

Where To Find/Buy:
Bookstores and libraries.

Overall Rating
★★
Primarily a nationwide employer directory; does include job search strategies

Design, Ease Of Use
★★★
Logical format; big and cumbersome

1–4 Stars

Author:
Adams Media Corporation is a publisher of career books and software products, including the online resource CareerCity.

Publisher:
Adams

Edition:
1997

Price:
$15.95

Pages:
919

ISBN:
1558507523

Media:
Book

Principal Subject:
Employer Research

Secondary Subject:
All Inclusive Job Search

★★

Overall Rating
★★
Free information is scarce; some helpful "excerpts" and articles

Design, Ease Of Use
★★
User-friendly format, but subject-headings are often deceptive

1–4 Stars

Author:
Vault Reports, Inc. is a producer and publisher of career related resources.

Publisher:
Vault Reports, Inc.

Edition:
1998

Media:
Internet

Principal Subject:
Employer Research

Employer Research

VAULT REPORTS
The Job Seeker's Secret Weapon

Description:

Vault Reports, Inc. produces print resources and extensive employer profiles based on ongoing employee interviews, surveys, and a "network of company infiltrators." Their web site offers visitors free access to over 60 "employer profile excerpts;" users can click on the company name (i.e. ARCO, Coca Cola) from a side bar on the home page, or view the alphabetized "complete list." (Vault Reports provides full-length profiles and 2–3 page "employer snapshots" for a fee.) The "excerpts" contain details on each company's culture, work force, working conditions, and pay rates. Similar "excerpts" of "law firm profiles" are also available. Other sections of the site include "Industry Guides" (brief excerpts from 6 print resources), "Employment Classifieds," and "Career Advice." In "Career Advice," users will find articles on such work-related subjects as "Evaluating the Job Offer," "Writing Scannable Resumes," and "Temping," as well as links, "celebrity interviews and profiles," and reviews of the "top 10 job-posting sites."

Evaluation:

As is too often the case with online resources, visitors are lured into the site by deceptive descriptions of the site's content only to discover, several clicks later, that the really juicy stuff isn't free. Unfortunately, that is precisely the scenario at the Vault Reports site. The home page employs misleading "bait and switch" tactics: only after clicking on such headings as "Employer Profiles" is it made apparent that the complete profile is available for a fee. There are "excerpts," and these "excerpts" do contain some helpful data for job seekers researching the specific companies they represent, but 60+ employers of widely varying types makes for limited browsing. (The employers range from Microsoft to Proctor & Gamble.) And don't even bother to click on the "Industry Guides," they're just advertisements. Overall, unless you're prepared to order the full-length employer reports, this site is only worth a quick visit. If the company you're researching is on the side bar menu, stay and read the "excerpt;" if not, move on.

Where To Find/Buy:

On the Internet at http://www.vaultreports.com/

Employer Research

HIDDEN JOB MARKET 1998
2,000 High-Growth Companies That Are Hiring At Four Times The National Average!

★

Description:

Manufacturers and developers of technology products are one of America's fastest-growing business segments. Since these companies are hiring at "nearly four times the national average," they represent myriad job opportunities for candidates with backgrounds in technology, engineering, chemistry, physics, and business skills (i.e. finance, human resources). To help career-changers with their job searching/researching, this guide offers profiles of 2,000 such "high growth" employers. The profiles provide contact information and the number of job openings in the past year; they're arranged alphabetically by state and by company. Readers can search entries by city or by industry (i.e. "pharmaceuticals"), via the indexes. Quick reference icons indicating industry "type" appear beside each listing. In addition to the profiles, the guide also includes interview "checklists," a discussion of hiring trends affecting high-tech and low-tech jobs, and tips for "Getting the Job You Want."

Evaluation:

Despite the presence of rudimentary job searching tips and interview "checklists," this is basically a directory of high-growth companies involved in manufacturing and developing technology products. Although the guide offers readers a list of 2,000 such companies, it offers little else. The "profiles" comprise an address (for contact), the company's industry "type," and a few basic statistics (number of job openings, annual sales, number of employees). That's it. The listings don't include any information on products, type of job openings, company history, etc. Recent graduates with suitable backgrounds (technology, engineering, etc.) may find this guide of use as a preliminary resource, but there are better resources for conducting employer research. Keep in mind that CorpTech's 45,000 employer database can be found online at www.corptech.com. Nonmembers can search similarly brief "profiles" by company name, while members (for a fee) can access more extensive data.

Where To Find/Buy:

Bookstores and libraries, or order directly 800-338-3282.

Overall Rating
★
A list of companies that manufacture and/or develop technology products

Design, Ease Of Use
★★
Directory-style format; search indexes can be difficult to use

1–4 Stars

Author:
CorpTech

Corporate Technology Information Services, Inc. (CorpTech) is a supplier of company information on America's manufacturers and developers of technology products. CorpTech surveys over 45,000 companies and updates its database annually.

Publisher:
Peterson's

Edition:
(7th) 1997

Price:
$18.95

Pages:
306

ISBN:
1560798343

Media:
Book

Principal Subject:
Employer Research

II. Career Exploration And Research

CAREER
TRANSITIONS

CAREER TRANSITIONS

Being in transition can be a disorienting, disconcerting experience. When the transition involves your career, anxiety and fear may accompany the change as well. Whether the transition emerges from a slowly building dissatisfaction with your present job, or results from a brutal round of layoffs, the experience can be difficult to negotiate.

Career transitions involve high stakes. Whether you are reentering the work force after a season away or leaving the security of corporate America to strike out as a consultant, the transition from the familiar through the unknown can be intimidating. The transition may bring up some deeply rooted, emotionally laden issues and concerns: financial security, self-esteem, family stability, relocation, self-identity, a sense of purpose, fear of rejection or fear of failure. On the other hand, transitions can be a time of exhilaration at finally "doing it," whatever that long awaited "it" might be. Usually it is a combination of both reactions.

The resources reviewed in this chapter approach the topic very differently. Some come across like a business school case study; others carry a poetic and therapeutic tone. Some coax you to embrace the transition period as a time filled with possibilities for all sorts of personal, emotional and professional growth. Others act like a road map for getting through to the goal at the other end as quickly as possible. Our descriptions and evaluations should help you find the type of guide you are looking for during this time of transition.

Some rules of thumb:

- It always takes longer than anticipated to make a transition, so plan ahead financially and move cautiously but with a clear direction.

- Don't leave your current position until you have a solid transition plan in place.

- Most real, dramatic career change takes a couple of years for all the planning, retraining and transition.

- Move towards your goal by upgrading skills and getting your employer to let you learn and practice new skills that support your new goals.

Career Transitions

THE CAREER CHASE

 Recommended For:
Career Transitions

Description:
Written for those facing career changes, whether by choice or circumstance, Dr. Harkness' guide focuses on the emotional and psychological factors related to the process. Part 1 details the "problems of change" inherent in the contemporary work world (i.e. feeling caught between the former Industrial Age and the "Age of Runaway Technology,") and the resulting "career shock syndrome." To combat these elements, a "new personality for the future" is needed and the "Type CC Career Chaser" is introduced. The "Career Chaser" thrives in chaos and possesses attributes necessary for "embracing change." Part 2 explores the "levels of career unrest," debunks the "12 deadly myths" that delay change, and analyzes "The Chaos of Change." Four steps for a successful career change are discussed in Part 3: self-assessment, career exploration (research), deciding "our future image," and developing and implementing a "strategic action plan."

Evaluation:
Like Dr. Kranchier's "Dare to Change Your Job and Your Life" (see review), Dr. Harkness' book can be described as both a self-help guide and a philosophical treatise on working. (Dr. Kranchier's guide is reminiscent of "Will to Power;" Dr. Harkness borrows elements from "chaos theory.") Despite differences in vocabulary, both books are, primarily, advocates for changing/developing personal attributes as the best way to stay "on top" of the constantly morphing 21st century work world. There's less "how to" in this guide. The "Type CC Career Chaser" (like Dr. Kranchier's "Quester") embraces change and reeks adaptability—the character trait hailed by both as the key to success in today's job market. The Chaser is also self-reliant, courageous and calm in the midst of chaos. The guide offers insight into today's work psyche, i.e. career identities, underlying fears. The author offers both a fascinating model of how it ought to be and a greater understanding of how it is.

Where To Find/Buy:
Bookstores and libraries.

Overall Rating
★★★★
An intelligent, insightful examination of psychological factors in career changing

Design, Ease Of Use
★★★★
Very well written and organized; engaging

1–4 Stars

Author:
Helen Harkness, Ph.D.

Dr. Harkness is the founder and Executive Director of Career Design Associates, Inc., a company which develops career management programs.

Publisher:
Davies-Black Publishing

Edition:
1997

Price:
$17.95

Pages:
222

ISBN:
0891060987

Media:
Book

Principal Subject:
Career Transitions

Secondary Subject:
Termination/Job Loss

★★★★

Overall Rating
★★★★
A sophisticated, psychological self-help book for changing your approach to work/life

Design, Ease Of Use
★★★★
Engaging, combines personal stories, advice, interactive exercises

1–4 Stars

Author:
Carole Kanchier, Ph.D.

Dr. Kanchier is a psychologist, counselor, instructor, and trainer who writes about career change for business and professional journals.

Publisher:
JIST

Edition:
2nd (1996)

Price:
$14.95

Pages:
332

ISBN:
156370224X

Media:
Book

Principal Subject:
Career Transitions

DARE TO CHANGE YOUR JOB AND YOUR LIFE

 Recommended For:
Career Transitions

Description:
Dr. Kranchier groups people into 3 work-types: "Traditional," "Self-Seeker," and "Quester." "Traditional" workers "passively commit" to work, value "advancement, position, salary," and have low mobility and adaptability. "Self-Seekers" work less and "pass up promotions or . . . business challenges that threaten their comfortable lives." Conversely, Questers take control of their careers, welcome change, have high mobility and adaptability, take risks, and find greater purpose in their work. In this 9-chapter guide, Dr. Kranchier shows readers how to make career changes by becoming Questers. Readers learn which attributes, i.e. self-confidence, Questers share, and how to develop those qualities. Career changing, "career cycles," and job satisfaction are then discussed from a Quester point of view. Finally, Dr. Kranchier examines the "psychological aspects of decision making" and offers a step-by-step plan for "daring to change." Quizzes and interactive exercises are used throughout for self-assessment.

Evaluation:
Dr. Kranchier presents an assortment of thought-provoking ideas in her self-help guide. Simply put, she suggests that changing/developing certain attributes—those she labels "Quester" attributes, such as self-confidence, autonomy, androgyny, innovativeness, etc.—enables you to "take control" of your life in a way that leads to both more satisfying work and to greater mobility/adaptability in today's job market. Her premise is occasionally undermined by a subtle glorification of Questors (she frequently mentions how attractive individual Questers are), but, by the end of the book, even the most hard-boiled cynic will be won over. In today's job market, Questing works. If you want to change not only your career but your attitude, this guide is a good bet; it's intelligent, eloquent, psychologically sound, and difficult to disagree with. A discussion of balance and the potential spill over of these career attributes into every aspect of one's personality would be a welcome addition.

Where To Find/Buy:
Bookstores and libraries.

Career Transitions

IN TRANSITION
From The Harvard Business School Club Of New York's Career Management Seminar

★★★★

 Recommended For:
Career Transitions

Description:

Authors Burton and Wedemeyer have taught the Career Management Seminar for the Harvard Business School Club of Greater New York for the past decade. They've distilled the essentials from their seminar in a dense, sophisticated, engaging paperback. Part I, Putting Things Into Perspective reassures displaced managers that they are not alone, that many competent professionals lose their jobs in today's economy. Part II, Getting To Know You—The Product, presents a series of exercises and questionnaires designed to reveal your "life mission," priorities, style, values, motivation, skills and organizational fit. These exercises require hours, not minutes. Results from the self-awareness process are recorded in a "product specification file." This file is referenced during the product marketing stage (the job search) to make help managers find a job that is both professionally and personally a good match. The final section addresses the job hunt, with detailed attention given to the elements most essential for upper-echelon professionals: interviewing (including the informational or courtesy interview), working with recruiters, networking and negotiating a compensation package.

Evaluation:

The antithesis of the spiritually leaning self-awareness guides on the market, this book reads like a case study with you as the product. Information is presented in bulleted text, under bold headings, with frequent summaries and outlines. In an effort to speak the language of their B-School alum audience, the authors use the you-are-the-product metaphor throughout the book, a habit that could grate someone not used to conceptualizing human development as product specs. The primary difference between this book and others with a similar table of contents is its penetrating coverage of each topic. For example, the self-awareness section goes beyond the common know-your-dreams exercises to include a discussion of first impressions, how you are perceived and the Johari Window. Similarly, the section on priority and goal clarification includes a discussion of the "phantom spectator," the shadowy person we imagine is looking over our shoulder and influences are stated goals, as well as the "hired detective" rankings (our priorities as they would be recorded by an outside observer). The analyses are very helpful in peeling away the "shoulds" and the "oughts" that keep us in jobs and careers for which we are ill-suited. An all around excellent resource. Its title is not misleading. This book is a fantastic tool for managers who are presently employed but anticipate a lay off or find themselves heeding an inner voice calling for a change.

Where To Find/Buy:
Bookstores and libraries.

Overall Rating
★★★★
Geared to managers and upper-echelon professionals

Design, Ease Of Use
★★★★
Clear, logical structure with headings to chart the path

1–4 Stars

Author:
Mary Burton and Richard Wedemeyer

The authors have taught the Career Management Seminar for the Harvard Business School Club of Greater New York since 1980. Ms. Burton provides career coaching to individuals and Mr. Wedemeyer consults to organizations on enhanced employee/employer relationships.

Publisher:
HarperBusiness

Edition:
1991

Price:
$14.00

Pages:
248

ISBN:
0887305717

Media:
Book

Principal Subject:
Career Transitions

★★★

Overall Rating
★★★
An excellent "all-in-one" guide to career-changing

Design, Ease Of Use
★★★★
Plenty of samples, exercises, lists, graphics and tips

1–4 Stars

Author:
William Charland

Dr. Charland is a career counselor and private industry consultant. He is also the author of "Life-Work: Meaningful Employment in an Age of Limits" and "Career Shifting: Starting Over in a Changing Economy."

Publisher:
Alpha Books

Edition:
1998

Price:
$17.95

Pages:
328

ISBN:
0028619773

Media:
Book

Principal Subject:
Career Transitions

Secondary Subject:
All Inclusive Job Search

Career Transitions

THE COMPLETE IDIOT'S GUIDE TO CHANGING CAREERS

 Recommended For:
Career Transitions

Description:
Charland's guide is divided into 4 parts: "Changes," "Directions," "Connections," and "Challenges." "Changes" offers an overview of the central issues in career changing, i.e. the causes of career dissatisfaction (unemployment, "misemployment," mismanagement), focusing on "skill sets" rather than job titles, and "surviving" change financially. It also includes chapters on employer loyalty, analyzing "hot jobs," and networking. Part 2 hopes to aim readers in the right "Directions." The shape of the "new" workplace is examined, as are changes in the economy, employer needs, self-assessment, and setting goals. Job searching is the subject explored in "Connections," i.e. researching, using the Internet, writing resumes, interviewing, etc. In "Challenges," there's advice for "older workers," "younger workers," and overcoming "bad breaks" (i.e. being fired). Lists of resources and "hot" industries, as well as sample letters and resumes, appear in the appendices.

Evaluation:
There's a ton of advice and information packed into this volume, and if it suffers (slightly) by trying to cover "every" aspect of career changing, the same can be said of any purported "all-in-one" guide. Though the resume section isn't as expansive as a "step-by-step" book dedicated to the subject, it provides a solid refresher course, and there are insightful tips for dealing with "problem backgrounds," i.e. being fired or convicted of an offense. The real "selling point" here is the terrific explanation and examination of today's changing marketplace and the issues facing career changers. To avoid the pitfall of trading one unsatisfactory job for another, Charland helps the reader understand how the "new," "outsourcing" marketplace works, how to evaluate "hot jobs" and employers, and how to think and market yourself as a "skills set," rather than a "job title"—a survival must! With this guide, you'll be better educated and better prepared to make a change. (And you don't have to be an "idiot" to take advantage!)

Where To Find/Buy:
Bookstores and libraries.

Career Transitions

CHANGE YOUR CAREER

★★★

Description:
Banning and Friday have combined theory, personal stories, and interactive exercises to create a workbook-style guide to planning and pursuing a second (or third) career. The authors focus on those elements of the job search which are "unique" to their target audience: career changers and those who are reentering the workplace after a long absence (i.e. raising a family). The forces affecting reentry and career change, including the "emotions of change" (i.e. fear, anxiety, anger, etc.), are explored in Chapters 1 and 2. To prepare for the job search, Chapter 3 helps readers "take stock" of their skills, Chapter 4 offers self-help guidance for "turning yourself around," and Chapter 5 examines "your prospects" and "your credentials." Preparation and job search advice comprise Chapters 6–10. Finding jobs through ads, networking, and employment agencies is discussed, as is interviewing, and there is an explanation of how employers use resumes. There are also tips on writing resumes and cover letters and samples of both. The final chapter, Chapter 11, looks at "Operating Your Own Business," i.e. business structure, financing, etc. An appendix of recommended reading is provided.

Evaluation:
Like other resources in the NTC LearningWorks "Here's How" family, this combination workbook/guide places a heavy emphasis on its interactive exercises. Not everyone responds to such a format; some seasoned veterans may find this approach pedantic at best, patronizing at worst. But for people who are reentering the work force after years away, this guide may be one of the better resources available. Think of it as a mini refresher course in career changing and/or job searching. Although the general tone may be considered "less sophisticated" than other guides, the advice and tips are on-target, practical, and strategically sound. All the major job searching issues, from networking to resumes, are addressed, and the exercises, however much they may feel like "homework," are effective and useful to job search preparation. The authors pay particular attention to the needs of women who are reentering the work force and to older career-changers; every section includes suggestions tailored to these two groups. For instance, in the interviewing segment, using maturity to your advantage is discussed, and examples of women who took time off to raise a family (or marry, or care for relatives, etc.) are frequently used to illustrate points. If you're a member of this guide's target audience, this is a resource well worth trying.

Where To Find/Buy:
Bookstores and libraries.

Overall Rating
★★★
Well tailored for women reentering the work force and older career changers

Design, Ease Of Use
★★★★
Easy to use; relies heavily on interactive exercises

1–4 Stars

Author:
Kent Banning and Ardelle Friday

Mr. Banning is a writer and job search consultant. Ms. Friday is a medical social worker who counsels people in career transitions.

Publisher:
NTC LearningWorks

Edition:
1995

Price:
$16.95

Pages:
171

ISBN:
0844266280

Media:
Book

Principal Subject:
Career Transitions

Secondary Subject:
All Inclusive Job Search

Of Interest To:
Returning To The Workplace

III. Career Transitions

★★★

Overall Rating
★★★
A psychological look at career change; good advice for women and minorities

Design, Ease Of Use
★★★
Straightforward organization and language

1–4 Stars

Author:
David P. Helfand, Ph.D.

Dr. Helfand is a professional career counselor and professor.

Publisher:
VGM Career Horizons

Edition:
1996

Price:
$12.95

Pages:
318

ISBN:
0844242748

Media:
Book

Principal Subject:
Career Transitions

Of Interest To:
Women

Career Transitions

CAREER CHANGE

Description:

Dr. Helfand offers two types of guidance for career changers: the universally applicable and the situation specific. Chapters "for everyone" discuss such issues as "adult development and how it affects your life," "conquering your fears," "identifying career options," and self-assessment, i.e. defining "your values." (Interactive exercises are used for evaluation.) Job search techniques, of use to all readers, are espoused in Part 2. "Getting Additional Education, Training, or Experience," time and money management (i.e. financing your job search), research, and networking are among the topics explored. Part 3, "Strategies for Groups with Special Challenges in the Workplace," provides tailor-made advice for career changers in specific situations. Chapters include "Women at Work," "Minorities," "People Over Age 50," "People with Disabilities," "Dual-Career Couples and Single Parents," and "Ex-Military Personnel." There's also a chapter on "Layoffs, Firings, Voluntary Separations, and Related Dilemmas."

Evaluation:

Despite the occasional tips on the practicalities of career changing, such as a few paragraphs on networking, a few on research, this can't be described as a "how to" guide. The author's goal primary goal is to explain and explore the psychology behind/involved with changing careers. If that's the type of information you want, this is a good, "quick-read." Dr. Helfand throws in enough psychological jargon to win readers' confidence, but his approach is more "down to earth" than "highbrow," which may appeal to readers who just want the "general idea." That isn't to say that he is simplistic; the chapter on adult development, for example, is both insightful and educational. Though Dr. Helfand makes an attempt to be "all-inclusive," not all of the "groups with special challenges" will find worthwhile advice. Women will benefit (Dr. Helfand is especially attentive to their needs), as will minorities and people over 50, but the other "special situation" chapters are too brief to pay for the book.

Where To Find/Buy:

Bookstores and libraries.

Career Transitions

THE CAREER DECISIONS PLANNER
When To Move, When To Stay, And When To Go Out On Your Own

★★★

Description:
Millions of people are, as Lloyd says, "vaguely dissatisfied" with their jobs. They're unhappy, but they're not sure why, or what would make them happy. To help such readers understand their situation/motivations and plan accordingly, Lloyd incorporates both interactive self-assessment exercises and case studies into her text. The case studies "teach by example" by presenting an individual's "dilemma," Lloyd's "diagnosis," the "decision" made (to stay, go, etc.), and "what really happened." The first 5 chapters begin by examining common causes of job dissatisfaction. Readers analyze their own job feelings in Chapter 1, while Chapters 2–5 discuss such issues as advancement (not getting promoted), "poisonous" bosses, sabotage via office politics/corporate culture, and "wrong job fit: squeezing size 10 skills into a size 8 job." Chapter 6 addresses the question, "When Is It Bad Enough to Call It Quits?" while Chapter 7 explores the entrepreneurial question: "To Be Boss or Be Bossed." In the final chapter, Lloyd provides tips and techniques for job searching, including advice on setting goals, writing resumes and cover letters, networking, and interviewing.

Evaluation:
Lloyd's guide best addresses the needs and situations of people who work in traditional office/corporate environments. If you fall into that category and are unhappy on the job, this book should help you pinpoint the reasons/causes of your discontent. The exercises are thorough, but not exhaustive; they're straightforward, logical, and on-target. Lloyd's goal is to generate self-knowledge. Thus, the presumption is: once you understand what you want, then you can make a decision. The decision itself is up to you. Lloyd won't tell you what to do, though the case studies she presents do offer a look at the outcome of decisions made by other individuals. (The case studies make up a fair portion of this guide; they're a joy to read and an effective "learn-by-example" device.) If you do decide to leave your job, you'll need another guide to help you along. Lloyd makes a minimal effort to provide job searching tactics and advice, but a single chapter can't compare with a resource solely dedicated to the subject. The same goes for the chapter on entrepreneurism, which only scrapes the surface of a serious, lifestyle-altering choice. This book was designed to be used before a career decision is made, and for that limited purpose, it's a helpful resource.

Where To Find/Buy:
Bookstores and libraries.

Overall Rating
★★★
A preliminary resource for self-assessment and help with career decisions

Design, Ease Of Use
★★★
Simple design; includes interactive exercises and case studies

1–4 Stars

Author:
Joan Lloyd
Ms. Lloyd is the President of Joan Lloyd, Inc., a company specializing in workplace issues. She is also a syndicated columnist.

Publisher:
John Wiley & Sons

Edition:
1992

Price:
$17.95

Pages:
257

ISBN:
0471547328

Media:
Book

Principal Subject:
Career Transitions

III. Career Transitions

★★★

Overall Rating
★★★
A "must visit" for military personnel looking for civilian employment

Design, Ease Of Use
★★★
Well formatted, easy to navigate,

1–4 Stars

Author:
TAO is a cooperative effort by DI-USA, Inc. and the Army Times Publishing Company. DI-USA is a software publishing company founded by former military members.

Publisher:
Army Times Publishing Co. & DI-USA, Inc.

Edition:
1998

Media:
Internet

Principal Subject:
Career Transitions

Secondary Subject:
Job/Resume Online Database

Of Interest To:
Military

Career Transitions

TRANSITION ASSISTANCE ONLINE

Description:
TAO (Transition Assistance Online) is a site specifically designed for service-members and veterans; though its job/resume bank is applicable to both groups, the majority of its features are aimed at those who have recently left the U.S. Armed Forces or who are expecting to leave within the year. All sections of the site, i.e. the job/resume bank, the "Transition Center" and the "Entrepreneur Center," are accessible from the home page. Visitors can search the job database by occupation, region, state, and/or keyword, or browse all employers and job postings. Profiles of "Featured Employers," which contain a brief description of the company and contact addresses, are also provided. In the "Transition Center," users will find articles and advice on "Preparing for Your Transition" and "Conducting Your Career Campaign," i.e. self-assessment, job hunting strategies, resume tips, etc. The "Entrepreneur's Center" offers information and links for investing in a franchise, business plans, and financing.

Evaluation:
For many service members, the U.S. military is the only employer they've had. A civilian job search can, therefore, be a daunting task. TAO is here to help. Its "Transition Center" offers advice that you won't find at "typical" job/career sites, i.e. information on transition assistance programs, preparation, etc., as well as job searching tips (resume writing, etc.) tailored to service members. While the job bank can't compete (in quantity) with the "big guns" at America's Job Bank or the Monster Board, keep in mind that the employers posting jobs here are open to/actively recruiting ex-military personnel. For that reason alone, it's worth a search. Although anyone who is making the transition from military to civilian employment can benefit from the TAO, this site will be most beneficial to those who have served for 10 years or less. (This isn't the best resource for service members who are looking for high-level or executive employment, or for budding entrepreneurs.)

Where To Find/Buy:
On the Internet at http://www.taonline.com

Career Transitions

ATHLETE'S GUIDE TO CAREER PLANNING
Keys To Success From The Playing Field To Professional Life

★★

Description:

The authors are psychologists with extensive experience helping athletes "transition" into careers. Their goal is to help athletes "learn the skills you need to plan effectively for future decisions and future careers." Part 1, "Transitions in Life and Sport," opens with a discussion of the transitions athletes are likely to encounter (i.e. retiring from a sport) with exercises to help readers learn how to manage them effectively. Part 2, "Exploration and Planning," is designed for self-exploration and goal-setting, again with a series of exercises to help athletes assess their values, interests, and skills. In this section, readers can also identify careers that appeal to them, and begin to develop an "action plan." Part 3 of the book, "Career Acquisition," contains information about the job search itself, with tips and strategies for finding a job, writing cover letters and resumes, and handling job interviews. Appendices include lists of career books and sport-related careers.

Evaluation:

For athletes at all stages of their careers, the "real world" lurks somewhere out of bounds, a reality that most will have to deal with sooner or later. Because their college and professional experiences are so unique, athletes may find that the average career guide does not really speak to them, leaving them in a sort of professional "limbo" when it comes time to find a job. This is a limbo which this book aims to fill: it manages to balance career advice with much needed supportive counseling. Exercises are designed to appeal to sports people (i.e. "Your Support Team"), and the writing is down-to-earth and straightforward. At times, the advice tends towards the simplistic, especially in the sections about the job search itself; there are better resources for writing resumes, cover letters, etc. Although this guide addresses the needs of younger athletes, i.e. recent college grads, it effectively addresses the issues facing professional athletes as well. For athletes "transitioning" into more "traditional" careers, this is real find.

Where To Find/Buy:

Bookstores and libraries.

Overall Rating
★★
A unique resource tailored for athletes' career needs

Design, Ease Of Use
★★★
Helpful exercises written in "sports" metaphor

1–4 Stars

Author:
Al Petitpas, Ed.D.; Delight E. Champagne, Ph.D.; Judy Chartrand, Ph.D.; Steven J. Danish, Ph.D.; Shane M. Murphy, Ph.D.

Al Petitpas, Ed.D., is involved in Athletic Counseling. Dr. Champagne is a professor of psychology, Dr. Chartrand is a research scientist for Consulting Psychologists Press. Dr. Danishis a professor of psychology. Dr. Murphy is president of Gold Medal Consultants.

Publisher:
Human Kinetics

Edition:
1997

Price:
$17.95

Pages:
226

ISBN:
0873224590

Media:
Book

Principal Subject:
Career Transitions

Of Interest To:
Athletes

III. Career Transitions

★★

Overall Rating
★★
A popular author dismisses the notion of mid-life crisis and celebrates the transition

Design, Ease Of Use
★★★
Relaxed, friendly style

1–4 Stars

Author:
Barbara Sher

Ms. Sher is a therapist and career counselor who conducts workshops throughout the world. Her best selling books include *Wishcraft, Teamworks!, I Could Do Anything If I Only Knew What It Was* and *Live The Life you Love.*

Publisher:
Delacorte Press

Edition:
1998

Price:
$22.95

Pages:
324

ISBN:
0385315058

Media:
Book

Principal Subject:
Career Transitions

Of Interest To:
Women

Career Transitions

IT'S ONLY TOO LATE IF YOU DON'T START NOW
How To Create Your Second Life After 40

Description:

According to the author, a popular writer, career counselor and regular on the Oprah show, mid-life is not a time of crisis. Turning forty may well be the time to "rediscover the inspired, enthusiastic adventurer you wanted to be before you became the responsible adult you had to be." Sher postulates that "Your first life belongs to nature. Your second life (which begins at forty or whenever you experience a mid-life crisis) belongs to you." The first half of her lengthy guide focuses on "Nature and Instinct" the governing forces of your first life. Chapters include: Don't Panic, It's Only A Midlife Crisis, You Are Not The Favorite and a series of Illusions, such as Time Limits, Age, Beauty, Love and Power. Other chapters in part one include "What's Your Score" with the sub-heading "What you need is a new score sheet, based on your quality as a human being" and Escape to Freedom which casts a warning glance toward succumbing to "road fever." The second half of the book, Reclaiming Your Original Self: Your Second Life, inspires readers with The Courage To Live Your Life, Turning Dreams Into Goals and Going for Greatness. The Epilogue begins, "Will you look at this splendid world!"

Evaluation:

Sher takes the stereotypical notion of a mid-life crisis and turns it on its head. Instead of your forties being a time for loss, confusion and regret (and bringing home a trophy wife in a red sports car), this pivotal decade can be the turning point when you begin to live your life purposefully and with renewed enthusiasm. Sher sets out to "deprogram" readers from the "illusions" (youth is good/age is bad; beauty lies in skinny thighs and wrinkle-free skin) that keep them bound in the limits of the first life. She attacks attitudes, values and ways of thinking that run counter to living a free, triumphant life. After explaining narcissism, fear, inertia and other ills, she uses questionnaires, exercises and anecdotes to prod the reader into spotting these maladies in their life. Once the ground is thus tilled, she encourages the reader to plant hopes, dreams and illusion-free fantasies. Readers contemplating changing jobs or even careers at forty may find in the gospel according to Sher the encouragement and support to make a major life change. Others may find themselves reevaluating their career and life choices and realize that the time for a shift in balance or direction is at hand. For anyone seeking a friendly, inspiring voice to shake them out of the college plus twenty blues, Sher just may be it.

Where To Find/Buy:
Bookstores and libraries.

MANAGING TRANSITIONS
Making The Most Of Change

★★

Description:

Bridge's guide could be paraphrased Zen and the Art of Firing. Part One: The Problem differentiates between change which is situational, and transition, which is "the psychological process people go through to come to terms with the new situation." It is in effectively shepherding their employees through transition that managers prove their mettle. In his section on The Solutions, Bridges explains the three stages of transition (Endings, The Neutral Zone and The New Beginning), and the proper attitudes and behaviors managers should adopt to lead their employees through the experience successfully. How To Get Them To Let Go, speaks to employees' tendency to hang on to the "good old days" in the face of change. Managing the Neutral Zone Successfully contains advice in essay form, with headings such as Acknowledge The Losses Openly And Sympathetically. Launching A New Beginning addresses the ambivalence many employees feel toward the new way of doing things, the new computer system, the new organizational chart, the new anything that displaces the status quo. It guides managers through sections such as Clarify and Communicate the Purpose and Two Things To Watch Out For.

Evaluation:

William Bridges is a respected leader in the field of transition management, writing and lecturing on the perspective of change from a human and organizational perspective. We have reviewed his book on managing career change from an individual frame of reference ("Transitions"). This book extends his analysis and applies his developmental theory of transition to organizations. Written to an audience of managers and organizational leaders, the book educates decision-makers about the effects of change on employees, and the effects of employees-in-transition upon an organization. His overall goal is to minimize the "distress and disruption" caused by change. The changes most salient for our readers are jolting employment shifts such as the firing, demotion or rapid promotion of an employee or group of employees. But the guide is equally valid in discussing changes following a merger or technological overhaul. Bridges uses case studies of both well managed transition and management missteps that wrought corporate disaster to teach the reader. If "touchy feely" books make you squirm, this one will cause convulsions. But Bridges would say that the emotive-phobes are exactly who will benefit most from reading his guide.

Where To Find/Buy:

Bookstores and libraries.

Overall Rating
★★
This one's for the manager, not the employee

Design, Ease Of Use
★★★
Anecdotes, quotations and pithy advice

1–4 Stars

Author:
William Bridges, Ph.D.

Dr. Bridges is a consultant and lecturer. Formerly a professor of English, he shifted to the field of transition management two decades ago. He is past president of the Association for Humanistic Psychology and is a popular executive development consultant.

Publisher:
Perseus Books

Edition:
1991

Price:
$19.00

Pages:
130

ISBN:
0201550733

Media:
Book

Principal Subject:
Career Transitions

Secondary Subject:
Moving Ahead

★★

Overall Rating
★★
Brief outlines of options facing people in mid-career transitions

Design, Ease Of Use
★★
Emphasizes realistic expectations; inspiring in the drill sergeant sense

1–4 Stars

Author:
Stephen M. Pollan and Mark Levine

Mr. Pollan is an attorney and career advisor; he is currently a commentator for "The Nightly Business Report." Mr. Levine is a freelance writer.

Publisher:
Warner Books

Edition:
1997

Price:
$10.99

Pages:
241

ISBN:
0446671665

Media:
Book

Principal Subject:
Career Transitions

Secondary Subject:
Entrepreneurship

Career Transitions

STARTING OVER
How To Change Careers Or Start Your Own Business

Description:

While other authors dwell on future predictions and the "workplace revolution," Pollan is determined to focus on the nuts and bolts: "your job and your pragmatic options." That's the promise he makes in Chapter 1 of his guide to career transitions (though he does provide a concise summary of job market changes in Chapter 2). The first step to solving job problems is to identify them, so readers begin by "Getting Specific" about the causes of their dissatisfaction. Once your problem is defined, Pollan offers 9 options and a "rating system" for weighing those options. The first 4 options are to get another job in the same career/industry, in the same career/different industry, in a different career/same industry, or in a different career/different industry. Or, you can start a business in the same industry or in a different industry, go back to school, stay where you are, or "downshift" (place less emphasize on your job, more on your personal life.) Each of the 9 options is discussed in its own chapter. Chapters on career-changing include advice on job searching, researching, and using technology. Chapters on starting a business provide tips on business plans. The chapter on staying at your job suggests ways to "regain the spark."

Evaluation:

One thing's for sure: Pollan doesn't pull any punches. As he says in his introductory first chapter, he's interested in quick, reliable results, not long-term health care for your career psyche. This isn't a "find your true career and be fulfilled" book. In some respects, this guide is more likely to burst you're bubble than to make your dreams seem viable. The exception is the chapter on entrepreneurism, which manage to be both inspiring and pragmatic. Many of the other chapters are dryly pragmatic. And don't look here for a sugar coating of all options. For example, if you choose to find a new career in a new industry, Pollan warns that this option is the "least feasible, riskiest, and most time-consuming." (You'll make less money and have a hard time finding a job.) He even implies that he would not have included this option had he not felt "duty-bound" to do so. It's important to understand the ramifications of your decisions, but a little light at the end of the tunnel would be appreciated. In general, all of the chapters suffer from brevity; none offer more than pithy "soundbytes" of advice. However, the "rating system" for realistically weighing your options is sound, and Pollan's practical tone may appeal to those thirsting for straight talk.

Where To Find/Buy:
Bookstores and libraries.

Career Transitions

TRANSITIONS
Making Sense Of Life's Changes

★★

Description:

This is guide is regarded as a classic in the field of transition management, written by a man rated by The Wall Street Journal as one of the ten most popular executive development consultants in the U.S. His expertise, and the book's focus, is on coping with unexpected transition. Though not written exclusively about career transitions, the book is included because it developed a framework for understanding the psychological reaction to transition that is widely accepted and absorbed into conventional wisdom about the subject. Divided into two sections, the book begins with an overview of our human Need For Change and a description of Being In Transition. He describes transitions encountered in a lifetime, particularly in "Love and Work." The longer second half of the book explores The Transition Process. According to Bridges, there are three stages of transition. Endings should be recognized as opportunities as well as losses, and even celebrated. The Neutral Zone can be the most uncomfortable stage, when one feels disconnected from the past and emotionally unconnected from the present. The New Beginning stage requires us to launch new priorities, and to listen to internal and external signs that point the way to our future.

Evaluation:

Sometimes during a stressful career transition, it is helpful to step back from the pressing circumstances at hand, the resume that needs to be rewritten, the interview thank yous to be sent, to reflect on how one is handling the process of change, and its effect on significant relationships. For these moments of reflection, Dr. Bridges offers a theory of personal development that can help make sense of the whirling feelings of disorientation, fear, exhilaration and anxiety which often accompany career change. His best-selling book lacks the practical exhortation of a self-help guide. It is more like a mini-course in human psychology, with a humanist's optimism woven throughout. Bridges views transition as a "natural process of self-renewal," something to be embraced rather than survived. His emphasis is not on the practical adjustments you'll need to make if you change careers or jobs, but rather on the process of "letting go of the person you used to be and then finding the new person you have become in the new situation." The overarching philosophy of the book is summed up nicely in the Ralph Waldo Emmerson quotation selected for the epilogue: "Not in his goals but in his transitions man is great."

Where To Find/Buy:

Bookstores and libraries.

Overall Rating
★★
May help make sense of the swirl of emotions which accompany career change

Design, Ease Of Use
★★
A humanistic, optimistic guide

1–4 Stars

Author:
William Bridges, Ph.D.

Dr. Bridges is a consultant and lecturer. Formerly a professor of English, he shifted to the field of transition management two decades ago. He is past president of the Association for Humanistic Psychology and is a popular executive development consultant.

Publisher:
Perseus Books

Edition:
1980

Price:
$14.00

Pages:
170

ISBN:
0201000822

Media:
Book

Principal Subject:
Career Transitions

Of Interest To:
Returning To The Workplace

III. Career Transitions

Overall Rating
★
General tips on conducting research, fairly superficial

Design, Ease Of Use
★★
Simple, straightforward style; includes samples and exercises

1–4 Stars

Author:
Jane Ballback and Jan Slater

Ms. Ballback and Ms. Slater are partners in The Baldwin Group, a Newport Beach consulting firm. They have over 15 years of experience designing and implementing programs in the areas of career development and management training.

Publisher:
Richard Chang Associates, Inc.

Edition:
1996

Price:
$14.95

Pages:
109

ISBN:
1883553792

Media:
Book

Principal Subject:
Career Transitions

Career Transitions

MAKING CAREER TRANSITIONS

Description:
Whether your career needs a "minor" tweak or a "major" upheaval, this book is designed to help you. Interspersing personal stories (from their clients) and advice with interactive exercises, Ms. Bellback and Ms. Slater have devised a step-by-step guide to planning a "gradual, no-risk career transition." Chapters 1 and 2 introduce the philosophy and purpose behind the authors' approach, i.e. "You Are Constantly in Career Transition" and "Why Create a Career Vision?" The next step is "labor market research," or finding out "what's out there." Chapters 3 and 4 explore ways to conduct research, i.e. online research, job fairs, etc., while Chapters 5 and 6 address the advantages of informational networking. The final chapters teach you how to "Put It All Together" by "creating an action plan" and starting a "career journal." Fill-in-the-blank action plans, self-assessment exercises, and journal sheets are included.

Evaluation:
The best parts of this guide are the chapters on conducting research (which, thankfully, comprise half the content). These chapters are by no means in-depth, but they are sensitive to the needs of people who haven't looked for a job in a long time and they do cover the basics: resources, networking, informational interviews, etc. Still, though they're the best this guide has to offer, they aren't good enough to compensate for the content's superficiality. The personal stories from the authors' clients are too brief and too pithy to demonstrate anything, the advice is general, and the authors have an annoying habit of referring to their other books, i.e. "We handed Phil a copy of 'Unlocking Your Career Potential,' and asked him to read it. . . ." and "If you need help with self marketing, read our book, 'Marketing Yourself. . . .'" The interactive exercises aren't insightful, either, i.e. "List all the careers you're interested in." For self-assessment and research tips, "Starting Out, Starting Over" is a better choice. (See review.)

Where To Find/Buy:
Bookstores and libraries.

MOVING AHEAD

Often career transitions involve moving up within the same company or field, making a lateral move to a similar job with a different employer, or to a different job with the same employer.

New employees have a training manual or the like to answer questions about their company's regulations, mission statement or benefits. But who can they ask about inter-office politics or promotion policies? Mentors are a terrific resource for learning how to effectively manage one's career. If you don't have one, where can you get advice on making a move. There are literally hundreds of guides on the market on how to succeed at work. The guides we selected for review all pay close attention to "unwritten rules" of business, especially the rules governing moving ahead.

These guides include advice on topics such as:

- How to take charge of your career

- How to position yourself for the career change you desire

- When to move and when to stay

- How to get what you want without compromising who you want to be

- How to cope with being the only minority in an office

Some rules of thumb: You decide when/if to move ahead; don't let others decide for you. Take your time. Make sure your goals are clearly defined and that you have a real plan of action for the transition. More planning is not going to be wasted. Think bigger and make small steps in that direction.

Overall Rating
★★★★
An absolute must for executives; focuses on strategic job-changing

Design, Ease Of Use
★★★★
Explicit contents, smartly written; includes samples

1–4 Stars

Author:
John Lucht

Mr. Lucht has recruited senior executives to major corporations since 1971, as head of the John Lucht Consultancy Inc., since 1977, and for 6 prior years at Heidrick and Struggles, New York.

Publisher:
Viceroy Press

Edition:
6th (1998)

Price:
$29.95

Pages:
621

ISBN:
0942785215

Media:
Book

Principal Subject:
Moving Ahead

Secondary Subject:
Job Search All Inclusive

Moving Ahead

THE NEW RITES OF PASSAGE AT $100,000+
The Insider's Lifetime Guide To Executive Job-Changing And Faster Career Progress

 Recommended For:
Moving Ahead

Description:
As Lucht says in Chapter 1, you are the person in charge of your career. Or are you? To help you take charge, the proceeding 19 chapters offer a rite of passage, a "cram course" in the techniques executives use to get to the "top." Though many of Lucht's strategies can be applied to getting a promotion within a company, his primary focus is on job-changing: moving from company to company as one climbs the ladder. Chapter 2 introduces the four main ways to find jobs: personal contacts (people you know), networking (referrals), executive recruiters, and direct mail. Chapters 3–4 explore using contacts and networks, Chapters 5–10 offer an in-depth examination of recruiters (i.e. recruiter agendas and "hunting patterns"), and Chapters 11–13 delve into direct mail and resumes. Chapters 14–16 tackle an assortment of issues, including outplacement and interviewing. Negotiating an employment contract is discussed in Chapter 17. Chapters 18–20 look at self-employment, problem solving, and increasing contacts.

Evaluation:
Lucht's book has been so well received it may be considered the ruling champion of executive job-changing guides. One of the many reasons for its stellar reputation is that it truly is the "inside track." As a top executive recruiter, Lucht knows the subject from the inside out. His "thorough taxonomy" of executive recruiters, both contingency and retainer, is surprising, enlightening, and imminently useful. By reading these chapters, you'll not only understand how the system works, but how to make it—and the recruiter—work for you. There are plenty of other highly valuable chapters, especially those addressing resumes, cover letters, and interviewing. Worthy of particular praise is the chapter on negotiating an employment contract, which combines advice on executive compensation devices with savvy negotiating techniques. If you're an executive who wants to keep moving up, this book is an absolute must!

Where To Find/Buy:
Bookstores and libraries.

Moving Ahead

WORK SMART
250 Smart Moves Your Boss Already Knows

 Recommended For:
Moving Ahead

Description:

The authors have divided their "250 smart moves" into three segments: Part 1 "How To Look, Think, And Act On The Job," Part 2 "How To Get Ahead," and Part 3 "How To Change Careers." Part 1 deals with "developing a professional identity," via image, clothes, attitude, and "workplace politics." Each of these chapters, like all of the chapters, begins with a "Work Smart IQ Quiz." Each "Quiz" involves differentiating between workplace "myths" and "realities." Other self-assessment exercises (i.e. a "Client Response Diary" for evaluating responsiveness to a client's needs) are used throughout, enabling readers to pinpoint their target "issues." Part 2 presents strategies for "marketing yourself," "making yourself the office 'MVP'," and "dealing with change in your organization." Topics discussed include: goals, performance reviews, networking, transferring, unemployment. Part 3 examines the decision to change careers, choosing "the best new career," and "making the transition."

Evaluation:

American culture has a lot of laughs at the expense of "the corporate world;" just look at the success of "Dilbert." For professionals, however, life at the office is no laughing matter. (Though the authors do encourage, and employ, a sense of humor.) Based on the trials and tribulations of their clients, both the successes and the "bloopers," Dr. Tullier and Ms. Taub have created a formidable tool for anyone who is new on the job, wanting to get ahead, or thinking about changing careers. Not only is there valuable, practical advice on everything from phone "shticks" and body language to taking credit and getting noticed, there are also real-life examples supporting the advice. It is easy to identify with these examples, which, in turn, makes it easier to imagine incorporating the skills/strategies into daily life. The interactive exercises are fun, quick, and insightful; career-changers in particular will benefit from such self-appraisal. A great book for beginning, surviving, and succeeding in the corporate world.

Where To Find/Buy:

Bookstores and libraries, or directly from the publisher at 800-793-2665.

★★★★

Overall Rating
★★★★
Well-written and engaging, interactive; great for corporate work environments

Design, Ease Of Use
★★★★
Straightforward, easy-to-use format: explicit chapter headings and an index of topics

1–4 Stars

Author:
Marci Taub, M.A., and Michelle Tullier, Ph.D.

Ms. Taub and Dr. Tullier are career counselors in private practice; they have successfully coached thousands of clients. They are also the authors of two titles in the "Job Notes" series, "Interviews" (Taub) and "Cover Letters" (Tullier), and co-authors of *Job Smart*.

Publisher:
The Princeton Review

Edition:
1998

Price:
$12.00

Pages:
223

ISBN:
0679783881

Media:
Book

Principal Subject:
Moving Ahead

III. Career Transitions

★★★

Overall Rating
★★★

Insightful, inspiring career guidance for minorities; not a "how to get a job" book

Design, Ease Of Use
★★★★

Easy to read and use; explicit chapter headings for "browsing"

1–4 Stars

Author:
Miquela Rivera, Ph.D.

Dr. Rivera is a psychologist in private practice and a regular contributor of pieces on minority and career issues to such publications as Hispanic Engineer and U.S. Black Engineer. She also offers workshops on a wide range of topics, including leadership.

Publisher:
Adams

Edition:
1991

Price:
$9.95

Pages:
272

ISBN:
155850012X

Media:
Book

Principal Subject:
Moving Ahead

Of Interest To:
Racial/Ethnic Minorities

Moving Ahead

THE MINORITY CAREER BOOK

Description:
Preparing for job success is the first step to succeeding. This guide, which combines career preparation/guidance with advice on such related issues as "dealing with stress" and "balancing family and professional commitments," has one primary aim: to prepare minority professionals for "the winner's circle." In Part 1, "Get Ready," Dr. Rivera focuses on the "importance of goal setting" and education. Part 2, "Get Set," examines workplace "expectations" and "values" from the minority point of view; discussion includes "understanding cultural diversity," "practicing discipline," "seeking opportunities," and "paying the price." The final part, "Go," offers techniques and strategies for surviving and thriving in your career. There are chapters on "Being the 'Only'," "Taking Risks," "Gaining Legitimacy and Recognition," and "Answering the Call to Leadership," as well as a chapter on changing careers. "The Basics of Job Winning," i.e. interviewing, are also detailed; sample resumes and cover letters are provided.

Evaluation:
In may be an understatement to say that there is a cultural "blind spot" to the workplace concerns and contributions of minority professionals. Certainly there are few "mainstream" career guides with portions dedicated to minority needs. Stepping into that breach is Dr. Rivera and her tough, touching, astute, and illuminating resource. How does one cope with being the "only" minority in a white-dominated business? In what way do cultural values and attitudes affect the workplace? Issues like these are so rarely treated by "career experts" that any discussion of such topics is laudable. Luckily, in the case of this book, the treatment isn't just commendable, it's practical and useful as well. Dr. Rivera provides insight and advice on "how to succeed at work," and her ideas are definitely worth reading. Although she does include tips on "job winning," this really isn't a "job hunt" resource; the tips are better suited to people interested in "getting ahead" than for job seekers. Best for "corporate" work environments.

Where To Find/Buy:
Bookstores and libraries.

Moving Ahead

THE CAREER COACH
Inside Tips To Getting And Keeping The Job You Want

Description:
Career management is more than just locating a job and getting it; it's an ongoing process that continues throughout a lifetime, changing and evolving in tune with the individual. As the "Career Coach," it's Ms. Kleiman's goal to help her readers through all aspects of their professional lives, from choosing a career path to succeeding on the job, "keeping current," and "moving up." Divided into four parts, the guide begins with advice on job searching: choosing the "right" job, resumes and cover letters, research, networking, interviewing. In Part 2, "Keeping Your Job," readers learn how to deal with problems at work (i.e. difficult bosses, interacting with management) and how to let "people know what you want." "Taking Charge of Your Career" is discussed in Part 3 (i.e. continuing to network, what to do if you're fired), while Part 4 helps readers prepare for a "second career." Succinct "Coach's tips" are scattered throughout the text of each chapter; appendices include a list of the "100 best jobs" and their salaries.

Evaluation:
As the "Career Coach," Ms. Kleiman is exactly that: a coach. She teaches you the strategies necessary to win the game, but she won't play for you. She doesn't coddle her readers the way some author's do; she isn't a cheerleader or your mother. If there's one message that comes through loud and clear in this guide, it's to temper (not hinder) ambition with a solid dose of realism. For example, you may be advised to take a lower paying, not-ideal job just to "get in the door." And those hard questions at interviews? Be creative, be sly, and learn how to say things they want to hear without saying anything at all. As for job security, Ms. Kleiman's message is clear there too: there are no "secure" jobs, only savvy job seekers. This is a guide to the politics of career management; it isn't a "hold your hand" guide with sample resumes and practice interview questions. For practical, pragmatic, blunt advice for succeeding at work (especially in a corporate or large office environment), this a valuable, insightful resource.

Where To Find/Buy:
Bookstores and libraries.

Overall Rating
★★★
Solid advice and good tips on successful job/career management

Design, Ease Of Use
★★★
Simple format, engagingly written; no "sample" resumes

1–4 Stars

Author:
Carol Kleiman
Ms. Kleiman, business columnist for the Chicago Tribune, is also the author of *The 100 Best Jobs for the 1990s and Beyond.*

Publisher:
Berkley Books

Edition:
1994

Price:
$5.99

Pages:
257

ISBN:
0425151956

Media:
Book

Principal Subject:
Moving Ahead

Secondary Subject:
All Inclusive Job Search

III. Career Transitions

★★★

Overall Rating
★★★
A hard-hitting self-help guide for taking yourself to the top

Design, Ease Of Use
★★★
Ambiguous chapter headings; browsing required to find chapters that fit

1–4 Stars

Author:
Laura Berman Fortgang

Ms. Fortgang is the president and owner of InterCoach, a company specializing in business and executive coaching. As a career coach, she has worked with hundreds of entrepreneurs, managers, and executives.

Publisher:
Warner Books

Edition:
1998

Price:
$13.99

Pages:
218

ISBN:
0446673773

Media:
Book

Principal Subject:
Moving Ahead

Secondary Subject:
Entrepreneurship

Moving Ahead

TAKE YOURSELF TO THE TOP

Description:
To help bridge the gap between where you are and where you want to be, this book combines self-assessment guidance with career coaching. The focus is on personal change. By showing you how to change personally, Fortgang promises that your career and life will change, too. The 14 chapters incorporate personal stories, interactive exercises and advice into the text. Chapters address such topics as "where you were, where you are now," overcoming hurdles, feeling stuck, burnout, and "having it all, but really wanting something else." Other chapters include "New to Entrepreneurship," "Overqualified and Underutilized," and "The Hero Syndrome" (e.g. taking on too many problems and trying to save the day). How to realistically "chase your dreams" is discussed, as is developing self-discipline. Fortgang also teaches readers how to nurture important relationships and thus network. Final chapters provide "Advanced Tools for Getting to the Top" and tips for the future.

Evaluation:
This guide falls into the ambiguous but interesting category of change-yourself-to-change-your-career resources, a type of resource that holds self-development as the key to career development. While other books of this type tend to be either philosophy-heavy or touchy-feely, Fortgang's guide is distinguished by its business-oriented practicality. Without suggesting that financial success is the only kind of success, Fortgang does focus on personal changes that help you in business, not that (necessarily) lead to euphoric personal fulfillment. For example, in the chapter on building relationships, the reader is advised to "let go" of people who "stopped contributing positively to your life," even if you share a history with them or feel loyal to them. As Fortgang says, "To get to the top of your game, you will have to become very selfish." Fortgang says her clients call her "edgy" because of her blunt honesty, you may have another word for it. If you want a career coach who'll tell it like it is, look here.

Where To Find/Buy:
Bookstores and libraries.

Moving Ahead

★ ★

ADVANCING WOMEN

Description:

At the AW (Advancing Women) home page, visitors will find links to numerous news/current event articles, as well as access to the career portions of Ms. Glasscock's site. (A site map provides an annotated "table of contents.") There's the "Workplace," a collection of articles on "getting ahead" at work and strategies for advancing your career, i.e. "overcoming barriers," finding a mentor, etc. The "AW Career Center" offers self-assessment articles, "Fast Facts" on "top markets" and job growth by region/industry, and access to CareerMosaic's job/resume bank. For advice on using the Internet to "advance yourself and your career," there's "Web," a section which includes "tools for the Web," tips on "developing your strategy," and a discussion of "women on the Web." Mentoring and networking are highly-touted by Ms. Glasscock, so there are message boards and chat rooms designed to champion "women helping women." The site also features "Latina," a segment on Latin American business, news and trends.

Evaluation:

The idea and the palpable passion behind AW is admirable: help women help each other and themselves with their career aspirations. The "Web" portion, dedicated to using the Web to network and "advance yourself," is interesting and apropos; women do need to take greater advantage of the Web. What better way to "get ahead" than to build an "old girls network?" The emphasis on mentoring, i.e. articles, message boards, etc., is equally welcome and timely. Unfortunately, while the site's content, from the insightful advice to the job/resume bank from CareerMosaic (see review), is terrific, its format leaves something to be desired. The home page doesn't list all of the site segments, nor does the site map. For example, neither the home page nor the site map mention the resume bank; it's hidden in the "AW Career Center," in small print on the side bar! Some sites aren't worth navigating difficulties; this one is. Be patient and you'll be rewarded.

Where To Find/Buy:

On the Internet at http://www.advancingwomen.com

Overall Rating
★ ★
Lots of advice for advancing women; good networking potential

Design, Ease Of Use
★ ★
Convoluted format, difficult to navigate; the site map should be better

1–4 Stars

Author:
Gretchen Glasscock

Gretchen Glasscock is the founder and Web publisher of *Advancing Women*; she's a writer, a consultant, and a frequent speaker at women's business and career events.

Publisher:
Gretchen Glasscock

Edition:
1998

Media:
Internet

Principal Subject:
Moving Ahead

Of Interest To:
Women

III. Career Transitions

★★

Overall Rating
★★
A few good tips on negotiating exit bonuses/ compensation and networking

Design, Ease Of Use
★
Convoluted and without a clear purpose

1–4 Stars

Author:
Julia Hartman, M.B.A.

Ms. Hartman jumped from being a $200-a-week musician to a six-figure corporate consultant in eight strategic leaps.

Publisher:
Prima Publishing

Edition:
1997

Price:
$13.00

Pages:
236

ISBN:
0761510230

Media:
Book

Principal Subject:
Moving Ahead

Moving Ahead

STRATEGIC JOB JUMPING
50 Very Smart Tactics For Building Your Career

Description:

A "job jumper" is Hartman's term for people who "take control" of their careers by planning and implementing strategic job "jumps:" changes, promotions, new positions within a company, etc. To introduce readers to the concept behind job jumping, Chapter 1 recounts Hartman's own jumping background (from $200 a week to $165,000 a year). Chapter 2 explores the "growth" of jumping due to outsourcing, downsizing, etc. Chapter 3 looks at the "whys" of jumping and presents the 14-point "Jumper's Credo," which includes "invest in the people you meet." Jumper's tricks-of-the-trade are examined in Chapters 4–9. There's advice on self-promotion, creating a contact database, interviewing, and networking to find jobs. There's also information on negotiating exit bonuses and compensation, employment contracts, and marketing your jumping experience as an asset. "Building Personal Wealth" and "Your Personal Life" are discussed in Chapters 10 and 11. Chapter 12 contains interviews with 9 successful jumpers.

Evaluation:

There are some valuable portions of Hartman's guide to job jumping, but they are often lost in the cluttered organization. This book jumps around, from topic to topic, haphazardly; even the author's introduction can't produce a concrete thesis. Ambiguous promises abound, such as "discover how to build your career and financial future," yet the "and-here's-how," never fully materializes. You can catch a glimpse of it, in the occasionally insightful tips on self-promotion, networking, and negotiating, but a glimpse isn't enough to see a whole picture. Maybe there is no "whole picture." Although Hartman offers advice on issues ranging from contracts to health insurance, she never gets around to the "planning" part of strategic jumping. Maybe the only strategy is to be continually prepared for change. In any case, if you have to play a guessing game to figure out a guide's purpose, forget it. "The New Rites of Passage at $100,000+," though written for executives, tackles similar subjects and is a better resource.

Where To Find/Buy:

Bookstores and libraries, or order direct from the publisher by phone 916-632-4400.

JOB LOSS OR TERMINATION

No matter how you phrase it—fired, terminated, laid-off, restructured, downsized or terminated—losing your job is a traumatic event. Your career represents more than just a paycheck. And losing it can be similar to losing a loved one. You may experience the full range, or a part of, the grieving process. Shock and denial; fear and panic; anger; bargaining; depression; temporary acceptance; these are some of the stages you may experience in the wake of job loss.

Allowing yourself to be driven by the whirling emotions during the crucial period before, during and immediately after a job loss can have lasting repercussions. In your anger you may feel like acting belligerent. However you have much to gain by parting company productively with your former boss and colleagues. You may feel overwhelmed by anxiety and depression. Yet allowing yourself to become lethargic, isolated or unproductive can contribute to a negative spiral of emotions and behaviors.

Being fired is one of life's situations that proves the maxim that knowledge is power. The more informed you are about your rights, antidiscrimination laws, and industry standards for severance packages, the better prepared you will be to either fight back or leave on your terms.

The resources we evaluate in this chapter vary considerably in their focus. Some emphasize legal issues. These guides can help you know when to get a lawyer and when you don't need one. You can research how to negotiate the best severance package possible, and the tax implications of any termination settlement.

Other guides focus on helping you move through the whole range of emotional and psychological issues that often accompany a firing, both for you and your family. Other resources focus on the practical realities of job loss, beginning with how to recognize when the writing's on the wall, to getting favorable job references after you leave, to signing up for unemployment compensation. Some resources touch on all of these aspects. Read through the reviews to find the best one for your particular situation.

If you need help coping with the loss get it sooner rather than later. If you are forced out of a job:

- Don't be too proud to get unemployment insurance—it's your money.

- Don't take the first job offered if you can wait, unless it really fits.

- Assess carefully why you lost your job and if you have adjustments to make, make them now!

Although job loss can be a difficult passage, it may also represent a golden moment to reinvent your professional self.

★★★★

Overall Rating
★★★★
Excellent legal and practical advice

Design, Ease Of Use
★★★★
No legalese, just plain English

1–4 Stars

Author:
Steven Sack

Sack is the author of seventeen books, including *The Employee Rights Handbook* and *The Lifetime Legal Guide*. He is a labor and employment attorney and lecturer with a private law practice in New York City.

Publisher:
Warner Books

Edition:
1999

Price:
$24.00

Pages:
370

ISBN:
0446522155

Media:
Book

Principal Subject:
Termination/Job Loss

Of Interest To:
Women

GETTING FIRED
What To Do If You're Fired, Downsized, Laid Off, Restructured, Discharged, Terminated, Or Forced To Resign

 **Recommended For:**
Termination/Job Loss

Description:
Mr. Sack is an articulate voice for the rights of the worker in a world where layoffs and downsizing are common. He speaks regularly on the subject, through a variety of media (including radio, TV and his seventeen books). As an attorney specializing in labor and employment issues, Sack guides readers on what to do to protect themselves if they sense they might be fired or have already received the dreaded pink slip. Part I, Determining When You Are Being Treated Illegally Or Unfairly, covers anti-discrimination laws and how to build a discrimination case if you chose that recourse. Sack offers in-depth treatment of age, gender, racial, handicap and religious discrimination and briefly addresses several dozen specific situations, such as hiring interviews, pregnancy discrimination and being fired for reporting accidents or for personal appearance. Part II, Negotiating The Best Severance Package After You Are Fired, coaches readers from "recognizing the warning signs" through "how to properly handle the news" to "getting the best package." The final section, Fighting Back, advises how to "resign from a job properly," what to do if you face slander or libel and employment litigation and alternatives.

Evaluation:
Dedicated to "abused and fired workers everywhere," Sack writes with empathy and a touch of righteous indignation. Having "Getting Fired" on your shelf is like having a lawyer in the family to guide you about your options and the without confusing legalese. He explains legal principles in plain English, empowering fired employees to take control of their situation. A practical manual, the guide presents real and created scenarios to illustrate legal principles. "Counsel comments" paragraphs follow each scenario and offer a lawyer's advice on each narrative. We highly recommend this legal guide for anyone who anticipates or has been fired for a bogus or suspect reason. Though the author frequently suggests that readers consult with an employment attorney (there is even a chapter on how to pick and effectively communicate with one), reading this guide can provide the kind of first-step information and advice needed to know before further steps are taken. It is especially valuable for workers who feel they may have been released for discriminatory reasons, but aren't sure what the law says in their particular circumstance. Readers will benefit from the detailed explanation of how to handle a firing, and the attention to often overlooked details such as how the termination will be presented to future employers.

Where To Find/Buy:
Bookstores and libraries.

Job Loss Or Termination

EXECUTIVE JOB SEARCH STRATEGIES
The Guide For Career Transitions

★★★★

 Recommended For:
Termination/Job Loss

Description:

In Chapter 1, Bruce describes the "Middle Manager's Crisis," the growing trend toward downsizing that has left many managers and executives wondering what to do next. Bruce calls these displaced workers "surplused executives;" it is to them and to career changers that this guide is addressed. (Chapter 2 recounts Bruce's own experience with downsizing.) The guide is designed to help readers manage their job search. In Chapter 3, readers evaluate their "standing" at work through quizzes, i.e. "Work Satisfaction Quiz," "Burn Out Quiz," etc. Chapters 4–5 discuss the emotional impact of being laid off and provide self-assessment exercises for creating a "personal profile." Chapters 6–10 cover job searching skills: resumes, cover letters, time management, "marketing yourself," and interviewing. Sample resumes, letters, interview questions, etc. are included. Developing telephone contacts, negotiating/evaluating job offers, and "FAQs" comprise the final 4 chapters.

Evaluation:

This guide is, above all, a response to the situation facing more and more people in middle-to-upper management: downsizing, "no-fault" termination, early retirement, etc. If you find yourself in such a situation and want a better understanding of the causes and personal/ emotional impact, this book can give it to you. It will also act as a refresher course on writing resumes, interviewing, negotiating, etc. Career changers can use Bruce's advice, too, but his sympathy to "surplused executives" is ever-present; this is, really, their guide. Bruce's own background—a downsized middle-manager who is now an executive in the financial industry—tends to color his text. Which, in most respects, is desirable; it's easy to identify with and trust Bruce. He is both teacher and peer. However, since his own experience was to move from one company to another, his book works best for those interested in similar routes. For more creative options, i.e. consulting, contract work, etc., try "The Portable Executive." (See review.)

Where To Find/Buy:

Bookstores and libraries.

Overall Rating
★★★★
Sympathetic guide for middle/ upper level executives who have lost their job

Design, Ease Of Use
★★★
Combines interactive exercises, advice and personal stories effectively

1–4 Stars

Author:
Robert C. Bruce
Mr. Bruce survived losing his job to launch a new career as an executive in the financial industry.

Publisher:
VGM Horizons

Edition:
1997

Price:
$16.95

Pages:
251

ISBN:
0844243752

Media:
Book

Principal Subject:
Termination/Job Loss

Secondary Subject:
All Inclusive Job Search

III. Career Transitions

★★★

Overall Rating
★★★
An emotionally supportive exploration of all aspects of the reemployment process

Design, Ease Of Use
★★★★
Clear headings, charts and graphics

1–4 Stars

Author:
J. Damian Birkel with Stacey J. Miller

Mr. Birkel serves as product marketing manager for a Fortune 500 company. Having lost a job as a result of downsizing and survived three company reorganizations, Birkel established Professionals in Transition to create a safe space to discuss unemployment issues.

Publisher:
American Management Association

Edition:
1998

Price:
$14.95

Pages:
162

ISBN:
0814479545

Media:
Book

Principal Subject:
Termination/Job Loss

Job Loss Or Termination

CAREER BOUNCE BACK
The Professionals In Transition Guide To Recovery And Reemployment

Description:
After experiencing his own brutal and demoralizing job loss and extended period of unemployment, the author hatched the idea of creating the job-support group he wished he had access to during his transition. Eventually he founded Professionals in Transitions. The organization's goals are to create a "safe space" where the unemployed can discuss the multiple issues of the reemployment process and to provide one another with "information, job leads, perspective and hope." Experience leading PIT led the author to research the psychological aspects of job loss, an under-researched and often neglected topic. He built upon the grieving process analysis of death and dying expert Dr. Kubler-Ross to establish a psychological framework for managing job loss. Birkel combined his practical experience counseling through PIT with this developmental scaffolding to create the career bounce-back program. His book reads like an Al-Anon guide, mixing practical advice with emotional support. In case it's been a while since you last hunted for a job, advice on the fundamentals of the job search (writing a resume, posting an e-resume, etc.) is included.

Evaluation:
The strength of this guide is its unflinching attention to the emotional issues which accompany job loss, especially for professionals facing sudden and unexpected termination. Although practical advice is included, the emphasis is on understanding, and normalizing, the emotional upheaval unemployment can bring. Shock, denial, fear, panic, anger, bargaining, depression and acceptance are explored and dissected. The author continually advises readers to develop a support group of friends and family to help them weather an extended period of unemployment, or to seek out an organized support group like PIT. Treatment of the nuts-and-bolts of the job hunt is brief but on target. Networking is appropriately given its own chapter, and the insights here are helpful. Advice throughout is geared to middle managers and other professionals, thus the networking chapter stresses the importance of informational interviews and other professional network based strategies. Attention is given to re-inventing yourself, or allowing yourself the freedom to use the period of unemployment as an opportunity to reflect and reconsider your career options. If losing your job has your world spinning, this guide can help you shake off the disorientation and launch back into the work force, a better, or at least deeper, person.

Where To Find/Buy:
Bookstores and libraries.

III. Career Transitions

Job Loss Or Termination

BEFORE YOU SAY "I QUIT!"
A Guide To Making Successful Career Transitions

Description:
You'd like to say "Take this job and shove it!" But is that the best decision? If it is, what's next? Holloway and Bishop designed their guide to help you answer the question "Should I stay or should I go?" The decision-making process begins in Part 1; first, you learn to "channel anger and frustration" into constructive action. Understanding the source of job dissatisfaction (via interactive exercises) comes next. In Part 2, "Considering What Will Make You Happier," chapters explore such topics as finding your job niche and changing careers. Part 3, "Determining Whether to Quit or Stay," examines job search considerations, provides tips for drawing up a career/life plan, and offers a "three-step guide" for making a final decision about quitting. The last and largest segment, Part 5, focuses on "What to Do After You Make Your Decision." If you choose to stay, there are "6 ways to improve your job." If you decide to leave, there are job searching and resume tips, as well as suggestions for evaluating offers, resigning, and handling exit interviews. Job interviews are also discussed, including what to say about quitting or getting fired. (Sudden job changes, i.e. being fired, asked to resign, etc., are dealt with in their own chapter.)

Evaluation:
Despite the title, this isn't just a book for people who are considering leaving their job. Readers who are dissatisfied at work are the primary audience, and most of the content is directed toward their concerns, i.e. the "three-step guide" to making a final decision about quitting, but there are lots of chapters that equally apply to people who are leaving by force, not by choice. Aside from the discussion of exit interviews, tips on making successful career changes and those that address the concerns of every job changer, there are special segments for those who have been fired, laid off, or expect to be dismissed. The authors include suggestions for how to best handle questions about both quitting and being fired at job interviews (a subject often neglected), and Holloway and Bishop offer a list of "warning signs" to let you know if you're in danger of receiving the "pink slip." The authors also repeatedly emphasize the notion that being fired is not the handicap it is perceived to be. Downsizing and changes in the marketplace have de-stigmatized termination; the employers quoted here say that they have no prejudice against people who have been fired. This is a helpful, straightforward, occasionally insightful resource for evaluating your current job, considering the practicalities of a change and facing change in whatever form it occurs.

Where To Find/Buy:
Bookstores and libraries.

★ ★ ★

Overall Rating
★ ★ ★
A helpful tool for considering career options; valuable tips for firings, lay offs

Design, Ease Of Use
★ ★ ★
Direct and to-the-point; includes self-assessment exercises

1–4 Stars

Author:
Diane Holloway, Ph.D., and Nancy Bishop

Dr. Holloway, a management consultant and psychotherapist, is a certified career counselor. Ms. Bishop is the author of *How to Get a Job in Dallas/Fort Worth* and a senior editor for the Southwestern bureau of *Adweek* magazine.

Publisher:
Macmillan

Edition:
1990

Price:
$10.95

Pages:
188

ISBN:
0020768818

Media:
Book

Principal Subject:
Termination/Job Loss

III. Career Transitions

★★★

Overall Rating
★★★
Good advice on firing/ job
loss and career management

Design, Ease Of Use
★★★
Straightforward format and
"no frills" design

1–4 Stars

Author:
William S. Frank

Mr. Frank is the founder and
President of CareerLab, a
consulting firm that specializes in
career, outplacement, and human
resources consulting. His career
articles appear in such publications
as *The Denver Post* and *Colorado
Business*.

Publisher:
CareerLab

Edition:
1996–1998

Media:
Internet

Principal Subject:
Termination/Job Loss

Secondary Subject:
Career Transitions

Job Loss Or Termination

CAREERLAB: THE CAREER ADVISOR

Description:

At the Career Advisor, CareerLab offers an array of free resources
from author (and CareerLab President) William S. Frank. These
resources include articles on a variety of career transition issues, as
well as a link to Mr. Frank's "200 Cover Letters." The articles are
arranged by topic on the Career Advisor's main page and the articles'
titles function as direct links. From within each article, readers can
use a menu bar at the bottom of the page to return to the "Article
List" or to move to the "Next Article." "Fired/Job Loss," "Job
Search," and "Career Management" are among the career topics
addressed; titles include "Make the Most of Your Outplacement
Program," "Before You Quit Your Job," "How to Ask For a Raise,"
and "Should You Consult While Job Hunting?" Other articles discuss
such job searching skills as networking, interviewing, and resumes.
There are also "Career Fitness Tests" and tips for "boosting" your
current career, i.e. "22 Career Basics."

Evaluation:

There are three "stand-out" sections in the Career Advisor: "Fired/
Job Loss," "Career Management," and "Consulting." The job search
portions, i.e. those dedicated to resumes, interviewing, etc., are fine,
but step-by-step guides will be better resources for people looking for
detailed instruction. (For cover letters, see the review of "CareerLab:
Cover Letters.") There are only 5 articles in "Fired/Job Loss," but
their high quality makes up for lack of quantity. Readers learn the
"dos and don'ts" of using their outplacement program, how to leave
gracefully (and without burning bridges), and what to do if you fear
a layoff. "Career Management" offers a greater number of articles,
all of which are valuable, and the "Consulting" section addresses the
interesting (and seldom-seen) question "Should You Consult While
Job Hunting?" Though the consulting articles are aimed at those with
salaries in the $100,000+ range, anyone can benefit from the advice.
For victims of job loss or general career transitions, try this site!

Where To Find/Buy:

On the Internet at http://www.careerlab.com/free.htm

Job Loss Or Termination

GETTING FROM FIRED TO HIRED
Bounce Back From Losing Your Job—And Get Your Career Back On Track!

★★★

Description:
The author walks the reader through the messy process of being fired, from "Twenty-One Clues That You May Be Fired" to "Hired Again . . . Hallelujah!" In between he pays close attention to the psychological trauma suffered by fired employees and their family. Though tips for the job hunt comprise half the book, even its advice on how to construct a resume is reflects the author's emphasis on the reeling emotions that often accompany sudden job loss. Two dozen chapters are divvied up into one or two page essays on each sub-topic. Set off by a bold heading, such as "Cleaning Out Your Desk" or "Headhunters," these sections allow for easing scanning and skimming. Beginning chapters discuss the global economic trends leading toward widespread downsizing and offer tips for knowing when the axe is about to fall. The next few chapters cover what to do as the firing process unravels—what to say and how to say it. Two reflective chapters, Are You A Failure? and How Does Management Evaluate Employees?, bridge into the second half of the book which is a detailed look at how to become employed again, quickly and on budget. A discussion of how to proceed when a job is offered and a look at self-employment round out the book.

Evaluation:
The tone and direction of Elkort's guide is clear from its dedication: ". . . to those wanderers in the purgatory of unemployment." Having been brutally fired himself, the author writes with a sense of empathy and support. His from-the-hip, irreverent style will appeal to younger workers and those who enjoy advice with a little attitude. What you won't find in this guide: legal advice or help with self-analysis to choose what kind of job or career you'd like to try next. The strongest sections are "Start Negotiating Immediately" which advises readers about severance pay and other post firing details and the two chapters on job interviews. These sections include factual information but they shine in their treatment of the often neglected areas of appearance and word choice. The author describes the importance of maintaining "grace under fire," and how to react in various situations. This is sage advice because caving into pressing emotions of anger or hurt can backfire and burn bridges. His encouragement to maintain a positive attitude and non-threatening, confident tone is right on target. These subtle attitude shifts can hold great sway when asking for more severance pay or explaining your job loss in a subsequent interview. Though job search advice is included, its strength is in helping to cope with the pain and confusion after a firing.

Where To Find/Buy:
Bookstores and libraries.

Overall Rating
★★★
Supportive, empathetic with plenty of advice on the job hunt

Design, Ease Of Use
★★★
Written in a series of mini-articles

1–4 Stars

Author:
Martin Elkort
An executive in the hospitality and travel industry with experience hiring, firing and counseling employees.

Publisher:
Macmillan

Edition:
1997

Price:
$14.95

Pages:
222

ISBN:
0028617371

Media:
Book

Principal Subject:
Termination/Job Loss

III. Career Transitions

★★

Overall Rating
★★
More sympathy than strategy

Design, Ease Of Use
★★★
Humorous and irreverent;
simple design

1–4 Stars

Author:
Tom Lonergan

Mr. Lonergan is an engineer and entrepreneur who has founded a computer hardware company, a computer software company, and computer services company.

Publisher:
Andrews McMeel

Edition:
1998

Price:
$9.95

Pages:
157

ISBN:
0836252101

Media:
Book

Principal Subject:
Termination/Job Loss

FIRED WITH ENTHUSIASM

Description:

Fired three times in the last 10 years, Lonergan understands the emotional ramifications of those two awful words: "You're fired." He also understands that firings and lay offs can be overcome. You have to get back in the game, and Lonergan's guide is designed to act as your "take-charge game plan." Divided into 11 chapters, Chapters 1–4 offer "pep talks," examine why you were fired, and answer the question "Why Does It Hurt?" There are checklists of "things to do," 4 rules for tackling money issues head-on, and self-help exercises for getting back on your feet. Chapters 5 and 6 provide advice for finding a new, better job, i.e. tips on interviewing, resumes, and evaluating employers, while Chapter 7 discusses starting your own business. Because unemployment is traumatic, Lonergan explores options for relieving stress and feeling better in Chapter 8, "Marathons and Long Walks." In a similar vein, Chapter 9 reminds you of "The Jerks You Left Behind" (so that you won't idealize the past). Chapters 10 and 11 include a summary of "things to remember" to help you through this crisis, such as "make a list of personal assets," "stay current," "focus on positive actions," and "don't give up when you hit the wall."

Evaluation:

There's no doubt that Lonergan's book will comfort fellow victims of job loss. He's understanding, nurturing, and frank about his own experiences. He's funny, too, though his humor is slightly bitter in flavor. For example, the chapter on "The Jerks You Left Behind" is populated by such Dilbert-esque figures as "The Emperor" (your boss), "The Sniper" (the guy who shot down all your ideas), and "The Go-Getter" (the guy who gets the credit, deserved or not). Reading this chapter is bound to provoke a smile; it may even make you feel better. Yet, while feeling better is definitely an integral part of rebounding from a job loss, there are another details to consider, too, like finding a new job. Lonergan doesn't offer much in the way of job search advice. There are some tips on interviewing and evaluating employers, but there aren't any suggestions for addressing your recent job loss in either your resume or the interview. (For guidance in this area, try "Before You Say 'I Quit!'" See review.) Also, some readers may be bothered by Lonergan's admission that he's still unemployed (that's why he's writing this book). Can this guy be trusted? Lonergan is a sympathetic pal, but his book is more likely to keep you smiling on the couch than to help you get back on your feet.

Where To Find/Buy:

Bookstores and libraries.

Job Loss Or Termination

REINVENTING YOUR CAREER
Surviving A Layoff And Creating New Opportunities

★★

Description:

When Adams was fired from his job in public relations, the future was uncertain and daunting. But being fired turned out to be a blessing in disguise. Adams went on to publish 3 novels and to start his own company; his former PR employer is now one of his clients! His story, as well as the stories of other people who have successfully overcome job loss, demonstrate that it is possible to "reinvent" yourself and your career; his guide is designed to show you how. The first three chapters explore the "downsizing/layoff phenomenon" and present case studies of 7 individuals whose lives were changed due to a sudden job upheaval. Because "there can be worse things than losing a job," Chapter 4 examines the cost of staying at the wrong job, i.e. workaholism, codependency. To prepare for job searching, Chapters 5–6 provide self-assessment tasks for identifying your "core competencies." Chapters 7–8 follow the composite character Jerry Davenport through the job search process, from motivating to "get off the couch" to constructing a personal mission statement for "self-marketing." Chapter 9 discusses such "alternatives" as starting a business and self-employment. Finally, "your life's mission" is addressed in Chapter 10.

Evaluation:

If nothing else, Adams represents a hopeful model of someone who reinvented their career after being fired. His book is so preoccupied with detailing his own path to success that it can only be considered a learn-by-example guide, rather than a "how to" resource. As such, it provides only a sketchy outline of the "reinvention" process for readers. For example, Chapter 5 emphasizes the importance of determining your work "purpose," explains how Adams arrived at his "purpose," then says "go do it" without further assistance. Chapter 6, which deals with self-assessment, explains which traits you should evaluate but doesn't provide any techniques for doing so; Adams himself took various personality tests at a reemployment center. (This guide often acts as a promotional device for professional career counseling.) As for job searching advice, there isn't much. Adams states that he isn't interested in "reinventing the wheel," so he purposefully includes only a few tips on networking and research. For a thorough treatment of job searching, he suggests you look elsewhere. (For tips on addressing firings in your resume or at an interview, try "Before You Say 'I Quit!'" See review.) Adams's guide may help generate ideas for reinventing your career, but, unless used in tandem with another resource, it's unlikely to generate results.

Where To Find/Buy:
Bookstores and libraries.

Overall Rating
★★
General guidelines for reinventing your career; more theory than "how to"

Design, Ease Of Use
★★
Too dependent on outside sources, references

1–4 Stars

Author:
Stephen P. Adams
Mr. Adams is the founder of Adams Business Communications, a former newspaper reporter, and a novelist.

Publisher:
Northfield

Edition:
1996

Price:
$9.99

Pages:
155

ISBN:
188127361X

Media:
Book

Principal Subject:
Termination/Job Loss

USING THE INTERNET TO FIND THE RIGHT JOB AND CAREER

GUIDES TO USING THE INTERNET

The world is at your fingertips. That is the promise of technology, and in the continuing evolution and expansion of the Internet we see the fulfillment of that promise daily. Presently, it is estimated that over 30 million people worldwide use the Internet regularly; by 2001, that number is expected to exceed 250 million. With so many users and myriad possible applications, Internet technology is rapidly changing the way we live our lives, including how we search for jobs and how we manage our careers.

When you log on to the Net, you step into a virtual library of career and job resources. On the World Wide Web alone, there are thousands of sites offering everything from actual job postings to career counseling tools, networking opportunities, in-depth company research, information on job and industry trends, salary surveys, and job hunting tips. No savvy job searcher is without e-mail, and more and more people are taking advantage of the convenience and speed of sending electronic resumes, either instead of or in addition to the traditional paper version. The advent of the Internet has had a substantial effect on hiring practices, too, with over 40% of employers and recruiters using the Net and the Web to advertise positions and make hires.

Having the world at your fingertips is an exciting, if heady, concept. It allows for endless possibilities, but, as many Internet users have already discovered, endless possibilities can feel as confining as limited ones. It's easy to make a choice between two options, but what if you have four options? Ten options? One hundred options? There are over 11,000 career-related sites on the Net.

What should you be looking for? How will you know when you find it? Which sites can best meet your specific needs? It isn't only Net newbies who can be overwhelmed by the dizzying array of career-related Internet offerings. Even savvy cybersurfers can waste time slogging through web sites in a fruitless search for career information. Learning to use the Internet effectively, and learning which URLs are bookmark-worthy, is a high priority in an electronic job search.

In this section, we review resources designed to help you make the most of your time online. Guides to using the Internet fall, broadly, into two categories: those that teach you how to use the Internet in all facets of your job search and those that function as Net guides, or directories of sites. (Some resources bridge both categories.) In the "how to" category, you'll find books that offer varying degrees of hand-holding as they take you from beginner basics—accessing the Internet, getting an e-mail account—to more advanced skills—such as translating HTML texts and building a web page. The reviews will help you match your skill level with the appropriate resource.

While the "how to" resources range in purpose and focus, the Net guides share a primary objective: to provide a directory of career-related sites. Most of the Net guides are themselves websites, often referred to as "portal" or "gateway" sites (Yahoo! is a famous example).

If you've done any topical searches on the Web, you've probably noticed that using the same keyword at various search engines produces different results. That's because the information on the Internet is decentralized; there is no central repository or registry for sites. Each search engine uses its own web crawler and "filter" system to find matches among the millions of sites on the Internet.

Online Net guides function along the same lines; they too send out web crawlers to collect sites that "match" their established criteria. But the online Net guide takes the process one step further than the search engine: it organizes the results of its search—the sites—into user-friendly categories, and, in many cases, includes descriptions and details of the sites' content.

A good online Net guide should speed up your search by offering a broad range of the types of links you need. When you find the link directory that works best for you, bookmark it! Since each guide has its own "filtering" criteria, be sure to take note of details such as target audience, types of sites listed, and scope of appeal, when reading the reviews.

Keep in mind as you explore the Internet, that most hiring continues to occur through the traditional path of networking. Although certain fields, such as technology and science, have developed Internet-centric hiring processes, the rest of the job market lags behind. So add the Internet to your arsenal, but don't rely on it as your only tool.

★★★★

Overall Rating
★★★★
A great guide for all aspects of online job searching; CD-ROM is packed with bonuses!

Design, Ease Of Use
★★★★
Written for all skill levels; CD-ROM is user-friendly and a valuable tool

1–4 Stars

Author:
Shannon Karl and Arthur Karl

Shannon Karl is an online public relations professional for a modem manufacturer. Arthur Karl is systems administrator for a major financial services firm in the Midwest. Together, they are online career correspondents for the national radio show, "Log On U.S.A."

Publisher:
Coriolis Group

Edition:
1997

Price:
$29.99

Pages:
420

ISBN:
1576101258

Media:
Book + CD-ROM

Principal Subject:
Using The Internet

Guides To Using The Internet

HOW TO GET YOUR DREAM JOB USING THE WEB

 Recommended For:
Using the Internet

Description:
The print portion of this guide is divided into 12 chapters, beginning with an explanation of "Why Using The Internet And Web Can Get You The Job You Want." Chapter 2 provides "An Internet Crash Course" which introduces readers to e-mail, mailing lists, newsgroups, navigating the web, etc. Chapter 3 helps readers "Get Connected." Chapters 4 and 5 detail job sites on the web. (The CD-ROM contains the same material, but with direct links to the sites.) Chapter 6 is dedicated to creating a "killer electronic resume." Networking on line is discussed in Chapter 7, while Chapter 8 (and the CD-ROM) offer instructions for "creating your home page." Chapter 9 deals with BBSes, Chapter 10 with advice from "job hunting experts." Chapter 11 describes "The Web's Best Job Hunting Resources" (these too can be found with direct links on the CD-ROM). Working at home is explored in Chapter 12. The CD-ROM also includes shareware programs for navigating the Net, career planning software, and resume builders.

Evaluation:
This guide is packed to the gills with practical, valuable information and advice for any computerized job search goal. It's written for all skill levels, in concise, everyday language; anyone with the least familiarity with computers can use this book. Still, as good as the print version is, it's the CD-ROM which makes this a recommended resource. There are three "parts" to the CD-ROM: "bookstuff," "internetstuff," and "jobstuff." The "bookstuff" contains the same descriptions of sites detailed in Chapters 4, 5, and 11, but with direct links to the sites. "Internetstuff" includes shareware ad freeware programs to help users navigate the web, and "jobstuff" is overflowing with easy-to-use, career-related software: creating home pages, creating resumes, career planning, scheduling, and interview simulators. (The CD-ROM works with Windows 3.1 or Windows 95.) This is a fabulous resource and an in depth course on using the Net, all rolled into one!

Where To Find/Buy:
Bookstores and libraries.

Guides To Using The Internet

JOB SEARCHING ONLINE FOR DUMMIES

 Recommended For:
Using the Internet

Description:

In the print portion of her guide, Ms. Dixon divides the online job search into five parts: "Getting Ready for Your Job Search," "Building Your Electronic Toolkit," "Communicating and Networking in the Digital World," "Finding and Choosing a Job Online," and "Parts of Ten," (e.g. "Top Ten" lists). These segments cover such topics as "winning online job search strategies," maintaining privacy, developing and using electronic resumes/cover letters, networking (i.e. via chat rooms), using e-mail, "marketing yourself with your web page," and "working" job databases. An Internet directory of reviewed sites is provided; a direct link directory is available on the CD-ROM. The CD-ROM portion (compatible with both Mac OS and Windows) offers a variety of tools, many of which are related to the book's central themes. Features include web browsers (i.e. Netscape Communicator 4.0), HTML editors, Acrobat Reader 3.01 (for opening PDF files), Eudora Light 3.1.3 (e-mail), and PageMill, a WYSIWYG editor for creating web pages.

Evaluation:

If you haven't been using the Internet in your job search because you've been "waiting for the manual to come out," you're all out of excuses now. The manual is here. The print portion of this guide is smart, effective, informative, insightful, and well-written; it also requires a basic familiarity with the Net. (Ms. Dixon will teach you everything else.) The number one reason to use this guide, however, has to be the CD-ROM. No matter how fantastic a print resource on the Web is, it can never compare to "hands on" learning. The CD-ROM is easy to install, and its software/freeware represents a variety of valuable tools: the direct-link directory provides URLs to visit, the HTML editors and PageMill will help you create electronic resumes and Web pages, the browsers (Netscape Communicator, Microsoft Internet Explorer) will enable you to do research, etc. Online job searching is the wave of the future. Pam Dixon doesn't just provide surfing instruction; her CD-ROM is a veritable surfboard!

Where To Find/Buy:

Bookstores and libraries.

Overall Rating
★★★★
All kinds of great tools and advice for conducting an online job search

Design, Ease Of Use
★★★★
Well written; the CD-ROM is user-friendly and easy to install

1–4 Stars

Author:
Pam Dixon

Ms. Dixon is a journalist, teacher, and the author of several books in the area of technology as it affects education, business, and culture. Her work includes *Be Your Own Headhunter Online*, *Virtual College*, and *Take Charge Computing for Teens and Parents*.

Publisher:
IDG Books Worldwide

Edition:
1998

Price:
$24.99

ISBN:
0764503766

Media:
Book + CD-ROM

Principal Subject:
Using The Internet

IV. Using The Internet To Find The Right Job And Career

Overall Rating
★★★★
Wide-ranging links, insightful advice; a valuable bookmark and "first step"

Design, Ease Of Use
★★★★
Simple and user-friendly; minimal graphics

1–4 Stars

Author:
Margaret F. Dikel

Margaret Dikel (formerly Margaret Riley) holds an MS in Library and Information Sciences. She is a private consultant, author of *The Guide to Internet Job Searching*, and an Internet columnist for *National Business Employment Weekly*.

Publisher:
Drake Beam Morin

Edition:
1998

Media:
Internet

Principal Subject:
Using The Internet

Guides To Using The Internet

THE RILEY GUIDE
Employment Opportunities And Job Resources On The Internet

 **Recommended For:**
Using the Internet

Description:

The Riley Guide originated in 1994 and was one of the first "gateway" sites for online job searching. It contains both links and original material from author Margaret Dikel. For locating "work opportunities," there are links to job listings from "general recruiters," "location-specific" resources/job sites, and sites for "specific occupational areas," i.e. engineering, recreation, etc. There are also links to online resume databases and other "meta-guides." For researching careers online, Ms. Dikel offers advice on and links for such subjects as career exploration, relocating, contacting a guidance counselor, and salary guides. She also helps users with electronic resumes, using/navigating the Internet, and choosing job search guides; relevant links are provided. A site map functions as a "table of contents;" it lists all of the pages found in the guide and briefly describes their "purpose." The site also includes information about the guide's history, a page on new additions, and an alphabetical "topic by topic index."

Evaluation:

Since it was designed for "everyone" (i.e. users with only a text-based browser and a slow connection), the layout of this site may seem overly simplistic to the seasoned Internet surfer: it's simple and contains almost no graphics. Despite it's less than exciting format, however, this is a valuable bookmark for any online job search. Users new to the Net will particularly benefit from this guide: it does not assume great technical acumen. In addition to the wide variety of links (which range from "major recruiting sites" to resources for users interested in law enforcement), Ms. Dikel offers plainspoken advice on how to use/navigate the Net effectively and how to continue the search "from here." Her original material is insightful and pertinent, and she always provides additional information. For example, the page on resumes includes her own tips and "points to consider," links to resume-building sites, and a list of print resources. This is great place for job hunters or researchers to begin their online search.

Where To Find/Buy:
On the Internet at http://www.dbm.com/jobguide/

Guides To Using The Internet

USING THE INTERNET AND THE WORLD WIDE WEB IN YOUR JOB SEARCH
The Complete Guide To Online Job Seeking And Career Information

★★★★

 Recommended For:
Using the Internet

Description:
The authors have prepared an updated edition to reflect recent changes on the World Wide Web. Chapters 1–3 introduce you to the Internet and tell you how to get connected, with introductions to commercial online services, bulletin boards, web browsers, search engines, and more. The WWW classifieds and career/job resources on commercial services are explored in the next chapters. Chapters 6, 7, and 8 discuss "venturing outside" the Web, with information on how to use such things as newsgroups and listservs; career resources and Internet support groups are explained as well. The following 4 chapters are devoted exclusively to the components of the job search: preparing and submitting an electronic resume, following job-hunting "netiquette," and dealing effectively with the Internet interview. The final chapters give advice for college students on the hunt, and advice for employers on electronic recruiting. A glossary of terms and software for submitting a resume to the IntelliMatch database round out the book.

Evaluation:
Experienced and novice Net surfers alike will find this an excellent guide to the new world of the electronic job search. Information on Internet resources, and especially, on how to use them, is presented clearly and effectively. Particularly useful are the plentiful graphics which allow you to actually see what a resource looks like onscreen; this is bound to be of help to new "Netters" who need a reassuring glimpse of what awaits them before plunging full-tilt into the electronic labyrinth. Also given are lots of step-by-step instructions for helping you perform such actions as subscribe to listervs and use gopher applications. An entire chapter is devoted to telling you exactly how to prepare an electronic resume, along with samples both good and bad; this is followed by 3 equally valuable chapters on submitting your resume, Internet job-hunting "netiquette," and dealing with the Internet interview. Overall a recommended resource for the electronic job hunt.

Where To Find/Buy:
Bookstores and libraries, or directly from the publisher at (800) JIST-USA, or by fax at (800) JIST-FAX.

Overall Rating
★★★★
A comprehensive guide to using Internet resources; great for employment "netiquette"

Design, Ease Of Use
★★★★
Graphics of actual Internet screens and explicit instructions make this "user-friendly"

1–4 Stars

Author:
Fred E. Jandt & Mary B. Nemnich

Fred E. Jandt is a communications professor at California State University, San Bernardino, and the author of *Win-Win Negotiating* and *The Customer Is Usually Wrong!* Mary B. Nemnich is an employment specialist with the California Employment Development Department, and producer of the T.V. show Job Connection.

Publisher:
JIST Works

Edition:
1997

Price:
$16.95

ISBN:
1563712924

Media:
Book

Principal Subject:
Using The Internet

Of Interest To:
Returning To The Workplace

IV. Using The Internet To Find The Right Job And Career

★★★★

Overall Rating
★★★★
A great directory of career resources, plus lots more!

Design, Ease Of Use
★★★★
User friendly, accessible, dynamic

1–4 Stars

Author:
The two developers of Yahoo!, David Filo and Jerry Yang, started their guide in April 1994 to keep track of their personal interests on the Internet. Today, Yahoo! contains information on tens of thousands of computers linked to the Web.

Publisher:
Yahoo! Inc.

Edition:
1998

Media:
Internet

Principal Subject:
Using The Internet

Guides To Using The Internet

YAHOO! BUSINESS AND ECONOMY: EMPLOYMENT

Recommended For:
Using the Internet

Description:
Yahoo!'s "Employment" section (a subdivision of "Business and Economy") has its own "table of contents." There are 23 job-related "areas," which range from basic career needs, i.e. "Career Fields," "Career Planning," and "Resumes," to the needs of certain job seekers, i.e. "Expatriates," "People of Color," and "People with Disabilities." Other "areas" include "Companies," "Jobs," "Mailing Lists," and "Organizations." The pages for each "area" offer an additional list of specific topics (for as narrow a search as possible), annotated links to relevant online resources, and access to subject-specific clubs. For example, in "Career Planning," "Veterans" can access online "veteran" clubs, while "People with Disabilities" can access related clubs from their "page." The annotated links are arranged alphabetically; a paragraph-length review is available wherever the word "review" appears. There are also message boards, news links, classified ads, relocation information, and a "salary comparison" calculator.

Evaluation:
Yahoo! is one of the best known and best loved organizational tools on the Internet; it's an enormous site, packed with lots of features (games, zines, events, etc.). At its most basic level, it is an accessible, comprehensive Net guide, and for job seekers, the "Employment" section functions as just that. Whatever the Net has to offer in terms of employment, from job banks to career planning assistance, users will find it at Yahoo! Despite a valiant attempt to "narrow" search perimeters (i.e. 23 job-related areas followed by more specific "titles," etc.), there is a huge amount of information to wade through. This is, however, a better designed and more user-friendly site than the average "meta-list." Plus, it offers features other Net "guides" do not, such as the message boards and the wide array of clubs (useful for online networking), as well as access to the rest of Yahoo!: a real estate/relocation guide (with maps), "Internet Life," "yellow pages," etc. Internet novices, in particular, will benefit from this fantastic guide.

Where To Find/Buy:
On the Internet at http://www.yahoo.com/business/employment

Guides To Using The Internet

★★★

JOBPOINTER

Overall Rating
★★★
A comprehensive bookmark collection for career and job search sites

Design, Ease Of Use
★★★★
Downloading is easy; the software is simple, straightforward, user-friendly

1–4 Stars

Author:
Jeff Rios

Publisher:
Dog-ear Development Company

Edition:
1998

Media:
Software

Principal Subject:
Using The Internet

Description:
JobPointer is a bookmark collection of more than 3,300 URLs to career and job search sites. The sites are organized into 5 databases (or directories) of links: "Job Search," "Job Hunt-Fields & Interests," "Job-Newsgroups," "Career Esources," and "Services & Tools." "Job Search" holds over 1,100 job search sites organized by location (i.e. U.S., Canada, etc.), while "Job Hunt" has 800+ links to job search sites for specific employment fields (i.e. technology, education, etc.) and "special interest" sites (i.e. minorities, people with disabilities, etc.). "Job-Newsgroups" contains 400 job newsgroups, "Career Esources" offers 800+ URLs to career guidance and counseling sites, and "Services and Tools" lists 150 "services," such as resume banks, online recruiters, job fairs, etc. Users click on a database icon, scroll through the contents, and click on the name of a site for a direct link. Both Macintosh and Windows users can download the software for free at www.dog-ear.com, which also provides an overview of the product.

Evaluation:
At www.dog-ear.com, the developers of JobPointer provide an overview of the bookmark collection (complete with pictures of the screens), as well as information on system requirements, installation, etc. The software is free to both Mac and Windows users; Mac's need a minimum of 2.9 MB free space (hard drive), Windows' requires a minimum of 4.3 MB free space (hard drive). Since the Net is constantly changing, users can choose to "sign up" for updates (new URL's, etc.), which are sent via e-mail. Downloading JobPointer is simple: just click on the "Download Job Pointer" (on the page "Get Your Very Own Dog") for automatic download. (It takes about 6 minutes.) Mac's will need "Stuffit Expander" to decode the file (free from Aladdin Systems); Windows' can use a utility such as the free "PowerZip." Online job searching can be arduous without a good Net guide; with its easy-to-use "point and click" format, JobPointer is a great choice. It's well organized and offers access to a wide variety of career/job search sites.

Where To Find/Buy:
On the Internet at http://www.dog-ear.com

★★★

Overall Rating
★★★
A good beginner's bookmark for all facets of the job search

Design, Ease Of Use
★★★★
User friendly, direct links to the sites reviewed, attractive

1–4 Stars

Author:
Richard Nelson Bolles

Mr. Bolles is the author of the best-selling *What Color Is Your Parachute?* He is listed in *Who's Who In America*, and *Who's Who In the World*. He is an acknowledged expert in the field of career planning.

Media:
Internet

Principal Subject:
Using The Internet

Guides To Using The Internet

WHAT COLOR IS YOUR PARACHUTE: JOB HUNTING ONLINE

Description:

There are two "parts" to this web site: "The Net Guide" and "Parachute Talk." "The Net Guide" is designed to help job searchers "surf" effectively by providing reviews/links to selected career-related sites. An introductory page outlines the "Guide" and the five "categories" of web sites: job listings, resumes, career counseling, networking, and research. Each "category" has its own page, accessible from the top of each screen, and begins with an explanation and advice on how to use the resources. Next, Mr. Bolles presents his choices for the "best" sites pertaining to that "category," i.e. the "best" sites for job listings, etc. Users can browse the reviews or use them as direct links to the described sites. (There is also a page for "links only.") "Gateway" sites, comprehensive general sites with thousands of links, are also reviewed. Highly recommended sites in each "category" are designated by a parachute graphic. "Parachute Talk" enables users to submit questions to the author and/or join a discussion group.

Evaluation:

There are, allegedly, over 11,000 career-related sites on the Internet. Searching through them can be time consuming, especially for users new to the Net. Hosted and maintained by WashingtonPost.com, this website is a good starting place for all facets of the job search, from locating actual job openings to networking via chat rooms, newsgroups, etc. Users can move easily between "categories," the format is user-friendly, and sites covered represent an introductory cross-section of available resources. (This isn't a huge site with hundreds of links.) Mr. Bolles also offers his honest opinion of "how effective" online tools are. For example, he estimates that only 1% of users looking for a non computer-related job will find a position as a result of their Internet search; for computer-related jobs, he estimates a 40% success rate. Mr. Bolles' book, "Job Hunting On The Internet," contains the same material as this website, but the online version is far superior: the site is updated regularly and allows immediate access to the reviewed sites.

Where To Find/Buy:

Online at http://www.washingtonpost.com/parachute

Guides To Using The Internet

CAREERXROADS
The 1998 Directory To The 500 Best Job, Resume, And Career Management Sites On The World Wide Web

★★★

Description:
The authors open with a brief introduction to new features in the 1998 edition, followed by a look at "trends to watch" in online employment. There are 10 brief essays written by consultants, entrepreneurs, and others to help employers and job seekers use the Web wisely. The bulk of the book is composed of the sites themselves, with information on costs to post/view jobs and resumes, industry, specialty, and location, and a brief review of the site itself. A sampling of sites includes: America's Job Bank; Asia-Net; CareerMosaic; Hard@Work; MonsterBoard; Talent Alliance; and Women in Technology & Industry-WITI. The authors have chosen 37 "Best of the Best" sites, and these they mark with the CAREERXROADS graphic. Sites are cross-referenced at the back of the book by Career Management Advice, College & Entry Level, Diversity, Industry & Specialty Niches, Jobs/Resumes for Free and for a Fee, and more. Intermediate to advanced knowledge of the Net is assumed throughout.

Evaluation:
Although suffering from poor editing/proofreading, this directory provides amazingly comprehensive coverage of the 500 "best" job, resume, and career sites on the Web. Sites are arranged alphabetically, and are easy to flip through IF you know what you are looking for. If you don't, the index at the back of the book provides some cross-reference help, including sites listed by career management, industry, and location (among others). While there is a lot here, one senses there is still a lot "out there," and that a book of this type can really only introduce you to some of the "biggies." However, as the Internet grows ever more vast and complex, research tools such as this become absolutely indispensable to smart navigating. If you're looking to find a job, this book will help you locate places to post resumes, research jobs and fields, etc. The effort to rate and review sites is especially useful— reviews are succinct and up-to-date, and the "Best of the Best" gives you quick access to the stand-out sites.

Where To Find/Buy:
Bookstores and libraries.

Overall Rating
★★★
Comprehensive, rated coverage of the 500 "best" career-related sites on the Web

Design, Ease Of Use
★★★
Some (but not a lot) helpful cross-referencing; could really use some editing

1–4 Stars

Author:
Gerry Crispin and Mark Mehler
The authors "have each been involved in the employment field for their entire careers." Gerry Crispin is currently vice president of Shaker Advertising Agency, Inc. Mark Mehler works as a consultant to major corporations on recruiting.

Publisher:
MMC Group

Edition:
3rd (1998)

Price:
$22.95

Pages:
373

ISBN:
0965223949

Media:
Book

Principal Subject:
Using The Internet

IV. Using The Internet To Find The Right Job And Career

★★★

Overall Rating
★★★
A good introduction for job seekers unfamiliar with the Net; includes lots of URLs

Design, Ease Of Use
★★★
Simple, nontechnical language; samples and "screens" are used for illustration

1–4 Stars

Author:
Steven Graber, Andy Richardson, Emily Ehrenstein

Adams Media Corporation is a publisher of career books and software products, including the online resource CareerCity.

Publisher:
Adams

Edition:
1998

Price:
$9.95

Pages:
306

ISBN:
1558507531

Media:
Book

Principal Subject:
Using The Internet

ELECTRONIC JOB SEARCH ALMANAC

Description:
The Internet is a valuable asset for today's job hunter because it offers so many tools and opportunities. So many, in fact, that many users don't know where to begin. To help readers use the Net effectively, this guide offers an introduction to "the concept of electronic job hunting," a glossary of terms, and advice on an array of job searching issues. In Part 1, "Reinventing the Traditional Resume," readers learn how to create and post an electronic resume. Part 2, "Finding Advertised Jobs," provides details and URLs for the "best" places to find job openings; discussion includes commercial online services, usenet newsgroups, the world wide web, and BBSs. Researching companies and employers is the subject of Part 3, wherein readers will find information on business databases and tips on locating a company's home page. Networking online is also explored. Finally, Part 4 examines other aspects of electronic job searching, such as job hunting and career management software and "computer assisted job interviews."

Evaluation:
Written primarily for the Internet novice, this guide takes pains to be easily understood: there's a glossary of terms, the language is simple and nontechnical, and technical terms (when used) are highlighted in boldface and quickly explained (in a style reminiscent of a high school text book). However what it lacks in style it makes up for in clarity: anyone can use this guide. Some chapters are more helpful than others, though. The sections on finding job openings, researching companies and networking online are excellent.
There are lots of URLs, including a great mini-directory of career-related web sites (complete with pictures of the home pages), and information on a variety of sources: gophers, newsgroups, BBSs, etc. These segments alone make this book a recommended resource.
The section on creating electronic resumes, however, suffers in comparison to online resources dedicated to the same feat.
Use the guide's web site list to find a better, online tool.

Where To Find/Buy:
Bookstores and libraries.

Guides To Using The Internet

THE QUICK INTERNET GUIDE TO CAREER AND COLLEGE INFORMATION

★ ★

Description:

This slim guide is designed as a quick and easy reference tool for navigating career-related sites on the Net. Chapters are designed to help you find information by subject, beginning with a brief introduction to the Net and its components (links, search engines, etc.) in chapter 1. Chapter 2 sets forth a list of sites related to career/job hunting, including "clearinghouses" composed of lists of other Internet sites ("a site of sites"), job and resume banks, and other sites that provide career-related information. Sites with Education and Financial Aid Information come next in chapter 3, broken down by secondary education, post secondary education and financial aid, and education planning/research. Chapter 4 contains a list of sites about the labor market and general economic information, such as employment statistics and projections, occupational data, and so on. The last chapter includes other resources such as sites for professional organizations, human development, and more.

Evaluation:

This guide is very useful for first-time or hurried users of the Net. For those with no time, patience, or ability to leisurely wend their way through the Web, it provides quick, lucid descriptions of what these sites contain, relatively jargon-free. An entire chapter is devoted to learning the basics of the Net and World Wide Web, a nice feature often overlooked by books of this sort. Also helpful is the grouping of sites into meaningful categories (e.g. clearinghouses, job and resume banks, education-related, etc.) which saves you having to slog through sites unrelated to your search. The reviews of the sites themselves are clear and thorough; the author gives you a good grasp of what they contain. (An added plus would have been a greater effort to rate these sites—particularly good ones are given special mention, but it is hard to assess the relative value of the rest.) We'd recommend this guide for busy professionals and newcomers to the Net who want a quick and easy career reference tool.

Where To Find/Buy:

Bookstores and libraries.

Overall Rating
★★
Quick, easy-to-use guide to career/job-related sites on the Web

Design, Ease Of Use
★★★
Reviews of sites are succinct and thorough; sites categorized by type and content

1–4 Stars

Author:
Anne Wolfinger

Anne Wolfinger is "a consultant and writer specializing in career information and issues."

Publisher:
JIST Works

Edition:
1998

Price:
$9.95

Pages:
49

ISBN:
1563704382

Media:
Book

Principal Subject:
Using The Internet

IV. Using The Internet To Find The Right Job And Career

Guides To Using The Internet

THE ARGUS CLEARINGHOUSE

Non-Rated Resource

Description:
The Argus Clearinghouse provides ratings and links for a variety of Internet resources. The resources are arranged by category, i.e. "engineering," "environment," and "communications." Within the "business and employment" category, users can click on such "keywords" as "career" or "resume" for a list of online "guides." "Guides" are rated on a 1–5 scale; "guide information" contains a direct link to the reviewed site and author/ sponsor name.

Publisher:
Argus Associates, Inc.

The Argus Clearinghouse was founded in 1993; its staff is made up of individuals who either have or are studying for Master's Degrees in Information and Library Sciences.

Media:
Internet

Principal Subject:
Using The Internet

Where To Find/Buy:
On the Internet at http:// www.clearinghouse.net

BEATRICE'S WEB GUIDE FOR WOMEN AND CAREERS

Non-Rated Resource

Description:
Beatrice's Web Guide is a directory of women-related websites on a wide variety of subjects, including "Fab Finds" for online career information. On the "Careers" page, visitors can choose from such topics as "Aptitude Tests," "Fired," "Maternity Leave," "Starting a Business," and "Starting a Job Hunt Working." Click on a topic for direct links to and descriptions of relevant websites. The site also offers online chat and message boards.

Publisher:
Women.com Networks

Media:
Internet

Principal Subject:
Using The Internet

Of Interest To:
Women

Where To Find/Buy:
On the Internet at http:// www.bguide.com/webguide/ careers

CAREER EXPLORATION LINKS

Non-Rated Resource

Description:
UC Berkeley's University Health Services' "Career Exploration Links" are links to over 700 career- and education-related (i.e. graduate school) Internet resources. Users can search by keyword, choose from topic headings (i.e. "Health," "Agriculture") or browse "all links." Icons representing the type of information users will find at each site—occupational, educational, or "special interest," appear beside each link for ease of reference.

Publisher:
University Health Services, UC Berkeley

University of California at Berkeley's University Health Services (UHS) provides a variety of mental health and occupational health services, including the online resource "Career & Educational Guidance Library," which features "Career Exploration Links."

Media:
Internet

Principal Subject:
Using The Internet

Where To Find/Buy:
On the Internet at http:// www.uhs.berkeley.edu/ CareerLibrary/links/ careerme.htm

IV. Using The Internet To Find The Right Job And Career

Guides To Using The Internet

CAREER PARADISE: COLOSSAL LIST OF LINKS

Non-Rated Resource

Description:
Emory University's Career Center's "Colossal List of Links" offers reviews of career- and job search-related Internet resources. It's divided into 4 categories: "Prime Sites" (the "top 12" sites), "Career & Job Search Web Sites," "Graduate & Professional Schools," and "Specialty Sites" (i.e. "Teaching Overseas"). Each review includes a direct link to the profiled site, a short description, and ratings for "functionality" and "artistic impression."

Publisher:
Career Center at Emory University

Career Paradise is an online product of Emory University's Career Center.

Media:
Internet

Principal Subject:
Using The Internet

Where To Find/Buy:
On the Internet at http://www.emory.edu/CAREER/Main/Links.html

CAREER RESOURCE CENTER

Non-Rated Resource

Description:
The Career Resource Center is an index of career-related web sites; it contains thousands of links for a variety of job searching needs. There are links to "major employers," job postings, career service professionals, colleges and libraries, and sites for small/home offices. Other "categories" of links include "Career Gems," CRC's top 100 career sites, and "Regional Pages," which organizes sites by location (e.g. U.S. state or Canadian province).

Author:
Marc D. Snyder

Mr. Snyder is both the director of Career Resource Center and its webmaster. He is co-author of *How to Get a Job in Seattle and Western Washington* (4th Edition) 1998 (Surrey Books).

Media:
Internet

Principal Subject:
Using The Internet

Where To Find/Buy:
On the Internet at http://www.careers.org/index.html

EMPLOYMENT INDEX

Non-Rated Resource

Description:
The Employment Index is a "gateway" site for online employment resources and contains hundreds of links; it also provides access to "Large General Search Engines," i.e. HotBot, Yahoo, etc., and to "Multiple 'META' Searchers," i.e. Ask Jeeves, MetaCrawler, etc. "Employment Search Categories" include Temporary Employment, Permanent Employment, GOV Jobs, Coll. & Univ. Jobs, HR Consultants, Retained Executive Search, Resumes, etc.

Publisher:
Employment Index

Media:
Internet

Principal Subject:
Using The Internet

Where To Find/Buy:
On the Internet at http://www.employmentindex.com

Guides To Using The Internet

THE FEMINIST MAJORITY FOUNDATION ONLINE

Non-Rated Resource

Description:
Professional associations are both important sources of career information and great venues for networking. To help women take advantage, this site offers lists of women's business, legal, and medical organizations. In "Business," entries range from "American Association of Black Women Entrepreneurs" to "American Society of Women Accountants."
Each entry contains contact information and a direct link to the association's website (where possible).

Publisher:
Feminist Majority Foundation

The Feminist Majority and The Feminist Majority Foundation are nonprofit organizations committed "to empowering women."

Media:
Internet

Principal Subject:
Using The Internet

Of Interest To:
Women

Where To Find/Buy:
On the Internet at http://www.feminist.org/gateway/womenorg.html

JOBHUNT

Non-Rated Resource

Description:
JobHunt is a "meta list" of online, job search-related resources; it offers annotated, direct links to over 700 sites. There are lists/links for "On-line Job Listings," i.e. classified ads, companies, "general" job banks, recruiting agencies, and for such "Other Job Resources" as reference sites, resume banks, and university career resource centers. A yellow, smiley-face icon indicates Mr. Spearing's choices of "Outstanding Job Resources."

Author:
Dane Spearing

Mr. Spearing began JobHunt in December 1993 as a personal "hot list;" today, the list includes over 700 resources.

Media:
Internet

Principal Subject:
Using The Internet

Where To Find/Buy:
On the Internet at http://www.job-hunt.org/

LATINOWEB

Non-Rated Resource

Description:
LatinoWeb is a gateway site dedicated to serving the needs of the Latino/Hispanic community. It provides annotated lists of direct links to Internet resources, including resources on business, government (i.e. federal jobs), education, publications, and nonprofits. The site also offers a chat room, free software (i.e. web browsers), and a database of jobs from companies specifically interested in hiring Latino/Hispanic employees.

Publisher:
LatinoWeb

LatinoWeb was designed "to empower the Latino community" by providing a gateway on the Internet for the free exchange of information.

Media:
Internet

Principal Subject:
Using The Internet

Of Interest To:
Racial/Ethnic Minorities

Where To Find/Buy:
On the Internet at http://www.latinoweb.com

Guides To Using The Internet

WEDDLE'S WEB GUIDE

Non-Rated Resource

Description:
Over 40 career-related Internet resources are profiled in Mr. Weddle's online guide. Each profile contains a brief "mission statement" and details about the site's job listings, resume database, and "other resources." Information on job listings includes the number available, the "top 3 fields," and primary salary ranges. For resume databases, there is data on the number posted, "posting period," and fees (if any). There are no links to the surveyed sites.

Author:
Peter D. Weddle

Mr. Weddle, a former business executive, is a freelance writer and the author of four books, including "Internet Resumes" (Impact Publications).

Publisher:
National Business Employment Weekly

Media:
Internet

Principal Subject:
Using The Internet

Where To Find/Buy:
On the Internet at http://www.nbew.com/weddle.html

INTERNET JOB AND RESUME DATABASES

There can be little doubt that the online job/resume database has come of age; this year, commercials for such job sites as The Monster Board appeared during the Superbowl! A few years ago, an ad for a website—any website—aired in one of television's costliest ad spaces would have been a phenomenon. Today, it barely raises an eyebrow.

As the Internet becomes as familiar as the newspaper, the television, and the telephone, its value to the job seeker increases exponentially. A positive spiral is in operation: as more and more companies post jobs online, more and more job seekers consider the Internet a practical place to look for work. Higher numbers of job seekers tempt more companies to invest in their own web sites or to advertise job openings in third party directories.

Today, almost 80% of employers have their own websites, and the majority of those employers post jobs online. Professional associations, non-profit organizations, government agencies, and special-interest groups are also using the Net to disseminate information, offer services, form networks, and post jobs. Internet watch groups estimate that over 3 million jobs were advertised online in 1997, with an average of 17,000 new job postings appearing every week.

Online job databases come in all shapes and sizes, from the enormous and all-inclusive, to the small and specific. Almost all of them provide a resume bank for posting resumes. Some of these sites are tailored to a special audience, like Saludos Web, which posts jobs for Spanish-English bilinguals, while others focus on certain industries, like CareerMosaic's emphasis on health care. Other sites, such as Career Path, cull want ads from newspapers across the country.

While the technical and engineering industries still hold the title for "most jobs offered online," the soon-to-be-booming service industry is poised to become a serious contender. Job openings in such fields as financial services, sales and marketing, health care, law, business and professional services, telecommunications, communications, public relations, and teaching are becoming increasingly common.

Though the numbers for online job postings are impressive, and no one can argue with the growth of job boards in the last few years, it's important to maintain realistic expectations. With the exception of certain technical and computer-related jobs, online job/resume databases are about as effective a means of job searching as scanning the Sunday newspaper. At this point, they are essentially electronic want ads. The expansion of the Internet hasn't changed the fact that 80% of jobs are never advertised; they are either filled internally or through networking. Networking, person-to-person contact, is still the number one way to find a job.

Visit the online job/resume databases, use them; but don't spend too much of your time there. Pick a few sites that regularly advertise the types of positions that interest you, bookmark them, and then visit them once a week. Or, use the "job search agents" offered by many of these sites. The "agents" search listings for you (based on a search criteria you establish) and then send "matches" to you, via e-mail.

The Internet's greatest use to the job searcher remains its incomparable wealth of up-to-date information; it has, in terms of convenience and scope, surpassed any other research tool. The Net has added a new dimension to the old find-a-job game, but the basic strategies for winning haven't changed: you must know yourself, know your value, know your choices, and know people who can help. The world at your fingertips can enlarge the world you inhabit; it cannot replace it.

Internet Job And Resume Databases

★★★★

Overall Rating
★★★★
The first site to visit if you want to work/volunteer/intern at a nonprofit!

Design, Ease Of Use
★★★★
Simple, straightforward format, user-friendly; excellent search interface

1–4 Stars

Author:
Idealist is a product of Action Without Borders, a nonprofit organization which provides information on worldwide nonprofits, publishes a biweekly e-mail newsletter, and trains nonprofit and community organizations on how best to use the Internet in their work.

Publisher:
Action Without Borders, Inc.

Edition:
1998

Media:
Internet

Principal Subject:
Job/Resume Databases

Secondary Subject:
Employer Research

Of Interest To:
Interested In Non-Profit Sector

IDEALIST
15,000 Organizations Under One Roof

 Recommended For:
Job/Resume Online Database

Description:
The Idealist's home page, which doubles as an annotated "table of contents," offers access to a series of databases which house data from thousands of nonprofits worldwide. (Currently, 15,000 organizations in 130 countries use the Idealist.) There are databases of jobs, internships, volunteer opportunities, services and programs, and "upcoming events" (i.e. workshops, fundraisers, etc.), as well as a database of materials and publications produced by nonprofits. The search mechanism for each database varies depending on the subject; most allow users to search by such fields as "area of focus" (i.e. "arts," "community renewal," etc.), location, keyword, and language. For jobs, internships, etc., a search results in a list of "matches;" click on a "match" for a short description of the position, skill and language requirements, a contact name and phone number, and (where possible) a direct link to the sponsoring organization's home page. Users can also locate specific organizations by name, location, or keyword.

Evaluation:
Nonprofits tend to be quieter about their needs and job openings than their private sector counterparts; many nonprofits advertise openings only in such "industry" newsletters as "Opportunity NOCs." If, as a job seeker interested in nonprofits, you've ever felt like an outsider with your nose pressed against the glass, perpetually wondering "How do I get in there?," wonder no more. This site is the inside tract. The Idealist is the doorway to nonprofit opportunity; it's free, easy to use, and should absolutely be your first stop on the Net. Not only are there plenty of job openings, internships (paid and unpaid), and volunteer postings to browse (keep in mind that many people use internships and volunteering to "get in the door"), there are lots of valuable research tools as well. For example, one of the best ways to learn about an organization is to read their own publications, and this site offers a database of just such materials. This is an "absolute must" for anyone who wants to work for a nonprofit!

Where To Find/Buy:
On the Internet at http://www.idealist.org

Internet Job And Resume Databases

THE MONSTER BOARD

Recommended For:
Job/Resume Online Database

Description:

The Monster Board is designed to help "top employers" connect with job seekers, but the site encompasses far more than the job listings. There's also a "Career Center," a "Recruiter's Center," weekly features, articles, and such free services as an online recruitment seminar and a "Personal Job Search Agent" named Swoop. "Monster Job Search," which provides access to 30,000–50,000 job listings, allows users to search for listings in the U.S. by location, category, and keyword, to search international listings, to research companies, and to find internships. Or, by completing a "profile," Swoop can find job matches for you. The "Career Center" offers advice (i.e. "interviewing insights"), relocation services (including apartment listings), links to other career sites, networking opportunities, and self-evaluation "tests." A "resume builder" helps you create, post (to the site), and edit an online resume. The "Recruiter's Center" enables employers to post job openings and provides employer-related services.

Evaluation:

Despite the size of this site, it's very user-friendly. A "menu" bar appears on a separate scroll at the left side of each screen, so it's easy to move from one area to another, and navigating is simple and straightforward. The search mechanisms for scanning the huge database of job openings is more precise than most: the occupational categories are relatively specific, there are keyword searches, and searches can be formatted to include only full time, part time, or contract positions. The process for creating and posting an online resume is equally easy: there's a fill-in-the-blank form. Another great "perk" is the "Personal Job Search Agent," Swoop. Swoop can find job matches for you and deliver them to you even when you're offline. The "Career Center" has advice applicable to any job searcher and helps users network online. The graphics are arresting, it's a fun site to visit, and it definitely has something for everyone. The Monster Board is online job searching at its best!

Where To Find/Buy:

On the Internet at http://www.monster.com/

Overall Rating
★★★★
A great site; a valuable "Career Center," lots of perks, tons of job listings!

Design, Ease Of Use
★★★★
Exciting, stimulating design, user-friendly and easy to navigate

1–4 Stars

Author:

The Monster Board was established in 1994 by Jeffrey C. Taylor. It is now the flagship product of the Interactive Division of TMP Worldwide, the 14th largest advertising agency in the U.S.

Publisher:
TMP Worldwide

Edition:
1998

Media:
Internet

Principal Subject:
Job/Resume Databases

Secondary Subject:
All Inclusive Job Search

IV. Using The Internet To Find The Right Job And Career

★★★★

Overall Rating
★★★★
One of the premiere online job banks; great search engine and bonus job market info

Design, Ease Of Use
★★★
User-friendly; "headings" can be misleading

1–4 Stars

Author:
America's Job Bank is a partnership between the U.S. Department of Labor and the state operated public Employment Service. The public Employment Service is a program that comprises a network of 1,800 offices throughout the U.S.

Publisher:
The Public Employment Service

Edition:
1998

Media:
Internet

Principal Subject:
Job/Resume Databases

Internet Job And Resume Databases

AMERICA'S JOB BANK

 Recommended For:
Job/Resume Online Database

Description:
America's Job Bank houses a database of hundreds of thousands of jobs. To search this database, users have a number of choices: a "menu" search, by keyword(s), by military code, or by job number. The "menu" search includes occupation categories, and/or location (zip code radius, city/state, nationwide, etc.), and/or such "advanced" options as only "new" (to the database) jobs and jobs requiring certain education levels (i.e. Ph.D., B.A.). For general/job market information on careers, the site offers "Career InfoNet." Again, users can search via "menu" (choose from job "families," than from specific titles) or by keyword. A brief "Occupation Report" is delivered, with data on employment outlook, earnings, training requirements, and a list of "employing industries." Click on an "employing industry" for an "Industry Report" (short description, industry projections). There are also "Geographic Profiles" (U.S.), which supply statistics on demographics and economic development, and charts on "occupational trends."

Evaluation:
The Public Employment Service is a state operated program that connects employers and job seekers through a network of 1,800 offices across the U.S. Since America's Job Bank is a product of that network, its job bank has no "bias." Unlike many online job banks, this one is not just for high-tech or health care positions. Besides that, the number of postings is enormous; at the time of this review there were 840,989 jobs! The search mechanism is one of the most detailed and easiest to use; the "menu" search, in particular, is incredible. If you're looking for a job bank, this is the preeminent choice. The rest of the site offers some nice "bonuses," too. The "Occupation" and "Industry Reports" are too brief to be of help, but the list of "employing industries" is very useful; it offers job seekers lots of ideas for possible employers. The charts depicting "occupational trends," i.e. "largest nontraditional female occupations," are fun and educational. The "instructions" can be confusing, but all in all, this is a top-notch site.

Where To Find/Buy:
On the Internet at http://www.ajb.dni.us/

Internet Job And Resume Databases

CAREERCITY
Cutting Edge Careers

★★★

Description:

Everything "to do" in CareerCity appears on (and is accessible from) its home page, which doubles as a site map. There is a place to post resumes, to search for regional job fairs (by city), and to search for "jobs in all professions." CareerCity is designed for both recruiters and job seekers, so they have their own database of job openings. Users can search the database by category (i.e. public relations, computers) and/or by state/region, or you can refine your search by using "job titles." There are also links to thousands of other job sites, U.S. employers, employment services, temp firms, and hi-tech firms. Other sections include original material on career planning, i.e. "explore careers," self-assessment, and career management, and job searching "skills," i.e. interviewing, resumes, and cover letters. The page on cover letters, for example, offers users a "complete cover letter tutorial," tips and samples. For recruiters, there is an "HR Center" for posting jobs. Adams Media products and software are also detailed.

Evaluation:

In most ways, any online job searcher can benefit from a visit to CareerCity. The sections which provide free advice on interviewing, networking, handling layoffs or firings, writing cover letters, etc., are applicable to everyone, as is the advice on career planning. There are tips for creating a resume and posting it, and a mechanism for easily editing/changing a previously posted resume. Much of the site's original material is reproduced from Adams Media's print resources, so be careful of the subtle (sometimes overt) advertising, particularly with regards to its software. Still, take advantage of these advice portions, for they do include valuable insights. Also, when searching CareerCity's database for job listings, don't be too disappointed if there are few results; many companies post listings only at their own sites. (Hence the thousands of "outside" links.) For finding actual job openings, this site is best for those users interested in hi-tech, government, health care, or education-related careers.

Where To Find/Buy:

On the Internet at http://www.careercity.com/

Overall Rating
★★★
Insightful, informative "general" advice; job listings cater to specific career interests

Design, Ease Of Use
★★★★
User-friendly; easy to navigate, post resumes, search database

1–4 Stars

Author:
Adams Media Corporation is a publisher of job search and career books. Its publications include the "Knock'em Dead" and "JobBank" series.

Publisher:
Adams Media Corporation

Edition:
1998

Media:
Internet

Principal Subject:
Job/Resume Databases

Secondary Subject:
All Inclusive Job Search

Internet Job And Resume Databases

★★★

Overall Rating
★★★
A good "mega site"; includes industry-specific info and job openings in health care

Design, Ease Of Use
★★★★
User-friendly, annotated links; attractive

1–4 Stars

Author:
CareerMosaic is a product of Bernard Hodes Advertising, Inc., a recruitment advertising agency.

Publisher:
Bernard Hodes Advertising

Edition:
1998

Media:
Internet

Principal Subject:
Job/Resume Databases

Secondary Subject:
All Inclusive Job Search

CAREERMOSAIC

Description:

Visitors to CareerMosaic's home page will find links CM employers, allied sites, and an annotated "table of contents" for the site's original material/databases. Users can employ the "job search agent," search the database of job listings by job description, job title, company, city, state, and/or country, or do a "USA radius search" (enter the zip code and distance in miles for jobs in a given radius). The site also features a resume database, with instructions on building/posting a resume in ASCII text, and a "Career Resource Center." The "Center" includes articles, a "Q&A" forum, ("CareerCoach"), relocation resources, a "resource library," salary information, and a "Resume Writing Center," which encompasses resumes, cover letters, and samples. For professionals in the health care industry, there is "HealthOpps," a page with job openings and industry-specific information. Other industries, finance and accounting, human resources, electrical engineering, and insurance, have available links/pages.

Evaluation:

There are a lot of career-related "mega sites" in cyberspace. Distinguishing one from another can be difficult; they include many of the same features: job and resume databases, "job search agents," etc. CareerMosaic is a good choice for people interested in the industries it highlights, especially the health care industry. The "Health Opps" section offers both advice for professionals as well as its own database of jobs; it's definitely worth checking out. The "Resume Writing Center," which offers instructions for creating both electronic and print resumes (there's a terrific explanation of ASCII text), as well as cover letters, is another valuable tool. The site also affords special attention to "novice" job seekers: there's an "employer" page for entry-level positions, tips on networking, and the section on interviewing provides sample questions for entry-level positions. Whether you're an inexperienced job searcher or someone returning to the workplace after years away, these "beginner" tips will serve you well.

Where To Find/Buy:

On the Internet at http://www.careermosaic.com/

Internet Job And Resume Databases

JOBOPTIONS

Description:

For the job hunter, JobOptions offers 5 main features: "Job Search," "Search Employers," "Post Your Resumes," "Job Alert," and "Career Tools." Click on "Job Search" to search the site's database of thousands of job openings; click on "Search Employers" for job openings at specific companies and/or direct links to employers' sites. Both databases use the same search interface: you can choose up to 5 state(s)/province(s) (or international) and/or up to 5 job categories (i.e. "education," "electronics"), or you can search by keyword. By completing a form, you can register for "Job Alert" and JobOptions will find job postings for you. To "Post Your Resume," there is a fill-in-the-blank "resume builder" and a resume bank. "Career Tools" provides annotated lists of links for such subjects as industry/business information, salary information, and relocating, as well as featured articles. Articles include "Resume Basics," "Choosing a New Career Path," and a "Practice Interview" with 16 sample questions and answers.

Evaluation:

Although JobOptions is ostensibly an "all-inclusive" site, its primary focus is definitely job openings. Therefore, the features associated with finding job openings—"Job Search," "Search Employers," "Post Your Resumes," "Job Alert"—considerably outshine the remaining feature, "Career Tools." In fact, "Career Tools" is so inadequate, it seems "tacked on." Not that there aren't a few good parts; the "Practice Interview" is well done, and the links are helpful. Still, the job openings are clearly JobOption's "bread and butter," and it is to those features they have dedicated their efforts. The search interface is one of the better ones; it allows users to broaden or narrow their search depending on the number of states/job categories chosen. Searching employers is equally effective, and there's "one-click resume forwarding." And what could be easier than a fill-in-the-blank "resume builder?" This isn't the biggest job database, but it is incredibly user-friendly. JobOptions is definitely worth a visit.

Where To Find/Buy:

On the Internet at http://www.joboptions.com/esp/plsql/espan_enter.espan_home

---

Overall Rating
★★★
Dedicated primarily to job postings; offers links and some articles on job searching

Design, Ease Of Use
★★★★
Easy-to-use search interface, user-friendly; includes a "resume builder"

1–4 Stars

Author:
Formerly known as E-SPAN, JobOptions is one of the pioneers of online employment recruiting; it began in 1991.

Publisher:
JobOptions

Edition:
1998

Media:
Internet

Principal Subject:
Job/Resume Databases

Secondary Subject:
All Inclusive Job Search

IV. Using The Internet To Find
The Right Job And Career

★★★

Overall Rating
★★★
Advice and articles for African American job seekers; worth a visit

Design, Ease Of Use
★★★
User-friendly, attractive

1–4 Stars

Author:
The Black Collegian Online is the electronic version of the 27 year old magazine of the same name.

Publisher:
Black Collegiate Services

Edition:
1998

Media:
Internet

Principal Subject:
Job/Resume Databases

Secondary Subject:
All Inclusive Job Search

Of Interest To:
Racial/Ethnic Minorities

Internet Job And Resume Databases

THE BLACK COLLEGIAN ONLINE
The Career Site For Students And Professionals Of Color

Description:

The Black Collegian Online combines articles from current and past editions of "The Black Collegian" with a database of job listings and a resume bank. The home page doubles as a table of contents, from which users can access the career, college or lifestyle portions of the site. In the career portion, "Career Related," there are lists of "Top 100 Employers," "Top Employers Contacts," and "Top Employers by Major." There are also articles and tools for "Career Planning," i.e. "Careers for the New Millennium," and "The Job Search," i.e. "How to Write an Electronic Resume." "Reports" on such featured industries and careers as "Financial Services" and "commercial artists" are included, as are "Relocation Resources." Users can search for job openings by employer (they're arranged alphabetically), or users can search the job database by keyword, job title, and/or state (U.S.). The site also provides "hot links" and reviews of other web sites, news, inspirational quotes, and commentary.

Evaluation:

Though The Black Collegian Online's job bank can't compete in size or scope with the enormous database of America's Job Bank (or similar "mega" sites), this is still a valid resource for African-American job seekers. In many ways it caters to the student/recent graduate crowd; most of the "Career Planning" articles are aimed at this age group. But there are also lots of informative "factoids," such as the charts of "Top 100 Employers," and helpful articles on all facets of job searching. The industry and career reports are well done, but since they cover only selected industries/careers, they may or may not be of help. This isn't the place to learn "how to" write a resume, cover letter, etc.; no "article" can replace step-by-step instructions and examples. However, the site does offer "bonus" features: commentary on topical issues, reviews of related websites, lifestyle pages, etc. It's a pity there aren't any chat rooms or "clubs;" this could be a great site for networking. Still, it's worth a visit in your online job search.

Where To Find/Buy:

On the Internet at http://www.black-collegian.com

Internet Job And Resume Databases

★★★

THE CAREERBUILDER NETWORK

Description:

The CareerBuilder Network is an independent site in partnership with other career sites; its "Personal Job Search Agent" can, therefore, search a number of databases for job openings. This site has its own "career center," full of original material, which addresses such subjects as "getting hired," how to "succeed at work," and how to "manage your career." In "getting hired," users will find handbooks, articles, "Q & A" forums, and recommended resources for writing resumes and cover letters (samples are included), interviewing, the "job hunting process," "marketing yourself," and "negotiating with employers." "Succeed at work" contains articles about "the workplace" and "getting ahead." For career management, there are articles, "Q&A" forums, and links for choosing a career, "career transitions," "working women," and relocating. The site also features a "salary calculator," to compare the cost of living between cities, an "e-zine," information on "hot companies," and research-related links.

Evaluation:

The original "job prep" material found at this site (the handbooks, articles) is well worth reading. There are some valuable insights and lots of samples of different resumes and cover letters; the interview segment is as good as most print resources on the same topic. In the career management "category," the articles and links for "working women" are a notable inclusion, since few "general audience" sites contain specific resources for women. This site also distinguishes itself by its attention to such issues as how to "succeed at work," which includes an article on interoffice dating, and its partnership with "diversity sites," i.e. "Hispanic Online" and "Black Enterprise Online." For users seeking prepatory information, this is a fine resource. As for format, it's generally easy to move around this site, but there are some minor nuisances. For example, you can't move from "resumes" to "cover letters" without returning to the "getting hired" main menu. And don't bother with the job database; it's too limited in scope.

Where To Find/Buy:

On the Internet at http://www.careerbuilder.com

Overall Rating
★★★
Worthwhile for the original handbooks, articles

Design, Ease Of Use
★★★
Generally user-friendly; some minor difficulty in navigating

1–4 Stars

Author:
The CareerBuilder Network is a product of CareerBuilder, Inc., a producer of Internet-based electronic recruiting products and services.

Publisher:
CareerBuilder, Inc.

Edition:
1998

Media:
Internet

Principal Subject:
Job/Resume Databases

Secondary Subject:
All Inclusive Job Search

IV. Using The Internet To Find
The Right Job And Career

★★★

Overall Rating
★★★
Search the want ads of 70+ newspapers from across the country

Design, Ease Of Use
★★★
Straightforward design; easy to use

1–4 Stars

Author:
CareerPath.com was founded in 1995 by six major newspapers: *The Boston Globe, Chicago Tribune, Los Angeles Times, The New York Times, San Jose Mercury-News,* and the *Washington Post.*

Publisher:
CareerPath.com

Edition:
1998

Media:
Internet

Principal Subject:
Job/Resume Databases

CAREERPATH.COM

Description:

Created by 6 major newspapers, including "The New York Times" and "The Washington Post," and funded primarily by their parent companies, CareerPath allows users to search the "want ads" of 70+ newspapers from all over the country. For example, there are newspapers from Boston, Chicago, Des Moines, Los Angeles, Nashville, Seattle, Charleston, and other mid to large cities. (A list of all participating newspapers is available by clicking on "About CareerPath.com" on the home page.) Users can search for want ads by job category, keyword, dates (i.e. "most recent Sunday"), and/or by newspaper. CareerPath also has a database of job postings from employers' websites. Visitors can search for postings by employer, state, job category, industry, and/or keyword; search results provide a copy of the job description plus a direct link to the original posting (at the employer's site). In addition to the job banks, this site offers a place to post resumes, a searchable database of one-page company profiles, and a selection of "Career Resources." The "Career Resources" include news articles, information on job fairs, tips on job searching (i.e. "phone interview 101"), and self-assessment exercises (i.e. the "career self-image quiz").

Evaluation:

The primary reason for visiting this site is also its primary reason for existence: the database of want ads from newspapers across the country. Although most job openings are not listed in the newspaper, this site is the best way to search those that are. Daily feeds of new jobs are incorporated regularly, and the entire database is updated with each newspaper's Sunday "Help Wanted" listings. For want ads, using this site really is like having 70+ papers delivered to your house—only, this way, you don't have to browse every ad to find what you want! The search interface is easy to use, and the newspapers cover enough of the U.S. to satisfy most job seekers. Plus, since the ads are from papers, they represent a wide-range of occupations. If you're looking for want ads from specific cities, this is a hassle-free way to find them. The site includes other useful features, too; you can search the bank of job postings collected from employer's websites, post your resume, or browse/search the database of employer profiles. The employer profiles are short and introductory, but they do contain direct links to the employer's home page. CareerPath isn't a site for job searching advice and guidance; skip "Career Resources," they're too sparse, too brief, and offer no practical "how to."

Where To Find/Buy:

On the Internet using the URL: http://www.careerpath.com

Internet Job And Resume Databases

SALUDOS WEB
Careers, Employment, Culture

★★★

Description:
Saludos Web is one of the first career websites dedicated to meeting the needs of the Hispanic job seeker. Both the database of job listings and the resume bank are for bilingual candidates, and there is an "Hispanic Resource Center" with links to Hispanic-related Internet sites. For general job searching advice and inspiration, the site offers a "Career Center" which is divided into three subject areas: "Exploring Career Options," "Going to College," and "Seeking Employment." "Exploring Career Options" features 12 profiles of such career fields as "Broadcasting" and "Computers and Engineering," 13 "mentor profiles" of successful Hispanics in a variety of occupations, and a range of "career" articles ("career guides"). Scholarship and internship listings, which include contact information, are found in "Going to College." "Job Search Information," i.e. resume writing tips, interview preparation, and a list (links) of "Internet Employment Resources" are provided in "Seeking Employment."

Evaluation:
Saludos Web isn't a head-turning, elaborate, graphic-filled site; its format, while user-friendly, is functional rather than eye-catching. Who cares? Saludos Web doesn't need artistry to mask deficiencies in content; its content speaks for itself. True, there are other "Metasites" with larger job and resume banks, and true, there are better sites for resume writing tips, interview strategies, and exploring careers. (The profiles of career fields are informative, but too few "fields" are represented.) No career website is "one-stop shopping." What Saludos Web does offer is an effective "starting point" for Hispanic job seekers. The job and resume banks are tailor-made for bilingual job hunters, the "mentor profiles" are inspirational and educational, and the "Hispanic Resource Center" provides links to Hispanic and Puerto Rican mailing lists, newsgroups, websites, and gopher sites (great networking possibilities). Used in tandem with other online resources, Saludos Web can be a valuable tool; it's definitely worth a visit.

Where To Find/Buy:
On the Internet at http://www.saludos.com

Overall Rating
★★★
Caters specifically to Hispanic job seekers; a good starting point

Design, Ease Of Use
★★
Simple, straightforward format; no graphics

1–4 Stars

Publisher:
Saludos Hispanos
Saludos Web is an offshoot of the print magazine, *Saludos Hispanos*.

Edition:
1998

Media:
Internet

Principal Subject:
Job/Resume Databases

Secondary Subject:
All Inclusive Job Search

Of Interest To:
Racial/Ethnic Minorities

IV. Using The Internet To Find The Right Job And Career

★★

Overall Rating
★★
Offers some uncommon features, but still needs to work out the "kinks"

Design, Ease Of Use
★★★
Basically user-friendly; includes a "guided tour"

1–4 Stars

Publisher:
CRC America

America's Employers was developed by CRC America, a network of professional career consultants.

Edition:
1998

Media:
Internet

Principal Subject:
Job/Resume Databases

Secondary Subject:
All Inclusive Job Search

Internet Job And Resume Databases

AMERICA'S EMPLOYERS
The Job Seeker's Home On The Internet

Description:

America's Employers provides a "guided tour" of its contents for first-time visitors, as well as an introduction-oriented home page. The site features a "job search essentials" segment with tips on resumes and "getting started," a "company database" of 44,000 employers, access to 55,000 "advertised positions," a resume bank, and information on recruiters and "entrepreneurial options." "My Job Finder" can be employed to select online job postings which match your skills, experiences, and preferences. For honing interview skills, there's a special "room" where users can submit interview "answers" for review ("YRUA Great Hire"), or, by posting a resume, users can download free "chat software" and participate in real-time "Internet Interviews" with representatives from "actively hiring companies." Electronic networking forums are available to help visitors make contacts or receive feedback on career-related issues; postings include such subjects as "starting your career" and "job seeking."

Evaluation:

In the overpopulated arena of career-related "metasites," America's Employers stands out as an innovator. It offers a variety of seldom-seen features, for which it should be commended; too bad the new features don't work very well. For example, offering networking forums whereby users can make contacts and share information is a great idea; eventually the Internet will play a key role in this facet of job searching. At the moment, however, too few visitors are participating in these forums to make them effective. (Most of the postings receive less than 3 responses.) An ironic "Catch-22," but a current truth. Submitting interview "answers" ("YRUA Great Hire") for "review" and participating in real-time interviews are other "cutting-edge" ideas; but, again, they're not well executed. Only chosen "answers" are "reviewed," and users must post a resume to download the software required for the "Internet Interviews."
In time, this may develop into a more valuable site, so keep it bookmarked.

Where To Find/Buy:
On the Internet at http://www.americasemployers.com/

Internet Job And Resume Databases

MINORITIES' JOB BANK
Career & Lifestyle Site For People Of Color

★ ★

Description:

The Minorities' Job Bank was created to assist minorities with both their job search and "self development" needs. Visitors to the site can post their resume and/or browse the database of job openings/internships; users can search by keyword and/or state (U.S.), or by employer/company name. An alphabetized list of employers is provided, as are brief profiles of each "employer member." Most profiles include a direct link to the employer's home page. For job search advice, there are career-related articles, i.e. "Tips for Finding the Right Job," "How to Write an Electronic Resume," and information on such resources as "Organizations Assisting People of Color." The site also features 5 "virtual villages," one for each ethnic group—African-Americans, Asian Americans, Hispanic Americans, and Native Americans—and a "Global Village." Each "village" has its own "Career & Employment" section, with additional, ethnospecific articles, as well as news briefs, announcements, and "village research library."

Evaluation:

Created by Black Collegiate Services to address the needs of a larger, more diverse group of minorities (African Americans, Asian Americans, Hispanic Americans, and Native Americans), the Minorities' Job Bank has the potential to be a great Web site. Unfortunately, at the time of this review, the site remains relatively underdeveloped. The "virtual villages" are only beginning to take shape (there's not much there right now), and the career articles (many of which originated at The Black Collegian Online) are too few and too sparse. The job listings are too limited to compete with such gargantuan databases as America's Job Bank or The Monster Board, but the concept is on-target: match job seekers with employers actively recruiting minorities. Currently, this isn't the best site at which to begin an online job search, but it is a site to watch. In the meantime, check out The Black Collegian Online or Saludos Web, post your resume here and at another, "mega" site, and keep coming back to visit.

Where To Find/Buy:

On the Internet at http://www.minorities-jb.com

Overall Rating
★★
Currently underdeveloped, but demonstrates exciting potential

Design, Ease Of Use
★★★
User-friendly, attractive; the "virtual villages" are colorful, enticing

1–4 Stars

Publisher:
Black Collegiate Services

The Minorities' Job Bank is a product of Black Collegiate Services, Inc., the producers of The Black Collegian.

Edition:
1998

Media:
Internet

Principal Subject:
Job/Resume Databases

Secondary Subject:
All Inclusive Job Search

Of Interest To:
Racial/Ethnic Minorities

IV. Using The Internet To Find The Right Job And Career

Internet Job And Resume Databases

GOOD WORKS ONLINE

Non-Rated Resource

Description:
Looking for a job with a nonprofit organization? From the producers of the print resource "Good Works" (see review), this site provides a database of job posting from nonprofits. Users can search for openings by state, then click on the job title of interest for a short description of the position.

Publisher:
Essential Information

Media:
Internet

Principal Subject:
Job/Resume Databases

Of Interest To:
Interested In Non-Profit Sector

Where To Find/Buy:
On the Internet using the URL: http://www.essential.org/goodworks

PHILANTHROPY JOURNAL ONLINE: NONPROFIT JOBS

Non-Rated Resource

Description:
The Philanthropy Journal Online is an industry journal for nonprofit foundations and organizations; its job page includes a database of nonprofit job openings. Users can search the database by U.S. region (i.e. northeast, southwest, etc.) and/or by job category. A resume bank is also provided, as are lists of annotated links to career resources.

Publisher:
Philanthropy News Network

Philanthropy News Network is a nonprofit group that publishes "Philanthropy Journal Online" and "Technology Report," a national newspaper for nonprofits.

Media:
Internet

Principal Subject:
Job/Resume Databases

Of Interest To:
Interested In Non-Profit Sector

Where To Find/Buy:
On the Internet using the URL: http://jobs.pj.org

RESUMAIL NETWORK

Non-Rated Resource

Description:
In addition to posting a resume, visitors to the Resumail Network can search for job postings in one of 25 "city hubs," by state/keyword, or by employer. Users can also download free resume software, for sending electronic resumes to positions advertised at the site. (The software is for Windows 95/98 and Windows NT 4.0, and for Windows 3.1+)

Publisher:
Resumail Network

Media:
Internet

Principal Subject:
Job/Resume Databases

Where To Find/Buy:
On the Internet using the URL: http://www.resumail.com/greatjobshere.html

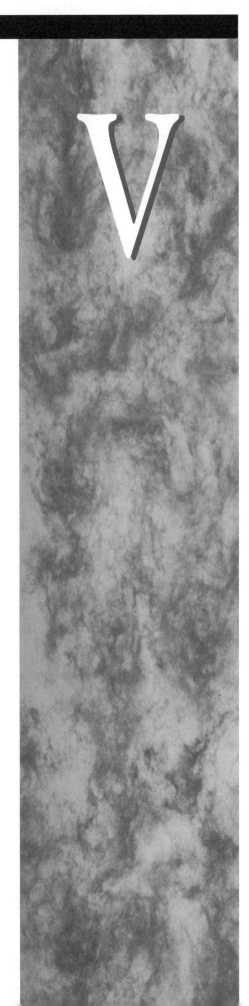

How To Land The Job You Want

OVERVIEWS OF THE JOB SEARCH PROCESS

The Internet has brought new resources for job seekers but the fundamentals of the job search have not changed. People hire people. It takes lots of time to find a job that is both a personal and professional fit. And you must work through the "nos" to get to the "yes." You may feel a little rusty when it comes to seeking a job, but it's time to dust off that resume, practice your interviewing skills, and try out that poker face for the salary negotiations.

The first section contains "all-inclusive" resources that can help you with your resume and cover letter, as well as coach you about the ins and outs of networking, interviewing and salary negotiation. As with any all-inclusive guide, the depth of coverage of each topic may not be as comprehensive as guides devoted wholly to just one aspect of the job hunt. However you may find it helpful to have one resource that offers tips and information on multiple subjects.

Following sections review resources tackling each individual topic, from resumes to salary negotiations.

Overviews Of The Job Search Process

CHANGE YOUR JOB, CHANGE YOUR LIFE

Recommended For:
All Inclusive Job Search

Description:

There are 21 chapters packed into this guide, along with interactive exercises, resource lists, charts and graphs, analysis, and advice. The subject is job changing, and Dr. Krannich covers all aspects, from preparation to research to job searching. To begin, Chapters 1–3 examines today's job market, while Chapter 4 "identifies" the "best jobs" and future trends. (Job lists are provided.) Next, acquiring "appropriate skills" and "planning your success" are explored in Chapters 5–6. Self-assessment and goal setting is the focus of Chapters 7–10, which offer interactive exercises for evaluating skills, interests, and "MAS" (Motivated Abilities and Skills). Chapters 11–15 concern job searching: i.e. resumes, letters, researching, networking, interviewing, negotiating salaries, etc. (Samples are included.) Advancing your career, relocating, and starting a business are discussed in Chapters 16–18. The final 3 chapters emphasize "taking action" and include resource lists/reviews and directions for using the Internet.

Evaluation:

If you're looking for an "all-in-one" guide to job changing, you've found it. Nothing is missing here. There are strategies for evaluating "hot job" lists, an exceptional discussion of today's economy, valuable advice for job searching, and smart self-assessment exercises. The chapter on starting a business can't compete in scope with resources solely dedicated to the subject, but that's nitpicking. This is a darn good book that will satisfy any reader. It's comprehensive, intelligent, and thought-provoking. Dr. Krannich never patronizes or "talks down" to his audience. Chapters of particular note include the absorbing and informative look at using the Internet, which offers one of the best succinct explanations of how the "electronic revolution" has affected job searching, and the educational analysis of future labor trends. Although there's (slightly) more theory than "how to," there's enough "how to" to make this book work on all levels.

Where To Find/Buy:

Bookstores and libraries.

Overall Rating
★★★★
A fantastic "all-in-one" guide for career changers; sophisticated yet practical

Design, Ease Of Use
★★★★
Dense but well organized, includes lots of graphs, charts, lists, samples, etc.

1–4 Stars

Author:
Ronald L. Krannich, PhD

Dr. Krannich is a former university professor who, along with his wife, Dr. Caryl Rae Krannich, now operates Development Concepts Incorporated, a training, consulting, and publishing firm.

Publisher:
Impact Publications

Edition:
6th (1997)

Price:
$17.95

Pages:
371

ISBN:
1570230668

Media:
Book

Principal Subject:
Job Search Overview

Secondary Subject:
Aptitude/Interest Analysis

★★★★

Overall Rating
★★★★
All-in-one job hunting guide; great advice, practical and useful

Design, Ease Of Use
★★★★
Graphics galore, well formatted; includes sample resumes

1–4 Stars

Author:
Marty Nemko, Paul Edwards, and Sarah Edwards

Mr. Nemko is a professional career counselor, columnist and author. Mr. and Ms. Edwards are the authors of several career books and the hosts of the Business News Network's one-hour show, "Working From Home."

Publisher:
IDG Books Worldwide

Edition:
1998

Price:
$16.99

Pages:
403

ISBN:
0764550950

Media:
Book

Principal Subject:
Job Search Overview

Overviews Of The Job Search Process

COOL CAREERS FOR DUMMIES

 Recommended For:
All Inclusive Job Search

Description:

Based on the work of its authors, this guide combines the "successful" job search strategies developed in Mr. Nemko's career counseling practice with the Edwards' self-employment "know how." The material is divided into five parts. Part 1 provides self-assessment exercises (i.e. "The 20 Most Revealing Questions") and "yellow pages" (brief profiles) of 512 "cool careers;" its goal is to help readers "Find the Right Career." In Part 2, "Getting Smart," readers learn where and how to get the education necessary for success in their chosen field; for example, if college/graduate school is the best choice, there are tips on choosing a school, "getting in," etc. Part 3, "A Better Way to Land the Job," tackles all aspects of job searching: writing resumes, narrowing the search, responding to want ads, networking, interviewing, and negotiating. Self-employment and "making any job better" are discussed in Part 4, "Customizing Your Career." Part 5 offers lists of additional resources, procrastination cures, and interview questions.

Evaluation:

There are very few "all-in-one" career resources that are truly worth recommending. Usually, one topic is dealt with better than another, or all topics suffer from "overcrowding." True, the "Find the Right Career" segment doesn't offer extensive multiple-choice personality testing, and the 512 brief career profiles can hardly compete with a huge resource like "The Enhanced Occupational Outlook Handbook" (see review), but it does provide more than the basics. The other segments, from "Getting Smart" to "Customizing Your Career," are illuminating. The advice is practical, realistic, thorough, and reasonable. This is a guide for normal job seekers, not the superhuman power brokers many career guides expect their audience to become. There are tips for procrastinators, for shy people who loath the idea of networking (and it's not just "get over it"), and for poor-planners who needed a job "yesterday." For "dummies" or anyone needing help finding their way down their career path, this book is a real find.

Where To Find/Buy:

Bookstores and libraries.

Overviews Of The Job Search Process

★★★★

EXECUTIVE JOB-CHANGING WORKBOOK

 Recommended For:
All Inclusive Job Search

Description:

Lucht devised this interactive workbook to function as a "tool kit" for executive job searchers. There are two parts to the workbook, literally; the halves can be physically separated. The first part, "The Front Pages" prepares you for your "campaign." Self-assessment exercises for mapping your campaign strategy are provided, as is instruction on writing resumes and cover letters. (Samples and "entry design sheets" are included.) Techniques for using personal contacts and networking effectively are next, followed by advice on interviewing and keeping tax/expense records. Information resources, such as retainer executive search firms and print resources, are also detailed. In the second part, called "The Attaché Pages" because Lucht recommends carrying it with you, there are tools for keeping track of the job search. Comprised of fill-in-the-blank forms, The Attaché Pages supply an "interview de-briefer" and devices for recording key networking contacts and tax-deductible expenses.

Evaluation:

Although Lucht's workbook supplements his guide "The New Rites of Passage at $100,000+," it is an independent resource; you don't have to read one to understand the other. ("Rites" is highly recommended; see review.) Some of the advice in this book resembles the advice in "Rites," but the workbook offers something its sibling doesn't: tons of interactive exercises, including self-assessment exercises and record-keeping devices. Also, while "Rites" is best for executives and near-executives, the workbook has greater cross-over potential. Any job searcher can use "The Attaché Pages:" the record-keeping forms. (You can put the data in your computer file later.) Still, executives are the target audience; the resumes and other samples are tailored to executive needs. If you think workbooks are only for new kids on the block, you haven't seen this one yet! It's smart, practical, and supremely useful.

Where To Find/Buy:

Bookstores and libraries.

Overall Rating
★★★★
Practical, functional workbook for executive job search

Design, Ease Of Use
★★★★
Inventive design; replete with record-keeping devices

1–4 Stars

Author:
John Lucht
Mr. Lucht has recruited senior executives to major corporations since 1971, as head of the John Lucht Consultancy Inc., since 1977, and for 6 prior years at Heidrick and Struggles, New York.

Publisher:
The Viceroy Press

Edition:
1994

Price:
$29.95

Pages:
576

ISBN:
0942785223

Media:
Book

Principal Subject:
Job Search Overview

Secondary Subject:
Moving Ahead

V. How To Land
The Job You Want

★★★★

Overall Rating
★★★★
Practical tips combined with discussions of academic and professional job markets

Design, Ease Of Use
★★★★
Clear, concise treatment of complex topics

1–4 Stars

Author:
English Showalter, Howard Figler, Lori G. Kletzer, Jack H. Schuster, and Seth R. Katz

English Showalter is professor of French at Rutgers University. Howard Figler is a career consultant. Lori G. Kletzer is assistant professor of economics at the University of California, Santa Cruz. Jack H. Schuster is professor of education and public policy at the Claremont Graduate School. Seth R. Katz is assistant professor of English at Bradley University.

Publisher:
The Modern Language Association of America

Edition:
2nd (1996)

Price:
$10.00

Pages:
156

ISBN:
0873526821

Media:
Book

Principal Subject:
Job Search Overview

Of Interest To:
Academics & PhDs

THE MLA GUIDE TO THE JOB SEARCH
A Handbook For Departments And For PhDs And Ph.D. Candidates In English And Foreign Languages

Description:
Professor Showalter opens with chapters devoted to "general advice" for the academic job hunt, such as ways to make yourself "marketable," i.e. by gaining teaching experience. He also brings up such practicalities as preparing for the cost of the job search, making up a vita, writing your letter of application, and the interview. Chapters 2–3 are directed to the job seeker and the various departments, respectively, consisting of advice and information for those involved in the hiring process (at both ends). Chapter 4 discusses opportunities available in the nonacademic job market, and how to translate academic skills into skills valued in the workplace. This chapter also contains advice about how to research employment fields and tailor your resume to fit a nonacademic job. Chapter 5 looks at general employment prospects in the professional labor market. The last 2 chapters contain discussions of the academic labor market and "job training" in graduate programs. Appendices include employment/salary statistics.

Evaluation:
At $10.00, "The MLA Guide To The Job Search" gives you a lot of "bang for your buck." Although PhD candidates may put it a little differently, they will still find an immense value packed in these pages. The academic job search is, as the preface points out, a stressful process, especially so for candidates in English and foreign languages who find themselves competing against ever-growing numbers of their peers for a relatively small number of places. This little handbook lays out the nuts and bolts of the process, as well as discussing opportunities in nonacademic job markets. PhD candidates will find this book opens up their eyes to the post-graduate school unknown, giving them a workable set of tools and a good sense of what's out there (and what isn't) for humanists. However, readers should be aware that this represents the "official" MLA version of the system, and that they may also want to avail themselves of other resources that provide different perspectives on the academic job hunt.

Where To Find/Buy:
Bookstores and libraries.

Overviews Of The Job Search Process

THE ULTIMATE JOB SEARCH SURVIVAL GUIDE
Find The Job You Really Want And Get Hired!

★★★

Description:
In his "survival guide," Mr. Dyer has divided the "journey" to job success into three phases: "Choosing Your Perfect Career," "Equipping Yourself for the Job Search," and "Conducting the Job Search." To help readers choose a career, there are chapters on motivation, "vocational identity," identifying "values and life's purpose," pinpointing "your marketable job skills," personality assessment, exploring options and defining "your objective." These chapters rely heavily on interactive exercises, tasks, and fill-in-the-blank charts, such as the "Mission Statement Worksheet" and "rating" personal adjectives to "[Assess] Your Vocational Personality." In "Equipping Yourself for the Job Search," there are samples, examples, and step-by-step instructions for writing resumes and cover letters, tips for conducting research, "the best job-finding methods," and techniques for interviewing. The final "phase" encompasses negotiating job offers and "career changing." Appendices provide additional samples, forms, and resource lists.

Evaluation:
Mr. Dyer's guide is more than an advisory text; it's an interactive workbook full of exercises, charts, tables, samples, forms, and planning tools. "Choosing Your Career" is the best section, offering lots of fun, engaging exercises and tasks for career/self exploration, many of which will be useful in resume writing (i.e. listing accomplishments, skills, etc.). Most of "Equipping Yourself for the Job Search," e.g. the chapters on resumes, cover letters and interviewing, is also valuable. The chapter on "the best job-finding methods" deals well with networking, but breezes over online job hunting. (In fact, online resources receive little attention throughout, though the appendix does provide 50 URLs.) The last segment, "Conducting the Job Search," is adequate, but misnamed; it primarily addresses post-job acquisition concerns (i.e. job offers). Overall, this is a fine choice for self-assessment and basic job search skills. Job seekers who find that fill-in-the-blank exercises encourage creative thought will benefit the most.

Where To Find/Buy:
Bookstores and libraries, or order directly from the publisher at 800-338-3282 or online at http://www.petersons.com/bookstore

Overall Rating
★★★
An interactive workbook; best for career planning and basic job search skills

Design, Ease Of Use
★★★★
Easy to use; lots of forms, examples, samples, planning tools

1–4 Stars

Author:
Paul L. Dyer
Mr. Dyer, a former human resources executive, is Director of the Rollins Consulting Group and Instructor of Organizational Behavior at Rollins College in Winter Park, Florida.

Publisher:
Peterson's

Edition:
1998

Price:
$14.95

Pages:
307

ISBN:
0768900093

Media:
Book

Principal Subject:
Job Search Overview

Secondary Subject:
Career Transitions

V. How To Land
The Job You Want

★★★

Overall Rating
★★★
A step-by-step approach to the academic job search for new PhDs

Design, Ease Of Use
★★★
Well-written; includes lots of sample vitas, etc. and a job search timetable

1–4 Stars

Author:
Mary Morris Heiberger and Julia Miller Vick

Ms. Heiberger is Associate Director and Ms. Vick is a Graduate Career Counselor at the Career Planning and Placement Service at the University of Pennsylvania.

Publisher:
University of Pennsylvania Press

Edition:
2nd (1996)

Pages:
194

ISBN:
0812215958

Media:
Book

Principal Subject:
Job Search Overview

Of Interest To:
Academics & PhDs

Overviews Of The Job Search Process

THE ACADEMIC JOB SEARCH HANDBOOK

Description:
Part 1, "What You Should Know Before You Start," prepares new Ph.D.s for their academic job search by examining "the structure of academic careers" and hiring practices. Part 2 offers suggestions for "Planning and Timing Your Search." A timetable is provided, which begins two years before one's dissertation is completed and extends until six months before the position's "start date." Deciding where and when to apply is the next step; readers learn what they "need to know" about the market, the target institution, their own competitiveness, etc. The importance of advisors, professional networks, conference presentations, and letters of recommendation is discussed, and there are tips for "learning about openings." Part 3 focuses on the "written materials," i.e. vitas, correspondence. Samples are included, as are guidelines for constructing a "Home Page." Aspects of the search, such as interviews and negotiating offers, are detailed in Part 4. Part 5 offers advice for "After You Take the Job," i.e. tenure, changing positions.

Evaluation:
"Uncapping" of the retirement age, which has reduced turnover, and cutbacks in public funding mean that new Ph.D.s face a daunting task: finding positions in a highly competitive job market. More than ever, it is important that Ph.D.s understand the academic job search and the process it entails: networking, researching positions, preparing vitas, etc. Enter Ms. Heiberger and Ms. Vick, who, as Associate Director and Graduate Career Counselor (respectively) at the University of Pennsylvania's Career Planning and Placement Service, are capable, knowledgeable mentors. Their handbook provides harried graduate students with the need-to-know basics: a practical timetable, sample vitas, interview strategies, etc. Though this handbook is designed to apply to any discipline, this guide shouldn't supersede any specific conventions of the reader's field. Use this resource as a supplement to information provided by faculty members in the field, national professional associations, etc.

Where To Find/Buy:
Bookstores and libraries.

Overviews Of The Job Search Process

HOW TO GET A JOB IN SEATTLE & WESTERN WASHINGTON

★★★

Description:

Surrey's "How To Get A Job In . . ." series is a combination job search guide and local resource "directory." The books are divided into 10 chapters which integrate area-specific data with "general" advice. For example, the chapter on "Choosing a Career" offers both self-exploration and assessment exercises as well as addresses for local career counselors, local women's resources, local colleges and universities, etc. Similarly, the "Network" chapter offers tips, techniques, "networking etiquette," and lists of in-area professional associations, trade groups, clubs, etc. The chapters on the "10-step job search," the "perfect" resume, and the "killer" interview follow the same pattern: advice plus relevant local addresses. The first and last chapters are dedicated solely to the target area. Chapter 1 examines employment projections, business trends, "fastest growing companies," etc., and lists local newspapers, Chambers of Commerce, etc.; the last chapter contains contact information on "major employers," by industry.

Evaluation:

Many job seekers have compelling reasons for focusing their search in a given geographic area; perhaps they want to find a job where they live or perhaps they want to relocate. Whether or not you're a local, this series provides lots of area-specific resources and addresses that are helpful for networking, informational interviewing, researching, and (in the case of newspapers) actually locating job opportunities. (Since the books often cover "large" regions, i.e. "Southern California," you may want to flip through the text before buying, just to make sure your area of interest is well represented.) The local information isn't as extensive as the employer directories found in Adam's regional "The . . . JobBank" series (see review), but these guides possess a quality other "directories" frequently lack: good job search advice. There are some great suggestions and tips on networking, resumes, and interviews, the "should I go back to school" question is well addressed (a rare inclusion), and there are lots of URLs for online assistance.

Where To Find/Buy:

Bookstores and libraries.

Overall Rating

★★★

A mini-directory of local resources plus good job searching advice

Design, Ease Of Use

★★★

Well formatted; addresses are often integrated into text

1–4 Stars

Author:

Robert Sanborn, EdD. and Marc D. Snyder

Mr. Sanborn is Dean of Student Affairs at Hampshire College and the recipient of the Chevron Award for Innovation in Career Planning. Mr. Snyder is Executive Director of Career Resource Center, which offers career and employer databases.

Publisher:

Surrey Books

Edition:

4th (1998)

Price:

$17.95

Pages:

397

ISBN:

1572840161

Media:

Book

Principal Subject:

Job Search Overview

★★★

Overall Rating
★★★
A good, all-inclusive site; includes "Catapult," a great Net guide

Design, Ease Of Use
★★★
Format is a little confusing; use the site map to navigate

1–4 Stars

Author:
JobWeb is a product of the National Association of Colleges and Employers (NACE). NACE is also the producer of the "Job Choices" publications.

Publisher:
National Association of Colleges and Employers

Edition:
1998

Media:
Internet

Principal Subject:
Job Search Overview

Secondary Subject:
Employer Descriptions

Overviews Of The Job Search Process

JOBWEB
Linking Jobs, Job Seekers, And Job Search Information

Description:

JobWeb is a career-related site sponsored by the National Association of Colleges and Employers, an organization dedicated to easing the transition from higher education to "the world of work." From the home page, users can access the "major segments" of the site or visit the site map for more precise navigating. In "Employment Information," users can search the database for job postings or employer profiles (profiles vary in length, most contain direct links) by keyword or location. For job searching advice, there's the online zine, "Job Choices." "Job Choices" includes featured articles (i.e. "6 Steps to Managing Job Offers"), samples and tips on resumes and cover letters, discussion forums, and "real life" career stories. For other online resources, there's "Catapult," a Yahoo!-style Net guide of annotated lists/links. Topic-specific pages from "Catapult" are incorporated throughout the site, but it's under "Career Service Professionals" (home page) that users will find "Catapult's" table of contents.

Evaluation:

NACE has done a good job of making JobWeb as "all inclusive" as possible. It has all the features: a database of job postings, employer profiles, and a fantastic guide to the Net's career-related resources, "Catapult." More experienced job seekers can skip "Job Choices," which seems to target first-timers; there are better sites for "how to" write resumes, cover letters, etc. However, do check out the employer profiles; they're definitely worthwhile. Most are informative and contain direct links to the employer's site. (For free employer profiles online, these are among the best.) Of course, the real reason to visit JobWeb is "Catapult." Like Yahoo!, it provides links for everything from general job searching to internships to "minority resources." Since "Catapult" and the site's original material are completely intertwined (a format choice which is both effective and messy), navigating can be difficult. The best way to navigate is to use the site map; bypass the home page and ignore the confusing table of contents.

Where To Find/Buy:

On the Internet at http://www.jobweb.org

Overviews Of The Job Search Process

KIPLINGER'S SURVIVE & PROFIT FROM A MID-CAREER CHANGE

★★★

Description:

Read by actor Dave Madden (best known for roles in "The Partridge Family" and "Laugh-in"), this two-tape audio guide has a running time of approximately 3 hours. Designed to help people who are changing jobs in "mid-career," either by choice or by circumstance, the tapes focus on re-learning and honing job search skills that may have grown rusty since the last time you looked for a job. Divided into 8 sections, Chapter 1 begins with advice on job searching while still employed, i.e. don't talk about your search with co-workers, and on job searching while unemployed, i.e. the job hunt is your job, so keep regular business hours. It also discusses such topics as age discrimination and the feelings, that a mid-career job loss can inspire. Chapter 2 explore the function, style, and content of resumes, while Chapter 3 offers suggestions for effective researching. The whats, whys, and whos of networking are examined in Chapter 4. Working with headhunters, and an explanation of retainer/contingency firms, is addressed in Chapter 5. Chapters 6–7 provide tactics and analyze scenarios for interviewing and negotiating job offers. Chapter 8 concludes with tips for succeeding at a new job.

Evaluation:

Mr. Madden has a wonderful voice, and, if you've been out of work for some time, it may be worth $18 just to hear him say, so calmly and earnestly, that you will find a job. His melodic voice is not the only reason to buy these tapes. Author Moreau offers a lot of constructive advice here, especially for those mid-career job changers who need a refresher course in job searching. The chapters on headhunters, interviewing, and negotiating job offers are particularly enlightening and educational, as is the chapter on networking. Also notable is the important discussion of age discrimination and the feelings inspired by a mid-career job loss. Moreau/Madden explain that, in your 40s and 50s, a job loss can inspire denial, confusion, and/or threaten your very identity. This rare inclusion typifies the content's attention to its target audience—older career changers—and it's that attention that sets these tapes apart from similar resources. Plus, there's a delightful, wry humor to these tapes that make listening enjoyable. There are a few sketchy suggestions to be wary of, such as having a friend check your references under the guise of hiring you, and the resume section suffers from the audio format. But if you've spent a long time at one company and/or fit the age group, this may be the perfect resource for you.

Where To Find/Buy:

Bookstores and libraries, or call 1-800-328-DOVE.

Overall Rating
★★★
Covers all the basics for mid-career job searching

Design, Ease Of Use
★★★
You'll have to rewind to take notes, but you can listen to it in the car

1–4 Stars

Author:
Daniel Moreau

Publisher:
Dove Audio

Edition:
1996

Price:
$17.95

ISBN:
0787106402

Media:
Audiotape

Principal Subject:
Job Search Overview

Secondary Subject:
Termination/Job Loss

V. How To Land
The Job You Want

★★★

Overall Rating
★★★
Essays paint a vivid and honest picture of the academic job hunt

Design, Ease Of Use
★★★
Each contribution is unique in style and scope, but highly readable

1–4 Stars

Author:
Christina Boufis and Victoria C. Olsen

Christina Boufis received her PhD in English literature from the City University of New Your, Graduate Center. She is an Affiliated Scholar at the Institute for Research on Women and Gender at Stanford University. Victoria C. Olsen received a PhD in English from Stanford.

Publisher:
Riverhead Books

Edition:
1997

Price:
$12.95

ISBN:
1573226262

Media:
Book

Principal Subject:
Job Search Overview

Of Interest To:
Academics & PhDs

ON THE MARKET
Surviving The Academic Job Search

Description:

A diverse array of PhDs confront the issue of academic employment in these essays, which tell their stories of the job search—failures and frustrations as well as hard-won successes. Authors come from a wide range of ethnicities and backgrounds, with fields ranging from art history to archaeology. The essays themselves are grouped into 8 sections, beginning with "First Words: The Application Process," which includes discussions of how contributors survived the job search process. Part 2, "Cattle Call," contains essays discussing aspects of the academic conference and interview. "The Aftermath and Beyond" has words of wisdom from academics who survived the job search, and the struggles they encountered and foresee for the future. In Part 4, essayists consider "identities and politics": affirmative action policies, gender and sexuality. "Different Paths" and "Alternative Careers" are considered in two sets of essays, and the final section takes a look at the future of the academy.

Evaluation:

It is notoriously difficult for new Ph.D.s to get a job. What is not so well known is how arduous the academic job hunt itself actually is. In these engrossing and (needless to say) extremely well written essays, recent Ph.D.s offer a candid picture of the "human side of the job search." Although these essays are not intended as "how-to" manuals for Ph.D.s searching for academic appointments, the reader will nevertheless glean a plethora of practical advice from reading these stories. An incredible amount of information is stuffed into these essays—and yet they read as excitingly as novels. Truly, anyone coming to this book will walk away with a full and vivid picture of the world of academia, as well as (perhaps most valuably) a sense of how the "personal" fits into the "professional" side the academic job market—how becoming an academic profoundly affects one's life. Highly recommended for those in academia for a realistic portrait of what awaits them in "the academic trenches," and how to survive.

Where To Find/Buy:

Bookstores and libraries.

Overviews Of The Job Search Process

★ ★ ★

WOMEN'S WIRE: WORK

Description:

Visitors to Women's Wire: Work will find tools and advice on an array of career issues. The site features articles on such topics as business travel and "9 to 5 fashion," several quizzes (i.e. a career assessment quiz), child care and elder care listings, chat rooms, message boards, and a Q&A forum called the "Career Coach." There are also "Management Tips," small business strategies, and profiles of "Women to Watch" and "Hot Careers." The "Hot Careers" range from "Buyer" to "Webmaster" to "Sleuth;" each profile contains segments on "what it's like," "stuff to know," "10 things to nail the job," and a "reality-check quiz." The "what it's like" segment relies heavily on interviews with women currently at work in the field. For example, Naomi Wolf discusses "what it's like" to be a writer. Users can find lists of "best places to work" (for women) by city, and a salary calculator is provided. A job database and resume builder are included, both of which are sponsored by the Monster Board.

Evaluation:

Just to be clear, the fact that the job database and resume builder are sponsored by The Monster Board means that these are the same features users will find at The Monster Board site (see review); they did not originate at Women's Wire. "Specialty sites" tend to have small job banks, so the advantage to this collaboration is obvious: since The Monster Board has one of the most extensive job banks on the Net, women get to have their cake and eat it too. And what a cake it is! The profiles of "Hot Careers," one of the best reasons to pay this site a visit, are both informative and entertaining, a seldom seen pairing. The child care and elder care listings are apropos, the chat rooms' message boards are good avenues for networking, and the profiles of "Women to Watch" are inspiring. Some of the "girlie" inclusions, i.e. "your work horoscope," can be annoying—this definitely isn't Ms. Magazine. Still, for working women, or women preparing to return to work, this is good advice and good company.

Where To Find/Buy:

On the Internet at http://womenswire.com/work

Overall Rating
★ ★ ★
Lots of advice and tips for working women; includes access to an extensive job bank

Design, Ease Of Use
★ ★ ★
Basically user-friendly; use the "site map" to find the "Hot Careers" segment

1–4 Stars

Author:
Women's Wire is one of the online products from Women.com Networks. Founded in 1992, Women.com was the first online media company to produce content specifically for women.

Publisher:
Women.com Networks

Edition:
1998

Media:
Internet

Principal Subject:
Job Search Overview

Of Interest To:
Women

V. How To Land
The Job You Want

★★★

Overall Rating
★★★
An exhaustive, step-by-step guide to job searching; effective and practical

Design, Ease Of Use
★★
Well organized; designed to take 7 days to complete

1–4 Stars

Author:
Peter K. Studner

Mr. Studner is a career counselor, former chief executive, and founder of Peter K. Studner Associates.

Publisher:
Jamenair

Edition:
3rd (1998)

Price:
$22.95

Pages:
318

ISBN:
0938667041

Media:
Book

Principal Subject:
Job Search Overview

Secondary Subject:
Career-Changing

Of Interest To:
Returning To The Workplace

Overviews Of The Job Search Process

SUPER JOB SEARCH
The Complete Manual For Job-Seekers & Career-Changers

Description:
As described by Studner, the "super search" program consists of "7 days of training sessions plus additional homework assignments." The program's goal is to prepare you for a "focused" job search. Chapter 1 offers tools and exercises for evaluating your situation and for planning the search, such as determining "family net worth," and "estimated job campaign costs." Day 1 begins with tools for self-assessment, goal-setting, and career planning. Tools include information about markets and advice on consulting/starting a business. Recording and analyzing accomplishments are Day 2's activities; writing resumes are Day 3's. Day 4 develops "your market plan," i.e. finding jobs, writing broadcast/cover letters, reaching your target company. On Day 5, you learn to network and on Day 6 you learn to "telemarket yourself." Finally, Day 7 tackles "The Interview/ Negotiations/Action Plan." Samples and lists of recommended resources are included in the appendices.

Evaluation:
Winner of the Benjamin Franklin Award for Best "How To" book (presented by the Publishers Marketing Association), Studner's guide isn't for lazy readers. It's an exhaustive, step-by-step, interactive approach to job searching. The program is designed to take 7 days to complete; this isn't a quick or easy exercise. It's demanding, though realistic. Studner expects dedication, both to the program and to your job search. As he says, you should spend at least 6 hours a day working on your search. This is an extraordinarily practical book, with every task serving a purpose, but due the time-consuming nature of the content, this is a better choice if you're currently unemployed or if you're returning to the work force after years away. There's no question that the program is beneficial, if taken seriously. If you need a job yesterday and can commit to following through with the "homework," this is may be the resource for you.

Where To Find/Buy:
Bookstores and libraries.

Overviews Of The Job Search Process

24 HOURS TO YOUR NEXT JOB, RAISE, OR PROMOTION

★★

Description:

Ryan, a self-styled "Career Coach," brings her tips and tools for getting a new job, raise, or promotion together in this "personal career coaching session." Chapter 1 begins by explaining the guide's premise and debunking the 9 "career killers," which include fear of failure and "letting 'no' stop you." Chapters 2–3 present survival tools for career success, with an emphasis on self-marketing strategies, and exercises for "defining your best skills and ideal job." Chapter 4 provides "The Persuasion Package:" tools to increase and support persuasiveness. These tools include the "60 Second Sell" ("a statement that directs attention to your top skills"), "The Salary Extractor" (to determine your highest possible salary), and the "Performance Chart" (to draw attention to your "growth" on the job). Chapters 5–7 focus on job searching, i.e. resources, researching, and interviewing, and getting promoted. Salary negotiations and job offers are discussed in Chapter 8. Finally, Chapter 9 offers motivation to "Go For It!"

Evaluation:

The title refers to Ryan's assurance that, by using this guide, readers can prepare to "convince an employer to hire you," "pitch your employer for a raise," or "land a promotion" in 24 hours. (To be clear, she doesn't say you can do it in 24 hours, just that you can *prepare*.) This book is an effective prepatory tool, because it offers many practical tools for self-evaluation and for getting organized. By using the "Persuasion Package," you'll know what to say in an interview, how much money you can ask for, and how far you've come at your current job. However, (with the exception of interviewing) the advice on job searching is largely perfunctory, i.e. a few paragraphs on temping, a two-page look at networking, etc. The chapter on getting promoted isn't particularly insightful either, though it includes solid advice along the lines of "continually improve skills." The "Persuasion Package" is the book's strongest feature, if the exercises appeal to you. If not, there are better resources for job changing and negotiating.

Where To Find/Buy:

Bookstores and libraries.

Overall Rating
★★
Perfunctory advice with a few good tools

Design, Ease Of Use
★★★
Straightforward; includes interactive exercises, checklists

1–4 Stars

Author:
Robin Ryan
Ms. Ryan is a frequent commentator on CNBC and the author of several career books, including *Job Search Organizer* and *60 Seconds and You're Hired*.

Publisher:
John Wiley & Sons

Edition:
1997

Price:
$10.95

Pages:
215

ISBN:
0471190667

Media:
Book

Principal Subject:
Job Search Overview

Secondary Subject:
Moving Ahead

V. How To Land
The Job You Want

★★

Overall Rating
★★
Addresses too many topics to treat any one in depth

Design, Ease Of Use
★★★
Well-written, straightforward format

1–4 Stars

Author:
Sharon F. Kissane, Ph.D.

Dr. Kissane received her PhD in education; she is the author of several books on career development.

Publisher:
VGM Career Horizons

Edition:
1997

Price:
$16.95

Pages:
248

ISBN:
084424175X

Media:
Book

Principal Subject:
Job Search Overview

Of Interest To:
The Disabled

Overviews Of The Job Search Process

CAREER SUCCESS FOR PEOPLE WITH PHYSICAL DISABILITIES

Description:

In Chapter 1, Dr. Kissane explains how new developments in technology and in the work place now offer expanded opportunities for people with physical disabilities. A disability is a challenge, but it needn't be an insurmountable obstacle in the path to success. The first step is to define "your dreams." Chapter 2 offers advice on finding "your pattern of interests" and on making the most of such resources as the HEALTH Directory. The next step is education. Chapters 3 and 4 examine such subjects as "high school skill development" and "optimizing your college experience." For career choice and job searching, Chapter 5 has tips on researching, networking, and government jobs and training, while Chapter 6 deals with resumes, cover letters, interviews, and disclosure. Chapters 7 and 8 explore "growth industries," "the changing complexion of work," and "hot prospects" for employment. The final chapter revisits the topic of assistive devices and technology, i.e. voice recognition software, vision enhancers, wheelchairs.

Evaluation:

There can be no question that there is a scarcity of career guidebooks for people with physical disabilities; perhaps that is why Dr. Kissane has attempted to cover so much ground at one time. The subjects detailed here range from Individualized Education Programs for children with special needs to interviewing tips to projected growth industries. Unfortunately, this wide variety of topics leads to more general guidelines than practical specifics. There are, however, some valuable inclusions. There's a "surfing guide" of disability-related websites, many of which are useful for job searching/researching, important information on assistive devices (especially software), and practical advice on when and how to handle disclosure. Had Dr. Kissane concentrated more on those issues which apply to her audience, rather than adding the "hot job prospects," etc., which readers could find in any career guide, this might have been a recommended resource. As it is, this book can only offer topics for further research.

Where To Find/Buy:

Bookstores and libraries.

Overviews Of The Job Search Process

★★

CAREERBABE

Description:

CareerBabe is a relatively small site primarily made up of original material from author Fran Quittel. There are 8 sections for job seekers, as well as a smaller section dedicated to employers interested in online recruitment. (All sections are accessible from the home page.) There are links to "Top Career Sites" and salary guides. CareerBabe's "Resume Tutorial" offers instructions and examples for writing resumes, and includes suggestions for job seekers who are changing fields. As "your personal career advisor," Ms. Quittel offers two "Q&A" forums. "Dear CareerBabe . . ." enables users to pose all types of career-related questions, which Ms. Quittel answers online. Past answers are arranged into subject categories, i.e. career counseling, home business, etc., and comprise most of the advice found in the site. Visitors can also have their salaries evaluated (anonymously) online in "What Are You Worth?" Strategies for handling career transitions or "emergencies" (i.e. firings) are also espoused.

Evaluation:

Unlike the larger "gateway" or "clearinghouse" sites, CareerBabe is a smaller, more intimate site which relies heavily on interaction with the user. The "Resume Tutorial" covers "the basics," but is not particularly in depth. The links are not a "selling point," either; they're fine, but there are better places for an index of career sites. There are some good strategies for coping and "surviving" such career "emergencies" as firings, but that's probably because Ms. Quittel's book, "FirePower," treats the same subject at length. For the "everyday" job seeker, the pertinent section is "Dear CareerBabe . . .," where most of the site's advice is found. Ms. Quittel's answers to career-related questions tackle issues as varied as "security within a start up company" and "military to civilian life." "Dear CareerBabe . . ." is the heart of this site, and the chief reason for visiting. It's a forum for sharing information and can be quite insightful. The ability to have your salary evaluated (anonymously) is a novelty worth checking out, too.

Where To Find/Buy:

On the Internet at http://www.careerbabe.com

Overall Rating
★★
Worth checking out for the "Q & A" forum, "Dear CareerBabe . . ."

Design, Ease Of Use
★★★
Simple, straightforward layout; explicit subject headings

1–4 Stars

Author:
Fran Quittel

Ms. Quittel is an Internet recruitment and technology staffing consultant. She is the author of *FirePower* (Ten Speed Press) and she writes a bimonthly High Tech Careers Column for *Computer Currents*, an online magazine.

Edition:
1998

Media:
Internet

Principal Subject:
Job Search Overview

Secondary Subject:
Termination/Job Loss

V. How To Land
The Job You Want

Overall Rating
★

Touches only on the basics of the job hunt; very quick treatment of essential skills

Design, Ease Of Use
★★

Friendly and straightforward tone; quick and readable

1–4 Stars

Author:
Ruby N. Gorter

Ruby N. Gorter has twenty years' experience in human resources. She owns a secretarial business and conducts job seminars for high school students.

Publisher:
Pilot Books

Edition:
1997

Price:
$8.95

Pages:
85

ISBN:
0875762018

Media:
Book

Principal Subject:
Job Search Overview

Of Interest To:
Women

Overviews Of The Job Search Process

HOW TO GET THAT JOB!
Tools, Techniques, And Strategies "Borrowed" From Successful Job Applicants

Description:
This is a slim guide to the essentials of the job search. Written with those reentering the work force and first-time job seekers in mind, it hopes to show the way to developing an effective job search. Chapters run chronologically from choosing a job/field to landing the second interview. In chapters 1–5 are discussions and advice about discovering what's important to you in a career; researching companies; setting up research interviews; and using referrals effectively. The next 2 chapters cover how to sell your accomplishments and skills in the resume and cover letter. Chapters 8–12 deal with the stages of the interview process: preparing, making a good first impression, anticipating the "twelve questions interviewers are most likely to ask of you," asking for the job, and negotiating the second interview. Readers will find sample resumes and cover letters, research interview requests and telephone conversations, and sample interview questions and answers.

Evaluation:
If you're pressed for time or need a quick refresher on the basic job search skills, you may find some help here. It is directed to those who have been out of the market for a while, with some advice tailored for women who have been raising children and/or managing a household. A book targeted to such an audience would be extremely valuable; unfortunately, this one doesn't delve into a lot of the issues women are bound to face when reentering the work force. Readers will only find basic coverage of researching jobs, writing resumes, and interviewing, but the treatment of these topics is not very in-depth. For instance, in the section about researching possible employers, there is no mention of the Internet. Advice about the interview runs along the lines of "clean your nails" and "don't slouch." On the other hand, there are some good sections on how to network, and how to sell your skills even if you've been off the job market. This resource skims, but does not delve into, most vital subjects.

Where To Find/Buy:
Bookstores and libraries, or directly from the publisher at (800) 79PILOT.

Overviews Of The Job Search Process

THE 12 ESSENTIAL LAWS FOR GETTING A JOB . . . AND BECOMING INDISPENSABLE

Description:

The author is president of Central Piedmont Community College in North Carolina, with experience in work force development. Stating that "belief drives behavior," he has amassed "twelve laws" or traits which employers want, focusing, for the most part, on positive attitude as the key to career success. Chapters 1–3 focus on attitude, communication, effort, and teamwork. Chapters 5–9 cover being a problem solver, being "customer-focused," being results-oriented, developing a plan to achieve career goals, and "putting your best foot forward," or selling yourself. Chapter 10 discusses the importance of being an active and continual learner, and chapter 11 focuses on getting the proper academic and technical skills. The final "law" is "emphasizing prior experience" when applying for a job. Each chapter defines its "law," includes short anecdotes, and ends with practical advice and a list of "points to ponder." Appendices include checklists for assessing interests and values, career goals, and skills.

Evaluation:

Dr. Zeiss, hoping to save job-seekers "wasted hours and dollars," has put together the "12 essential traits" that employers look for in an employee in only 166 short pages. There are advantages and disadvantages to this concise approach. The advantages are that, yes, it takes only a short time to read through and absorb the material in this book. The disadvantages are that you probably will need to do more than simply follow these 12 steps in order to get a job. Such crucial aspects of the job search as writing a resume and cover letter, for instance, are (deliberately) not covered. On the other hand, the author writes persuasively about the need for a positive attitude and communication skills. But he doesn't do more than simply state that you must have these traits ("make a conscious decision to be cheerful and optimistic") without a lot of help for getting you there. Chapters end with "points to ponder," which are really just rules to swallow.

Where To Find/Buy:

Bookstores and libraries.

Overall Rating

★

12 "laws" are too broad to be of much real help in the job hunt

Design, Ease Of Use

★★

Concise, but narrow treatment of employment success

1–4 Stars

Author:

Dr. Tony Zeiss

Dr. Zeiss is an author and president of Central Piedmont Community College in Charlotte, North Carolina.

Publisher:

Thomas Nelson

Edition:

1997

Price:

$5.99

Pages:

166

ISBN:

0785275649

Media:

Book

Principal Subject:

Job Search Overview

V. How To Land
The Job You Want

Overviews Of The Job Search Process

CAREERS ON-LINE

Non-Rated Resource

Description:
Careers On-Line is designed to provide career-related assistance to people with disabilities. There are job and internship postings, a database of "Adaptive Technology Products & Resources" (currently under construction), and a "Job Accommodation Handbook." The "Handbook" includes a review of the Americans with Disabilities Act, employer "profiles," and resources for additional information.

Publisher:
University of Minnesota

Careers On-Line is a federally funded project administered by Disability Services in cooperation with Distributed Computing Services at the University of Minnesota, Twin Cities.

Media:
Internet

Principal Subject:
Job Search Overview

Of Interest To:
The Disabled

Where To Find/Buy:
On the Internet at http://disserv3.stu.umn.edu/COL/

RESUMES

Nobody has ever hired a resume, they hire people and enthusiasm. A good resume is an ad focused specifically on what you want versus a simple history of what you have done. The only time historical data is useful in a resume is if you are really just wanting another job doing exactly the same thing you have done before.

Don't put personal information in a resume such as what hobbies you have, or what car club you belong to, or that you bet on the horses. That type of information, unless it is specifically associated with the job you are applying for is misleading and often negatively viewed.

Never lie. The research says that two-thirds of resumes have some form of a lie in them. It is not worth it. Just tell the truth and let the employer choose. Good reference checking is done and they will find our and either not hire you or even fire you after you got the job.

Use cover letters and interviews to expand on specifics. Just give them a focused and clear advertisement with lots of white space as a resume. Traditional print-based resumes should be attractively formatted and easy on the eye. Use good quality bond paper in a neutral color. Match resume paper, cover letter paper, and envelope.

Since technology has become standard in many human resources offices, it's useful to plan ahead by preparing four versions of your resume: scannable, web-based/HTML, email, and traditional. Keep in mind that many resumes are now scanned by machine, and such scanners often cannot decipher unusual fonts or layouts, italics, underlining, or bold face. When in doubt as to whether your resume will be scanned, it pays to ask the human resources office. Be sure, moreover, to include lots of industry/organizational keywords suited to the position you are seeking.

Posting your resume online at one of the resume banks we review in Chapter IV may be useful for those interested in jobs in the technology sector. Look for sites which are free to job seekers, are password-protected, and which allow you to preview and edit your resume once it's up. You'll do well to post the resume about three months before the time you'd like to start working.

Five Tips For Great Resumes

- Never lie.

- Keep your resume to one or two pages.

- If you are applying for jobs in different career fields, consider two or more resumes, each indicating a particular career objective and related experience.

- When describing past job experience, use "action verbs" in active voice. Indicate related and most important duties first.

- It is helpful to prepare four versions of your resume: traditional, scannable, HTML/web-based and email.

ASHER'S BIBLE OF EXECUTIVE RESUMES
. . . And How To Write Them

★★★★

 Recommended For:
Resumes

Description:

The executive resume, whether used to get new positions, promotions, investors or civic and philanthropic appointments is a breed apart from other resumes. It has a different purpose, sells a different type of candidate, sets a different tone. In this 14-chapter "Bible," Asher explores the unique qualities of the executive resume (Chapter 1), offers advice on constructing one, and presents one of the largest collections of sample resumes ever published for the public. Chapter 2 provides a "training session" on how to write executive resumes and how to handle problems such as being "too old," recent demotion, long period of unemployment or consulting. Chapters 3–12 organize the samples by type, from general management to presentations for specific professions, a section which includes curricula vitae. Types include legal, military, headhunter resumes, and nontraditional, i.e. "soprano." Tips on cover letters comprise Chapter 13; Chapter 14 covers salary histories and reference sheets.

Evaluation:

Most resume guides discuss first jobs and career changing, but few explore the executive resume. Executives in search of advice on preparing a senior level resume should consider Asher's "Bible." This tome is confident, reliable, exciting (in what it promises), intelligent, and, above all, practical. There's enough how-to to help you through the writing process, but not so much as to patronize or bore. The samples, aside from being vast in number, are terrific examples to learn from and be inspired by. The guide's easy to use, too; there's an explanatory introduction and an explicit table of contents. Unlike "100 Winning Resumes for $100,000+ Jobs" (see review), another resource tailored for executives, these samples are more varied in purpose, addressing such situations as curricula vitae, appointments, soliciting investors, etc. For its sophistication and clarity, this is the best resume guide on the market for experienced executives.

Where To Find/Buy:

Bookstores and libraries.

Overall Rating
★★★★
Truly a Bible for executive resumes; use this book!

Design, Ease Of Use
★★★★
Easy to use, sophisticated

1–4 Stars

Author:
Donald Asher

Mr. Asher is a contributing writer to *National Business Employment Weekly* magazine and the author of several career books. As principal of Asher Associates of San Francisco, he provides job-search coaching to executives and staffing transition assistance to corporations.

Publisher:
Ten Speed Press

Edition:
1997

Price:
$29.95

Pages:
554

ISBN:
0898158567

Media:
Book

Principal Subject:
Resumes

V. How To Land
The Job You Want

★★★★

Overall Rating
★★★★
A comprehensive and user-friendly guide to creating all types of resumes

Design, Ease Of Use
★★★★
Helpful icons illustrate major points; good sample resumes; info. presented clearly

1–4 Stars

Author:
Susan Ireland

Susan Ireland owns a consulting firm that "specializes in helping job seekers keep pace with the job market."

Publisher:
Alpha Books

Edition:
1996

Price:
$16.95

ISBN:
0028610938

Media:
Book

Principal Subject:
Resumes

Resumes

THE COMPLETE IDIOT'S GUIDE TO THE PERFECT RESUME

 **Recommended For:**
Resumes

Description:
Anyone, from a "complete idiot" on up to an experienced professional, will find information and advice about writing a resume in these pages. Designed to be an easy-to-read resource, it includes lots of graphics and highlighted sections, as well as sample resumes illustrating the author's points. Divided into 4 major sections, part 1 opens with a brief introduction to "important principles for making your resume work." Part 2, "Navigating Your Way," discusses strategies and formats for each section of the resume, such as choosing between the chronological and functional format; writing a strong job objective; creating a "summary of qualifications" section; and handling your work history and education sections. Part 3 focuses on "special resumes," such as achievement resumes and "hybrids," as well as how to write a curriculum vita. In the last section you'll find advise about how to make your resume scannable, and show to conduct an electronic job search.

Evaluation:
In the tradition of "user friendly" resumes, "The Complete Idiot's Guide To The Perfect Resume" tells you everything you need to know about creating a resume, with plenty of entertaining graphics and sympathetic advice. Susan Ireland's guide is fuller than most, and thus takes longer to work through—but she delves into issues that other guides skip over. Along with the absolute basics (how to list your name and phone number) you'll also find advice about the functional vs. chronological formats, the job objective, and what is called here a "summary of qualifications" section. The intent is to make a resume that will jump out at an employer, so the author advises using both a job objective and the qualifications section to create a kind of "mini-resume" that employers see first. (Some of her advice is questionable, however, such as telling professionals who wish to appear younger to lop off older sections of their resumes). A thorough "how-to" resume writing resource.

Where To Find/Buy:
Bookstores and libraries, or directly from the publisher at (800) 428-5331.

Resumes

DAMN GOOD RESUME GUIDE
A Crash Course In Resume Writing

 Recommended For:
Resumes

Description:

In this self-described "crash course in resume writing," readers will find concise, down-to-earth advice about writing a resume. The author moves step-by-step through the process, starting from step 1, "choosing a job target" (also known as a job objective). Steps 2–4 discuss finding out what is needed to do the job, making a list of your strongest skills, and then coming up with several accomplishments to illustrate each key skill. Step 5 involves turning each accomplishment into an "action statement." Steps 6–7 tell you to make a chronological list of jobs you've held and a list of relevant training/education. The next two steps discuss how to choose a resume format (chronological or functional) and arranging your action statements into that format. Step 10 discusses how to strategically summarize key points in the resume. 24 sample resumes, and employer responses, are included. Throughout, the author answers potential "yes, but . . ." questions that you may face at each step.

Evaluation:

Yana Parker first published her "Damn Good Resume Guide" in 1983. Since then, she's revised it four times to "keep up with changing times and the current needs of job hunters." At $7.95, readers will find this to be a both a great resource and a great bargain. A potentially dull subject is brought alive by the author's humor and spirit, and if you've ever had a case of the "yes, buts . . ." when reading resume writing advice, this is the book for you. It brings the advice home, making every tip and strategy relevant to your own case. Plus, it targets potential weaknesses and helps you turn them into strengths, such as gaps in your work history, or if you've had lots of short-term jobs. The 24 sample resumes are wide-ranging and diverse, from a supermarket checker to a marketing consultant, and show you different formats in which you can work. The appended "The Acid Test" in which employers evaluate the sample resumes is less helpful—they all contradict each other on likes and dislikes, proving that "one size does not fit all."

Where To Find/Buy:

Bookstores and libraries, or direct from the publisher at (800) 841-BOOK.

★★★★

Overall Rating
★★★★
Straightforward, quick "how-to" manual for writing a "damn good" resume

Design, Ease Of Use
★★★★
Very concise and action-oriented; drawings and humor enliven each page

1–4 Stars

Author:
Yana Parker

Yana Parker "manages a small team of resume writers who work in the 'damn good' style to help individual job hunters." She is involved with many other career-related activities, including publishing a newsletter and leading seminars in resume writing.

Publisher:
Ten Speed

Edition:
4th (1996)

Price:
$7.95

Pages:
79

ISBN:
0898156726

Media:
Book

Principal Subject:
Resumes

Resumes

REBECCA SMITH'S ERESUMES & RESOURCES

Recommended For:
Resumes

Description:

Rebecca Smith's website features a variety of job search tools: articles on trends and the job market, interactive exercises and tips for job searching on the Internet, and a "coffee break" segment which includes humorous anecdotes and a quiz for determining "your emotional intelligence quotient." The site's primary focus, however, is to provide "how-to" instructions and information on electronic resumes. In "eResumes 101," users will find a general introduction to electronic resumes, advice on posting resumes online and sending electronic cover letters, and 5 resume-specific "tutorials." The tutorials offer step-by-step instructions for creating a "Keyword Resume" (from scratch) and an "ASCII Resume," guidelines for preparing a "Scannable Resume," design strategies for hypertext "Web Resumes," and basic HTML tag strategies ("HTML Resume"). Samples of each type of resume can be found in the "Gallery." There are also links to related resources and suggestions for using/navigating the site.

Evaluation:

Wow! Click here for an excellent resource on electronic resumes!! There are simple, step-by-step instructions for creating or converting a resume in/to ASCII text, as well as "before and after" examples, and a thorough, step-by-step "manual" for building a resume from scratch using "keywords." There are guidelines for making paper resumes "scannable" and straightforward design strategies for hypertext "Web Resumes." Not only are the "tutorials" great, the database of samples is one of the most extensive and varied. Then too, there are the articles, the humorous anecdotes, the "emotional intelligence quiz," and the interactive exercises designed to make "job searching on the Internet" fast and effective. It's incredibly easy to navigate this site, and, for users with browsers that won't support frames, there are always corresponding "text-only" versions. It's worth mentioning, too, that, unlike most sites, there's practically no advertising. This is a first class web site; check it out!

Where To Find/Buy:

On the Internet at http://www.eresumes.com

★★★★

Overall Rating
★★★★
A wealth of valuable information on creating electronic resumes

Design, Ease Of Use
★★★★
Dynamic design, user-friendly; lots of original material with little advertising

1–4 Stars

Author:
Rebecca Smith

Ms. Smith is the author of *Resumes, Resumes, Resumes* (Career Press) and a contributing writer for *CareerMagazine* and *ComputerBits Magazine*. She also teaches adult education in Applied Web Technology.

Edition:
1998

Media:
Internet

Principal Subject:
Resumes

Resumes

RESUMES FOR DUMMIES

 Recommended For:
Resumes

Description:

Joyce Lain Kennedy, a syndicated journalist specializing in career related topics, focuses on creating a "KickButt" resume in this 310 page guide. Her goal is to help readers produce a resume that "pounds on the table and shouts, 'Don't pass me over—I'm the one who can do the best job in this job!'" She begins with a step by step process for writing and laying out a resume, providing guidelines for developing a resume that successfully presents the individual's skills, experience and personality. Worksheets are used in the third section "Creating Your KickButt Resume" to personalize the process and define specific qualities about the individual. Additions from the first edition include discussions on using Internet job services to post resumes and resume scanning. Chapter 13 lists a number of Web sites including specialty sites and sites that recruiters visit. Chapter 12 outlines a variety of specific criteria that should be used when creating an online resume such as which fonts work best and how to set up tabs.

Evaluation:

This is an extremely easy to use work that contains a large amount of quality information. The language is humorous and light hearted though still capable of transmitting serious content. For example, in "Deadweight: Kick It Out!," job seekers are advised to unload facts that weaken their resume just as they "would toss out chipped drinking glasses that might cut [their] lips." While the author strongly advises readers not to inflate experience or skills, since these misrepresentations will most likely be realized by the employer after the individual is hired, she does include a helpful chapter on how to handle a less than perfect job history. Chapter 16 "Spin Control against Special Issues" deals with resume predicaments such as employment gaps and guarding against negative information. For those readers who are returning to the workplace after a prolonged absence, such specific advice can be invaluable. (It'll help you gain confidence, too!) This is an informative, entertaining, "from the hip" guide!

Where To Find/Buy:

Bookstores and libraries.

Overall Rating
★★★★
A very user friendly book, an informative job hunting tool

Design, Ease Of Use
★★★★
Zippy graphics ease the reader through the work

1–4 Stars

Author:
Joyce Lain Kennedy

Joyce Lain Kennedy is the author of the *Los Angeles Times* syndicate's column CAREERS, which appears in more than 100 newspapers. She is the author of eight books, including *Cover Letters for Dummies*.

Publisher:
IDG Books

Edition:
2nd (1998)

Price:
$12.99

Pages:
310

ISBN:
0764551132

Media:
Book

Principal Subject:
Resumes

V. How To Land
The Job You Want

Overall Rating
★★★
An inspiring alternative for job searchers and up-and-comers

Design, Ease Of Use
★★★★
Step-by-step advice, clear language, easy-to-use

1–4 Stars

Author:
Anna Graf Williams, PhD, and Karen J. Hall

Publisher:
Prentice-Hall, Inc.

Edition:
1997

Price:
$19.95

Pages:
88

ISBN:
0137543670

Media:
Book

Principal Subject:
Resumes

Secondary Subject:
Freelance/Consulting

Resumes

CREATING YOUR CAREER PORTFOLIO
At A Glance Guide

Description:
Chapter 1 answers the basic question "What's in a portfolio and why do I need one?" as it presents an overview of the "portfolio process," the supplies needed to get started, and the potential uses in job searches/job reviews. Among the items contained in a portfolio are: a statement about career goals, a resume, a "skills area" (i.e. work samples, letters of recommendation), quality copies of awards, degrees, etc., and references. Some inclusions are discretionary, such as community service work samples, professional memberships, and an academic plan of study. Each of these components are separately explored in Chapter 2. Details examined include various resume formats, evaluating work samples, and methods of organizing skills. A 5-step approach to assembly follows. Elements of style, i.e. fonts, margins, etc., are discussed, as are production tips for photographs, videos, and other visual media. There is also advice on using the portfolio during an interview, at a performance review, or to get a promotion.

Evaluation:
There are two major benefits to a portfolio. First, there is the end product, the portfolio itself. Not only does it provide "proof" of skills, experience, etc., to (potential) employers, it also promotes distinction, since very few non-artists have one. Second, the creative process behind the portfolio requires a great deal of self-analysis (defining goals, organizing work experience into "categories"), which simultaneously prepares one for interview questions and job searching. True, making a portfolio requires time and effort, but the payoff may be worth it. (Be sure to check with contacts in your field/business to ascertain whether a portfolio would be welcomed; some employers may not appreciate the novelty.) Keep in mind, too, that consultants could use the principles set forth in this guide to create a marketing/business proposal forum. If you have more "non-traditional" experience than professional experience, or if you're dissatisfied with your resume, check out this book!

Where To Find/Buy:
Bookstores and libraries.

Resumes

★★★

ELECTRONIC RESUMES
A Complete Guide To Putting Your Resume On-Line

Description:

The printed text and the accompanying software are designed to work in tandem; the book acts as an introduction and as written instructions for using the "Resumes Online" and "Resumaker" programs. To give readers an overview of the guide's purpose/ electronic resumes, Chapters 1–5 discuss such topics as electronic vs. traditional resumes, text file resumes, multimedia resumes, the advantages of electronic resumes, and distributing electronic resumes online. Subsequent chapters offer an "Electronic Resume Checklist" and details about the "Necessary Equipment." Chapter 9, "How to Create an Electronic Resume," contains directions for installing and using "Resumes Online," the first half of the software package. The chapter includes pictures of the screens as they appear on the computer, to help users through the process step by step. Chapter 10 functions in the same capacity, guiding users through "Resumaker," the software provided for creating multimedia resumes. Sample resumes and cover letters are supplied.

Evaluation:

Basically, the print version of this guide has two functions: to offer an introduction to the advantages of electronic resumes and to act as a technical manual for the enclosed software package. This is not a book about "how to write resumes," nor does it advise users on job searching on the Internet. What it does do is enable readers to produce functional electronic or multimedia resumes quickly and efficiently, with only a minimum of familiarity with the medium. The software, "Resumes Online" and "Resumaker," is simple and user-friendly. "Resumaker," for example, allows users to create a multimedia resume, with text and graphics, by personalizing a supplied "template." There isn't much room for creativity, but what the software lacks in dynamism it makes up for in ease: it's almost like "fill-in-the-blanks." The "manual" chapters provide clear, step-by-step instructions and lots of "screens" as illustrations. For a "quick fix" electronic resume, this is a fine choice. (Software is IBM compatible.)

Where To Find/Buy:

Bookstores and libraries.

Overall Rating
★★★
A fast, efficient way to create electronic/ multimedia resumes

Design, Ease Of Use
★★★★
Straightforward, user-friendly software; appropriate for novice users

1–4 Stars

Author:
James C. Gonyea and Wayne M. Gonyea

James C. Gonyea is the creator of America Online's Career Center, Help Wanted-USA, and the Worldwide Resume/Talent Bank. He is also the author of *Career Selector 2001*. Wayne M. Gonyea specializes in the uploading of electronic resumes.

Publisher:
McGraw-Hill

Edition:
1995

Price:
$19.95

Pages:
255

ISBN:
0079121667

Media:
Book

Principal Subject:
Resumes

V. How To Land
The Job You Want

★★★

Overall Rating
★★★
Helpful exercises and practical advice; a variety of format choices

Design, Ease Of Use
★★★★
Direct and well-written; charts are included for clarification

1–4 Stars

Author:
Tim Haft, M.A.

Mr. Haft is a career counselor and resume consultant; since 1988, he has helped thousands of people find jobs. His own resume includes authoring *Trashproof Resumes*, *Crane's Guide To Writing an Effective Resume*, and co-authoring *Job Smart*.

Publisher:
The Princeton Review

Edition:
1997

Price:
$4.95

Pages:
87

ISBN:
0679778721

Media:
Book

Principal Subject:
Resumes

Resumes

JOB NOTES: RESUMES

Description:
To help readers "get started," the first two chapters explain the general purpose of a resume and the benefits of self-assessment. Readers are encouraged to complete a short series of exercises, such as listing their "five greatest strengths." Thus begins the "step-by-step" process of building a resume. Fill-in-the-blank worksheets enable readers to create a "qualifications bank" upon which any resume can be based. Once this "raw material" is compiled, the next step is to pick a format best suited to one's own work history. Six different formats are examined, i.e. the traditional "reverse-chronological" format and the "skills-based" format. Examples of each are provided, as is a chart of "pros" and "cons" for each strategy. For instance, "skills-based" is a good choice for those with a limited or "spotty" work history. Content issues discussed include: the objective, educational history, inclusions and omissions, "power verbs." There is also advice on typefaces, fonts, "bulleting," and handling Applicant Tracking Systems.

Evaluation:
Mr. Haft faces a difficult task: to guide people with varying backgrounds through the highly-personalized process of writing a resume. (Hence the inclusion of six different resume formats.) In general, he succeeds: he answers commonly-asked questions, addresses typical problems (spotty work history, etc.), and offers practical advice. The worksheets and exercises are particularly useful, since they encourage self-analysis and provide a facility for recording qualifications. Of course, due to the format (the book was specifically designed to be a portable, "quick reference), Mr. Haft cannot dwell on any one topic. For many people, however, the "need-to-know" basics are just that: all they need. Harried professionals looking for a cheap, quick refresher will benefit the most from this book. For consumers with less-than-perfect work histories, however, "The Resume Doctor" or "Conquer Resume Objections," both of which treat "problem" resumes, will be a better choice. (See reviews.)

Where To Find/Buy:
Bookstores and libraries, or direct from the publisher at 800-793-2665.

Resumes

100 WINNING RESUMES FOR $100,000+ JOBS
Resumes That Can Change Your Life

★★★

Description:
Enelow, a Certified Professional Resume Writer, has collected 100 "winning" resume samples for professional, management and executive job search candidates. Chapter 1 (of 3) offers a brief introduction to resumes, addressing what type of information should be provided, as well as a "quick guide" to the writing process. Chapter 2, which comprises all but 16 pages of the book, contains the 100 resume samples. The samples are categorized by job function/type, and includes: non-profit association, consulting, health care, project management, finance, general management, senior management, public relations, risk management and sales. The categories are arranged alphabetically in the table of contents; page numbers appear on the right. (The number of samples in each category varies.) Chapter 3 contains lists of action verbs and keywords (a.k.a. "buzz words") for use in resume writing.

Evaluation:
If you're a professional, management or executive job search candidate, chances are you've written at least a few resumes over the course of your career. Designed under that general assumption, this isn't a hand-holding, step-by-step, beginners guide to writing a resume. Though Chapter 1 does offer a few basic tips and short descriptions of resume components (i.e. "professional experience," "technology skills," etc.), there's no advice on format choice or how to handle "problem" issues, such as firings. This is a learn-by-example guide for busy professionals who need a refresher, inspiration, and/or tactical strategies. Some of the categories, such as "food & beverage/ hospitality," have only one sample, so browsing for ideas in other categories is advisable; besides, it gives readers more choices for style and format. This isn't as sophisticated a guide as "Asher's Bible of Executive Resumes" (see review), but it does offer great variety (of job types) and may appeal to those in search of a "quick read."

Where To Find/Buy:
Bookstores and libraries.

Overall Rating
★★★
100 sample resumes for professional/executive candidates, plus a few quick tips

Design, Ease Of Use
★★★
Some categories contain only one sample resume

1–4 Stars

Author:
Wendy S. Enelow
Ms. Enelow is president of The Advantage, Inc., an executive resume firm. She is a Certified Professional Resume Writer and is the author of *100 Winning Cover Letters for $100,000+ Jobs.*

Publisher:
Impact Publications

Edition:
1997

Price:
$24.95

Pages:
210

ISBN:
1570230706

Media:
Book

Principal Subject:
Resumes

V. How To Land
The Job You Want

★★★

Overall Rating
★★★
A useful, illustrative appendage to the "Damn Good Resume Guide"

Design, Ease Of Use
★★★
Wide range of resume types and styles

1–4 Stars

Author:
Yana Parker

Yana Parker is a public speaker on the topic of resume writing, writes books and a newsletter devoted to the subject, and provides a resume critiquing service.

Publisher:
Ten Speed

Edition:
2nd (1996)

Price:
$15.95

ISBN:
0898158915

Media:
Book

Principal Subject:
Resumes

Resumes

THE RESUME CATALOG
200 Damn Good Examples

Description:

In "The Resume Catalog," you'll find 200 sample resumes arranged into 13 job categories. Following a brief description of how to make your resume "scanner-friendly," the samples begin in the category of management. Resumes for positions in human resources, administration/ coordination, office/program support, finance/accounting, and technical/computers follow. Education, therapy/social work, and health resumes come next, followed by marketing and sales. A "potpourri" of resumes follows on pages 199–256, with samplings from the fields of product development, film, TV, editing/writing, and religion, among others. Fifteen "one-of-a-kind" resumes are also included, such as fire fighter, private investigator, apprentice baker, and cruise staff/activity director. Finally, you'll find six resumes for youth and students, from age 8 up through high school and into college. A brief section about cover letters, with samples, and a list of "25 tough problems" addressed by the resumes, round out the book.

Evaluation:

Whether you've Yana Parker's "Damn Good Resume Guide" in hand or another "how-to" guide, you'll find plenty of resume examples in here to look at and learn from. The 200 resumes are arranged into useful categories, making searching for an appropriate level/field an easy matter. One nice thing here is the inclusiveness of these resumes—they represent a broad range of talents and experience, from students to ministers to teachers to executives. It's hard to think of anyone who is excluded here (there's even a resume for a 14-year-old babysitter). You won't, however, find much advice about resume writing, except for a few tips about how to make a resume scannable. Short sections at the back address the cover letter, and problems such as "what can I do about an embarrassing job in my work record?" are matched with examples that grapple successfully with those same problems. But the meat of the book lies in the range and number of its examples—you can learn a lot just by looking.

Where To Find/Buy:

Bookstores and libraries, or direct from the publisher at (800) 841-BOOK.

Resumes

THE RÉSUMÉ DOCTOR
How To Transform A Troublesome Work History Into A Winning Résumé

★ ★ ★

Description:
Chapter 1 lays out the "key components of a resume": purpose, job objective, "the profile," education, and work experience, and explains how to use each section effectively. Chapter 2 focuses on overcoming problems in a resume, with eight examples and solutions for: a history of unrelated jobs; lacking required experience; having undergone a recent decrease in responsibility; having an embarrassing position on your resume; having periods of unemployment; a record of job-hopping; being currently unemployed; and nearing retirement age. Each has a "before" and "after" resume to show how the functional format can highlight skills and strengths while downplaying drawbacks. Chapters 3–4 deal with such "secondary sections" as honors and awards and computer skills, and discuss resume style/appearance. In chapter 5 you'll find advice for unique situations/job hunters. Final chapters discuss cover letters, the "resume-letter," and where to take your resume—contacts, prospective employers, resume databases.

Evaluation:
For those readers with a checkered or otherwise "troublesome" work history, this might be just what the doctor ordered. Although it covers many issues about resumes, its focus is how to "fix" resumes so that employers see your qualifications, and not shortcomings. You'll find plenty of "before" and "after" examples, plus very clear, detailed instructions on how to overcome common problems such as job-hopping, having an "embarrassing" job on your resume, nearing retirement age, and periods of unemployment. The solutions the author puts forth revolve around using the functional format to emphasize what you did over *when* you did it, or to highlights skills while minimizing potential drawbacks such as age or inexperience. This is a more serious guide to resume writing than others we've seen; it's geared toward adults with less-than-perfect work histories, rather than "hip" recent grads. It may be especially helpful to those returning to the workplace after a prolonged absence and to victims of job loss.

Where To Find/Buy:
Bookstores and libraries.

Overall Rating
★★★
A thorough, serious guide to "fixing" troublesome resumes

Design, Ease Of Use
★★★
Advice is very clear and direct; "before" and "after" resumes show solutions in action

1–4 Stars

Author:
John J. Marcus
The author has extensive experience in the employment field. He is a contributor to *The Wall Street Journal's National Business Employment Weekly*, and the author of *The Complete Job Interview Handbook*.

Publisher:
HarperPerennial

Edition:
1996

Price:
$12.95

ISBN:
0062733699

Media:
Book

Principal Subject:
Resumes

Of Interest To:
Returning To The Workplace

★★★

Overall Rating
★★★

A great, "how to" guide for posting resumes, creating home pages, online job searching

Design, Ease Of Use
★★★

Plain, nontechnical language; lots of samples, illustrations, thousands of URLs

1–4 Stars

Author:
Pat Criscito, CPS, CPRW

Ms. Criscito is a Certified Professional Resume Writer with over 25 years of experience. As president and founder of ProType, Ltd., she writes more than 1,000 resumes a year. She is also the author of Barron's *Designing the Perfect Resume.*

Publisher:
Barron's

Edition:
1997

Price:
$14.95

Pages:
323

ISBN:
0812099192

Media:
Book

Principal Subject:
Resumes

Resumes

RESUMES IN CYBERSPACE
Your Complete Guide To A Computerized Job Search

Description:
As the title implies, Ms. Criscito's primary goal is to teach readers how to design and post an electronic resume. Scannable resumes, e-mailable resumes, and multimedia resumes are first introduced in broad terms: what they are, how they work, etc. Step-by-step directions for creating such resumes follow, i.e. how to create an ASCII text file. For scannable resumes, there is a "complete guide to style, fonts, paper, and so on," sample scannable resumes, and an examination of Applicant Tracking Systems. The chapter on e-mailable resumes explores such topics as what e-mail is, sending a binary file, and e-mailing directly to a company's recruiter. Next, readers learn how to post their resumes. There are extensive lists of online resources for posting and/or searching for job openings; the resources are categorized by industry and "type" (i.e. accounting, academia). There are also instructions for creating a home page and advice on where and how to "upload." To help users find "new" sites, search engines and gophers are discussed.

Evaluation:
This is a highly valuable asset to job hunters who are interested in a "computerized job search" but who are new to or unfamiliar with Internet technology. In "plain," nontechnical language, Ms. Criscito demystifies the entire process, from creating a scannable paper resume, to how to save a file in ASCII text, to using online HTML reference guides (which offer guidance free of charge). She uses lots of sample resumes, illustrations, and pictures of "screens" to supplement the straightforward directions; even the novice user will quickly "catch on." She also provides thousands of URLs for companies, career counseling centers, job listings, newsgroups, etc. Since many companies post job openings at their own sites, readers learn how to post their resumes directly to a company's home page. This is a great resource for online job searching! Keep in mind, however, that the majority of jobs are filled before the "resume game" begins; this book will get you online, but old-fashioned networking still counts.

Where To Find/Buy:
Bookstores and libraries.

Resumes

CONQUER RESUME OBJECTIONS
Triumph Over Barriers: Job History, Career Objectives, Resume Format

Description:
Despite the title, there are three parts of this five part guide which do not directly involve resumes. Part 1, "Getting Out From Under," explores the five "predicaments" which preceded the need for this book: job loss, eminent job loss, dissatisfaction with current job, recent graduate, or returning to the job market after years away. In addition to offering situation-specific advice, this section also provides self-evaluation exercises to define interests and needs. Part 2, "Getting Organized," addresses financial issues, i.e. health insurance and unemployment compensation, as well as time management strategies. In Part 3, "The Flexible Resume," readers are taught to create a master "template" and master cover letter; "refitting" for a target audience follows. Each component of the resume is discussed; lots of sample resumes are included. Techniques for "Developing an Effective Marketing Plan" (i.e. "job seeker as product") are espoused in Part 4. Part 5 examines "Resume Objections" with "before-and-after" examples.

Evaluation:
In the pantheon of resume guides, this one is relatively sophisticated; it includes issues such as unemployment and termination for "cause," and employs business-school terminology, i.e. "market segmentation." The benefit of this "adult" orientation (verses recent graduates) is that career changers, people returning to the workplace after years away, and unemployed adults have a resume guide appropriate for people with a work history. They don't have to feel as though they've borrowed their son/daughter's guide. But that's not the best reason to buy this book. While almost all resume guides attempt to address a variety of work histories, few address the problematic ones, like firing, as well as this one does. The authors are smart, insightful, and, when necessary, blunt. While some people (the lucky few) want a resume guide for format or design instructions, most people look to these books for one major reason: to help them present the "bad parts" in the best light. For such consumers, this is a fantastic choice!

Where To Find/Buy:
Bookstores and libraries.

Overall Rating
★★★
A sophisticated choice for people with a work history; includes lots of samples

Design, Ease Of Use
★★
Well-written, but dense; requires reading rather than browsing

1–4 Stars

Author:
Robert F. Wilson and Erik H. Rambusch

Mr. Wilson is the author of the best-selling *Better Resumes for Executives and Professionals*. Mr. Rambusch is the principal of Rambusch Associates, a career consulting firm. They are co-authors of *Conquer Interview Objections*.

Publisher:
John Wiley & Sons

Edition:
1994

Price:
$10.95

Pages:
205

ISBN:
0471589837

Media:
Book

Principal Subject:
Resumes

V. How To Land The Job You Want

★ ★

Overall Rating
★★
Most useful for new resume writers who need extra help designing a "look"

Design, Ease Of Use
★★★
Highly user-friendly software; a wide variety of resume layouts to choose from

1–4 Stars

Author:
Yana Parker

Yana Parker works as a mentor for Roving Resume Writers, "a group of volunteers providing free resume writing for San Francisco homeless and low-income job hunters."

Publisher:
Ten Speed

Edition:
1995

Price:
$29.95

ISBN:
0898157331

Media:
Book + Software

Principal Subject:
Resumes

DAMN GOOD READY-TO-GO RESUMES

Description:

Three disks, complete with 28 different resume styles and formats, are included, one each for WordPerfect (PC), Microsoft Word (PC), and Microsoft Word (Macintosh). The accompanying text tells you how to use the resume templates on the software, as well as how to select between formats (chronological or functional). Ten examples of a chronological resume are followed by ten functional resumes, one page showing the template you'll see on the software, and the facing page containing an actual sample of a resume using that template. A section about when to use an "alternative resume" template comes next, with examples of a "combination resume," "accomplishment resume," "new graduate resume," "scanner-friendly resume," and "draft resume." A chapter explains how to "tweak" your resume into shape by customizing the wording and graphics. Final sections include cover letter templates and examples, a reference worksheet form, and a "crash course" in resume writing with solutions to common problems.

Evaluation:

There are two parts to every resume: what you say, and how you say it; in other words, form and content. In this book/software duo, the second of these is addressed—with some (minimal) attention to the "how-to" portion of resume writing. Thus, it's best used in conjunction with a resource that will help you actually compose the content of your resume. If you've done that work, but still feel you need to "spice up" the visuals, then you might turn here for help. The user friendly software essentially lays it all out for you; all you really have to do is choose a format (chronological or functional) and style by leafing through the samples provided in the book, and then just "fill in the blanks." While this isn't the most creative solution to laying out a resume, it might come in handy for hurried professionals or nervous newbies who don't particularly trust their software/layout skills yet. But that leaves a good portion of others who may be beyond this template-style of arranging a resume.

Where To Find/Buy:

Bookstores and libraries, or directly from the publisher at (800) 841-BOOK.

Resumes

HEART & SOUL RESUMES
Never-Before-Published Secrets To Capturing Heart & Soul In Your Resume

★ ★

Description:
Resumes are often the first impression a job candidate makes on a potential employer. Many resume guides seek to help candidates present themselves in the best light. Heart & Soul resumes aim to "communicate who we really are and why we are just the person the interviewer has been looking for—in a way that is positive and original." The book begins with the Seven Secrets to creating a successful resume; each receives a chapter's worth of explanation. Chapter titles are: Creative Visualization; Planning Career Strategies to Guide Your Job Search; So You Want to Be a Brain Surgeon; Attending to Attention; Doodle Your Way to Details; The Attitude of Gratitude and Appealing to the Heart. In the second half of the book, the authors offer before and after examples of resumes with and without Heart & Soul. An appendix contains the Myers-Briggs Type Indicator and the Strong Interest Inventory. The authors offer insider advice from their years of assisting in resume writing in graphic boxes called "Heart & Soul" tips. Some attention is given to cover letters, signature booklets and other job search documents.

Evaluation:
A Dale Carnegie quotation appearing in Chapter seven captures the rationale behind this book: "When dealing with people, let us remember we are not dealing with creatures of logic. We are dealing with creatures of emotion . . ." The authors, both professional resume writers, feel that most job seekers spend too much time focusing on the style of their resume, and not enough time developing its content. This guide distinguishes itself by offering help in developing the content of a resume, and guiding the job seeker through the often difficult work of recognizing who they are, who they want to be and what are their relevant skills, talents and experience. They help the job seeker ask and answer for themselves the fundamental questions that need to be addressed before choosing a chronological or skill format. These questions range from, What do I really want to do with my life? to How does my past experience relate to what I want to become? Sophisticated readers may roll their eyes at some of the folksy advice—such as doodling in margins to dissolve writer's block. And many of the Heart & Soul tips can give you heartburn (such as "Love yourself throughout your journey, and enjoy living in the moment"). But if your resume exudes the warmth of a dead fire, this book may help create one that allows your true self to shine through.

Where To Find/Buy:
Bookstores and libraries.

Overall Rating
★★
Tips for creating a resume that reflects your values and interests

Design, Ease Of Use
★★★
Before and after resumes help readers transform their own resume

1–4 Stars

Author:
Chuck Cochran and Donna Peerce

Mr. Cochran is founder and president of the Heart & Soul Career Center in Nashville. Ms. Peerce is vice president of writing services for the Heart & Soul Career Center. She is a published author with experience in writing for television, advertising and ghostwriting.

Publisher:
Davies-Black Publishing

Edition:
1998

Price:
$15.95

Pages:
219

ISBN:
0891061134

Media:
Book

Principal Subject:
Resumes

★★

Overall Rating
★★

Interesting sampling of diverse resumes, but with little advice about how to write one

Design, Ease Of Use
★★

Resumes alphabetized for easy reference

1–4 Stars

Author:
Jay A. Block and Michael Betrus

Jay A. Block is a Certified Professional Resume Writer, and contributing co-founder of the Professional Association of Resume Writers (PARW). Michael Betrus is the author of *The Guide To Executive Recruiters*.

Publisher:
McGraw-Hill

Edition:
1997

Price:
$10.95

ISBN:
0070328935

Media:
Book

Principal Subject:
Resumes

Resumes

101 BEST RESUMES

Description:
Opening chapters discuss such issues as where to look for a job, taking inventory of your skills, resume styles and formats, as well as what to include in each section. The "5 Ps of Resume Writing" address such issues as packaging, positioning of information, punch, personality, and professionalism of the resume. Advice about cover letters—format and types—is also found here, with examples. Most of the book is composed of the 101 resumes, spanning a variety of fields and skill levels. A sampling of these includes: actor; architect; banker; chef; forestry; human resources; karate instructor; librarian; nurse; photography; physician; pilot; real estate; sales; singer; social worker; teacher; and writer. A last chapter contains 25 resume, cover letter, interviewing, salary negotiating, networking, references, working with executive recruiters, and "what do I do now that I have my resume?" tips. The sample resumes are alphabetized in the index.

Evaluation:
What you see is what you get, literally, in these pages. 101 examples of good resumes may or may not be what you're looking for: if all you want to do is see a variety of resumes, then this is for you, but if you are unsure about how to translate your own skills and abilities into a "best resume," this book won't really help you out. Although introductory pages do include advice about various styles and formats, the advice is not particularly good, and seems intended rather to throw you headfirst into the 101 resumes. There are both good and bad things about such "example" resume books. While it's nice to be able to see how other people have handled graphics and wording, etc., but it's debatable whether you can learn much from an accountant's resume if you're, say, a teacher, or by looking over the resume of a cartoonist if you're a doctor. While there's a great breadth of resumes here, there's not a lot of depth in each field, so you may end up with only 1 "best" example from your field of employment.

Where To Find/Buy:
Bookstores and libraries.

Resumes

PROVEN RESUMES.COM
40 Free Online Resume & Job Search Workshops

Description:

Proven Resumes.com's "table of contents" divides the site's contents into "categories." (It also functions as a site map.) There are four resume-related "categories:" "Resumes that Sell in Seconds," "Blow Away Your Competition," "Electronic Resumes," and "Resume Tips For . . ." Under "Resumes that Sell in Seconds," users will find such segments as "6 easy steps to create resumes," "design and content," and "identify your skills." In "Blow Away Your Competition," segments include "marketing the 10 hottest skills" and "solving employers hidden needs." "Electronic Resumes" explores creating scannable resumes, "e-mail resumes," resume banks, and "homepage resumes." The advice offered in "Resume Tips For . . ." is situation-specific, i.e. "military resumes," "management resumes," etc. The site also features other job-related "categories:" "dynamic cover letters," "effective thank-you letters," strategies for online job hunting, articles from "career experts," and 100s of career-related links.

Evaluation:

The problem with this site is that the quality of the material found in each segment varies dramatically. Some segments may be text-only, while others include graphics, charts, and/or examples; some may comprise several pages, while others comprise two paragraphs. Some segments, such as "creating scannable resumes," offer genuinely helpful tools: there's a step-by-step guide for converting your resume to ASCII text and an explanation of how scanners work. Other segments, however, are "teases:" the "headings" are either misleading or the segment is mostly an advertisement for Ms. Pontow's print resource. For example, click on "marketing the 10 hottest skills" and you'll find 2 "hot skills" and a promotion for the book which contains the other 8. Many segments also suffer from the lack of samples. "Homepage resumes" provides some fine tips, but it desperately needs visual aids. Finding the worthwhile elements of this site is akin to panning for gold: there's a lot of sand to sift, and only a few nuggets.

Where To Find/Buy:

On the Internet at http://www.provenresumes.com

Overall Rating
★★
The quality of each segment varies; too much advertising

Design, Ease Of Use
★★
Easy to navigate, but "headings" can be misleading

1–4 Stars

Author:
Regina Pontow
Ms. Pontow is the author of *Proven Resumes and Confidence Builders*. She is a professional resume consultant with over 10 years of experience in resume writing.

Edition:
1997

Media:
Internet

Principal Subject:
Resumes

★★

Overall Rating
★★
Average resume samples and below-average cover letter samples

Design, Ease Of Use
★
Poorly organized; there's no index/table of contents for the samples

1–4 Stars

Author:
The Editors of VGM Career Horizons

Publisher:
VGM Horizons

Edition:
1996

Price:
$9.95

Pages:
151

ISBN:
0844241555

Media:
Book

Principal Subject:
Resumes

Secondary Subject:
Cover Letters

Resumes

RESUMES FOR MIDCAREER JOB CHANGERS
With Sample Cover Letters

Description:
To help "midcareer" job changers write successful resumes, the editors of VGM Horizons have compiled "nearly 100" samples. There are 6 chapters in this guide, beginning with 3 chapters of advice/explanation. Chapter 1, "The Elements of a Good Resume," explains such elements as the heading and the objective, and provides worksheets for gathering personal data. Chapter 2, "Writing Your Resume," offers before-and-after examples and a list of action verbs, while Chapter 3 explores "Assembly and Layout." The sample resumes are housed in Chapter 5 and illustrate a variety of format, style, and content choices. General management, production management, technical writing, and "communications director" are among the types of resumes presented. In addition to resumes, this guide also includes tips on writing cover letters (Chapter 4) and 20 cover letter samples (Chapter 6). The letter samples address such situations as answering ads, submitting resumes, and "follow-up."

Evaluation:
Even though Wendy Enelow's books "100 Winning Resumes for $100,000+ Jobs" and "201 Cover Letters for $100,000+ Jobs" target (ostensibly) a different audience than this guide, they're better choices for both resume and cover letter samples. (See reviews.) Enelow's books are for professional, management and executive candidates, but that doesn't mean they can't be used by "midcareer" changers. Enelow's samples are far superior to these. VGM's sample cover letters have good ideas, such as end with a follow-up "I'll call you," but they aren't very well written. (They're strikingly unoriginal: "I am writing to apply for . . . position. . . . Enclosed is my resume. . . .") The resumes are better, but only average compared to what's available in similar guides. And alas, the resumes aren't organized. There's no index of jobs or table of contents, just a wide variety of resumes you have to flip through. There are better resources for both samples and guidance.

Where To Find/Buy:
Bookstores and libraries.

Resumes

RESUMES THAT GET JOBS
With Resume-Writing Software

Description:

The software allows you to select a resume template and fill in your own data. Five templates are provided, each of which emphasizes qualifications, experience, accomplishments, skills, and profile, examples of which are included in the book. Also included on the disk are sample cover letters that you can edit to fit, as well as help for creating new ones. The book opens by addressing different sections of the resume. Chapters on personal skills, qualifications, work experience, accomplishments, and job skills provide fill-in-the-blank worksheets to generate lists, and show you how use action words and "facts and figures" to enliven and quantify these sections on the resume. Chapter 6 describes the qualifications summary, a "capsule description of who you are and what you have to offer an employer." Other chapters address education, awards, and job objective sections. Chapter 14 tells how to make your resume scannable. The second half of the book consists of sample resumes and a few "before and after" resumes.

Evaluation:

The software part of this book/software duo is clearly a late addition. No mention of it is made of it in the text, past a brief "user's manual" describing how to use the software. References to the templates and how to fill them are not made in relevant chapters of the book addressing work experience, education, job objective, and so on. There is clearly room for improvement in terms of integrating the software into the text, so that both parts can work in tandem. The software provides five resume templates and cover letter templates, samples of which are included in the book. You simply clear the existing data and fill in your own. Of course, you must first LIKE the existing template, because you can't change it. The book shows you how to list skills, qualifications, etc., with "action" words and "facts and figures." It's pretty much just fill-in-the-blank; you won't be lavished with lots of advice. The sample resumes are helpful and diverse, but overall, it's lacking in comparison to its peers.

Where To Find/Buy:
Bookstores and libraries.

Overall Rating
★
Skims the basics of creating a resume; little relationship between software and book

Design, Ease Of Use
★★
Simplistic "fill in the blank" exercises; resume template software is easy to use

1–4 Stars

Author:
Ray Potter

Ray Potter is a professional career consultant, and the coauthor of *100 Best Resumes For Today's Hottest Jobs*, also from Arco.

Publisher:
Arco

Edition:
9th (1998)

Price:
$24.95

ISBN:
0028621956

Media:
Book + Software

Principal Subject:
Resumes

V. How To Land
The Job You Want

COVER LETTERS

A cover letter, which always accompanies the resume you send to employers of interest, introduces you and asks them to consider your resume. We've recommended several books in this section that can help you to craft effective cover letters to potential employers.

The one-page cover letter should be tailored to a particular job and organization. Obvious form letters are rarely effective. Make sure you are very specific as to what you are applying for and where you got the information about the job. If you were referred by someone, indicate their name and title at the beginning of letter.

Next, let them know that you've researched their company, and why you believe your qualifications, interests, and career goals would make you an excellent candidate for a position with them. Relate your prior experience and skills to emphasize the concept of a good fit. Remain positive and upbeat. Give a few specific examples of successful achievements, taken from prior work experience.

Finally, tell the company know how you plan to follow up on your letter and resume. Let them know when you plan to call to arrange a time to interview, or to further discuss the position/ organization and your qualifications. And then do be sure to call as you've promised!

Five Tips For Great Cover Letters

- When possible, address your letter to a specific individual, with their exact title.

- Use words from the ad or job description to describe yourself when possible.

- Tell them why your skills and qualifications match what they are looking for in a job candidate.

- Let them know you've done your research about their organization.

- Tell them how you plan to follow up, mentioning that you would appreciate the opportunity to discuss your qualifications and the organization at a mutually convenient time.

COVER LETTERS FOR DUMMIES

★★★★

 Recommended For:
Cover Letters

Description:

Ms. Lain Kennedy, who is also the author of "Resumes for Dummies," is determined to make cover letter writing "painless." She maintains that this book showcases "the fun and easy way to create Red-Hot cover letters with impact." According to the author, Red-Hot cover letters are "an electrifying personal advertising tool that short-circuits the competition." The process for creating a Red-Hot letter is outlined in five sections. The first section disposes of cover letter myths and discusses the various types of cover letters. In the second section, interactive worksheets guide the reader through the writing process by identifying an individuals most marketable features. Part III focuses on writing the letter and includes a large section on language usage. Cover letter "dos and don'ts" are sprinkled throughout the book and approximately 50 sample letters are included. Internet resources and digital technology are also fully explored.

Evaluation:

In keeping with its title, this is an extremely easy to use book. The informal language and bold headlines add to its "for Dummies" charm. Icons are used throughout the work to flag points that the author believes are "too hot to ignore." The icons are defined in the introduction and include a bomb to indicate "mistakes that could end up costing you the job" and a chili pepper to highlight tips that "will make your cover letter burn all the rest." Although the "for Dummies" series is very popular, sophisticated readers may not appreciate the irreverent, sometimes juvenile style. Sample letters include resume letters, blind ad reply letters and employment service letters. These letters are categorized by type and also by career field. Unlike similar guides which merely present sample letters, Ms. Lain Kennedy offers highlighted tips and explanations along with every letter. If you're looking for a little humor and visual interest with your cover letter advice, this book's for you!

Where To Find/Buy:

Bookstores and libraries.

Overall Rating
★★★★
Great tips presented in a clear and humorous manner.

Design, Ease Of Use
★★★★
Easy to use with bold headlines

1–4 Stars

Author:
Joyce Lain Kennedy

Joyce Lain Kennedy is the author of the *Los Angeles Times* syndicate's column *CAREERS*, which appears in more than 100 newspapers. She is the author or co-author of eight books, including *Resumes for Dummies*.

Publisher:
IDG Books

Edition:
1996

Price:
$12.99

Pages:
237

ISBN:
156884395X

Media:
Book

Principal Subject:
Cover Letters

★★★★

Overall Rating
★★★★
An excellent resource for experienced job hunters who just need "models" to learn from

Design, Ease Of Use
★★★
Excellent letter samples but little step-by-step instruction

1–4 Stars

Author:
William S. Frank

Bill Frank is a career consultant to major U.S. corporations.

Publisher:
Ten Speed

Edition:
1993

Price:
$19.95

ISBN:
0898155584

Media:
Book

Principal Subject:
Cover Letters

Cover Letters

200 LETTERS FOR JOB HUNTERS

 Recommended For:
Cover Letters

Description:

The author states at the start, "Interviews produce job offers, but letters produce interviews." To help you write the kind of letter that gets results, he begins by stressing the unique importance of the cover letter in the job hunt process. Believing that most jobs are obtained through those you know, he helps you make a "Friendship Checklist" of contacts to send letters to, and gives tips about obtaining lists of employers for targeted mailings. Part Two contains a list of general principles for writing a great letter. Finally, Part Three contains the letters themselves, indexed in the back by situation (e.g. "Arrange informational interview," "Answer want ad," "Sell your way into a company," "Target favorite company"), some of which contain commentary. These are examples of real-life letters—letters the author wrote himself, letters that were written to him, and letters he co-wrote in collaboration with clients. Part Four includes the notes/commentary on selected letters.

Evaluation:

Mr. Frank emphasizes using emotion and passion in the cover letters over stale, hackneyed sentiment and expressions. Thus, in the introductory "principles," he steers the reader away from such greetings as "Dear Sir" and endings such as that old stand-by, "Sincerely," and towards fresher, friendlier vocabulary. He advises writing letters with "advertising appeal" and to "make your letters electric." "200 Letters," finally, is really just that: 200 good to excellent cover letters covering a variety of letter situations, and displaying an unconventional, direct charm. This is no line-by-line "how-to" however; there is little hand-holding beyond the few pages of general "principles." Experienced job hunters and those who learn best by models will find help simply by studying the tactics used in the excellent sample letters and adapting them to their own situations, but readers new to the job scene may find the "no-hands" approach a trifle disconcerting. (Mr. Frank's letters also appear online at CareerLab; see review.)

Where To Find/Buy:

Bookstores and libraries.

Cover Letters

175 HIGH-IMPACT COVER LETTERS

★ ★ ★

Description:

Richard H. Beatty is president of a corporate outplacement consulting firm, and a published author in the field of career literature. In the belief that "the cover letter is far too important a document to be left to chance or to be written hurriedly at the last minute," he has put together a book that provides professional letter models that "can be rapidly deployed as needed." The six cover letter models, addressing a variety of situations, include: the employee broadcast letter; the search firm broadcast letter; the advertising response letter; the networking cover letter; the "increasingly popular" resume letter; and the thank-you letter. Following an introductory chapter discussing the importance of the cover letter, a chapter is addressed to each letter type, with explicit instructions, advice, and some illustrative samples. Chapter 4, about writing letters in response to an ad, includes thirty sample letters along with the sample advertisements.

Evaluation:

Mr. Beatty's guide is nicely put together: each type of letter is given its own chapter, with instructions followed by samples illustrating the various formats. It is a very straightforward, step-by-step resource, with has its advantages (such as user-friendliness) and disadvantages (not a lot of encouragement to be creative). Basically, what you get is very good, concise information about putting together some of the most effective cover letter formats—you've probably seen most of them before, but that doesn't mean they don't *work*. The attitude here is serious—no gimmicks or cartoons—which should appeal to serious job hunters, and the sample letters are believable and persuasive. A key strength is the inclusion of six different types of letters; not all "cover letters" are intended to simply "cover" a resume. And the six letter "occasions" included here are well-chosen, each a potential opportunity to signal to an employer that you are "a highly desirable candidate worthy of an employment interview."

Where To Find/Buy:

Bookstores and libraries.

Overall Rating
★★★
A very good, serious-minded approach to all types of "cover letters"

Design, Ease Of Use
★★★★
Well-organized chapters include instructions and samples for each type of letter

1–4 Stars

Author:
Richard H. Beatty

The author is President of the Brandywine Consulting Group, a corporate outplacement consulting firm. He is the author of several other books on careers and the job search.

Publisher:
Wiley

Edition:
2nd (1996)

Price:
$10.95

ISBN:
0471123854

Media:
Book

Principal Subject:
Cover Letters

★★★

Overall Rating
★★★

A wide variety of letters are included in addition to cover letters

Design, Ease Of Use
★★★★

Great software enhances the book's value

1–4 Stars

Author:
Robert L. Adams

Robert L. Adams is the Senior Editor of and Adams Cover Letter and Laura Morin is the managing editor.

Publisher:
Adams

Edition:
1996

Price:
$19.95

Pages:
735

ISBN:
1558506195

Media:
Book

Principal Subject:
Cover Letters

Cover Letters

ADAMS COVER LETTERS
Almanac And Disk

Description:
The editors of this 735 page guide believe that the cover letter is the most important aspect of an individual's job search. Topics covered include marketing your skills, what potential employers focus on in a cover letter, and writing the type of cover letter that best matches your job search needs. Part III, the largest section of the book, contains over 600 sample cover letters. Two bulleted points appear along with every letter to highlight what works particularly well in the letter. The samples are divided into 23 chapters based on different letter types. Chapters include "Letter to an Employment Agency," "Response to a Classified Advertisement" and "Networking Letter." Within each chapter the letters are organized by careers. The accompanying disk is designed to create personalized cover letters and works as a template. The user selects the type of cover letter desired and then enters the appropriate information into the designated fields. The software then creates an actual cover letter.

Evaluation:
The FastLetter software that accompanies this guide streamlines the letter writing process. FastLetter is easy to use and even individuals who have very little computer experience should not have any problems loading the PC-formatted software or maneuvering through the program. An advantage this software has over similar programs is the Letter Tutorial section which gives a brief and informative presentation about the process of writing different types of job search letters. The Fast Letter section of the program provides a number of different templates that can be utilized to create unique letters. While the actual amount of information covered in the text is minimal, since the majority of the work consists of sample letters, the editors did include contact information for various agencies and organizations that either offer career development counseling or job placement. This book and software package is a great value.

Where To Find/Buy:
Bookstores and libraries.

Cover Letters

★★★

JOB NOTES: COVER LETTERS

Description:

In "Getting Started," Dr. Tullier introduces readers to the basics behind cover letters: what they are and who reads them (i.e. Human Resource recruiter, network contact). Cover letters, though they can be used for many different purposes, generally fall into three categories: letters for a definite opening, unsolicited letters, and "resume letters." Examples of each "type" of letter appear in the "samples" section, as do letters for a variety of situations. Letters for internships, "career-changers," exploratory interviews, responses to an ad, follow-ups, and networking are among the samples included. Yet there is more to letter writing than following examples. "Power tools" are taught, such as identifying the reader's needs, identifying your objectives, and preparing a "job search sound bite." In "Getting Down to Writing," step-by-step instructions for composition are provided. Content, language, and format choices are also discussed. There are "practice letter" worksheets; pertinent "FAQs" (Q & A) are interspersed throughout.

Evaluation:

Though this booklet was ostensibly designed for a broad audience (students to career changers), it is best suited to less experienced job seekers. People who have had previous success with cover letters, or who have their own successful strategies, may find this information rudimentary. However, for anyone with questions about the fundamentals, or for those who are returning to the work force after an extended absence, Dr. Tullier's advice is right on target. She provides answers to pertinent questions, such as "How do I address salary history [when I have none]?" and "What should I say if I'm relocating?" By confronting (almost) every conceivable situation, including "career changing" and networking, readers are given both practical tools and confidence. One of this book's greatest assets is its calm, authoritative voice: follow these guidelines and everything will be OK. Considering the methods taught, readers can heed that voice without reserve.

Where To Find/Buy:

Bookstores and libraries, or direct from the publisher at 800-793-2665.

Overall Rating
★★★
A great introduction to cover letters and how to write to them; lots of samples

Design, Ease Of Use
★★★★
Well-written, straightforward and accessible

1–4 Stars

Author:
L. Michelle Tullier, Ph.D.

Dr. Tullier has been a career counselor since 1985; her Ph.D., from UCLA, is in Counseling Psychology. Currently, she has a New York-based private practice and is on the faculty of New York University's School of Continuing Education. She is co-author of *Job Smart.*

Publisher:
The Princeton Review

Edition:
1997

Price:
$4.95

Pages:
86

ISBN:
067977873X

Media:
Book

Principal Subject:
Cover Letters

V. How To Land
The Job You Want

★★★

Overall Rating
★★★
Lots of samples for executive-level cover letters; quick, effective "tips"

Design, Ease Of Use
★★★
Basically well organized; may take "flipping pages" to find the letter you want

1–4 Stars

Author:
Wendy S. Enelow

Ms. Enelow is president of The Advantage, Inc., an executive resume firm. She is a Certified Professional Resume Writer and is the author of *100 Winning Resumes for $100,000+ Jobs.*

Publisher:
Impact Publications

Edition:
1998

Price:
$24.95

Pages:
264

ISBN:
1570230889

Media:
Book

Principal Subject:
Cover Letters

Cover Letters

201 WINNING COVER LETTERS FOR $100,000+ JOBS
Letters That Can Change Your Life

Description:

There are 2 chapters in Enelow's book on cover letters for $100,000+ jobs. (All of the 201 letters are written for management, senior management and executive job search candidates.) Chapter 1 discusses the fundamentals of "Writing Winning Cover Letters," such as critical messages and critical concepts to communicate, i.e. "your ability to quickly assimilate into their culture and organization." "Five critical rules and regulations to live by," i.e. "ask for the interview at the end of each letter," cover letter vocabulary words, and answered "FAQs" are also provided. Explanation and examples of various types of cover letter follow; types include "advertisement response," "targeted letter for companies, recruiters, and venture capital firms," and "network contact letters." The 201 sample letters comprise Chapter 2; the letters are organized into job function/ profession categories. Categories include "banking," "consulting," "health care," "human resources," "law," "marketing," and "senior management."

Evaluation:

Designed for management, senior management and executive job search candidates, Enelow assumes her readers have a basic understanding of what a cover letter is, its use, etc., and that they already know how to write well; thus there's no hand-holding or "step-by-step" instruction. The tips that are provided are straightforward, pointed and often appear in the form of bulleted lists. For example, there's a list of points to "highlight" in your letter, i.e. industry credentials, and a list of "high-impact" phrases, i.e. "accelerating revenue growth" and "cross-culturally sensitive." Each category of letters has its own list of action verbs, keywords, and phrases, too; in "marketing," these include "cross-functional team leadership" and "new market penetration." The variety and number of samples in each category varies, but you may find inspiration in other categories as well as your own. A winning collection of quick, timely pointers and impressive samples.

Where To Find/Buy:

Bookstores and libraries.

Cover Letters

NATIONAL BUSINESS EMPLOYMENT WEEKLY COVER LETTERS
Proven Techniques For Writing Letters That Will Help You Get The Job You Want

★★★

Description:

Taunee Besson bases her belief that cover letters are the most important element of a job search on her years of experience as career counselor. She maintains that "Cover letters and thank-you notes play a bigger role in attracting employers' attention and convincing them to hire candidates than do most resumes." Her book is organized in a process oriented manner. The first chapters present the basics and the final chapters offer sample letters that may be used as models. The final chapter focuses on follow-up letters such as thank-you letters, acceptance letters and rejection letters. Also discussed are letter writing tips, hints on how to gather information about employers and openings, and alternatives to traditional cover letters and resumes. Tips on how to make letters stand out from the competition and how to handle "negative" information are included. As the title suggests, actual letters are provided; scattered throughout the work are letters from real individuals who were successful in their job searches.

Evaluation:

Both individuals who are returning to their careers as well as career changers will enjoy the insider tips and expert advice Besson provides. Her book offers practical suggestions for individuals needing to turn negative job history information into positive assets. Special situations that are discussed include career changes and women returning to work after time off from the employed work force. Few cover letter books address these situations specifically, so consumers should take advantage! The author writes like the seasoned columnist she is, in an informal and easy to read style. Individuals with very little work experience may find the first chapter especially useful because of its discussion of the myths concerning cover letters. This is done through the inclusion of a twenty question quiz. The letters she includes as examples are interesting, and some are thought-provoking; however, the book does not contain as many sample letters as similar guides. For more samples, check out CareerLab online (see review).

Where To Find/Buy:

Bookstores and libraries.

Overall Rating
★★★
Author offers a lot of practical advice

Design, Ease Of Use
★★★
Easy to read writing style and well organized

1–4 Stars

Author:
Taunee Besson

Taunee Besson is president of Career Dimensions, a Dallas consulting firm that helps individuals and companies with issues such as career change, career pathing, small-business strategies, spouse relocation/employment and outplacement.

Publisher:
John Wiley & Sons

Edition:
1995

Price:
$10.95

Pages:
262

ISBN:
0471106720

Media:
Book

Principal Subject:
Cover Letters

★★

Overall Rating
★★
200 sample letters and valuable advice on letter writing; for sample lovers

Design, Ease Of Use
★
Can be difficult to navigate; no search engine for the letters (only "sections")

1–4 Stars

Author:
William S. Frank, M.A.

Mr. Frank is founder and President of CareerLab; he is also the author of *200 Letters For Job Hunters* (Ten Speed Press). He created the *RED HOT Cover Letters* collection in the Career Center at America Online.

Edition:
1998

Media:
Internet

Principal Subject:
Cover Letters

Cover Letters

CAREERLAB: 200 LETTERS FOR JOB HUNTERS

Description:

The portion of CareerLab dedicated to job-related letters, "200 Letters For Job Hunters," contains two segments: the letters themselves ("200 of the World's Best Letters") and "How To Write a GREAT Letter." The "How To . . ." segment is a collection of tips, "dos and don'ts," advice and guidelines for 13 letter-writing topics. The topics include "What To Do for a Quick Job Search," "Writing to Strangers," and "How to Select a Mailing List." Networking is discussed in "The Most Important Letter You Will Ever Write," which provides a "friendship checklist" and addresses common "objections," i.e. "I don't want to use my friend." "Common Mistakes," such as "using the word 'I' too much" and spelling errors, are also detailed. The 200 letters, which range from answering want-ads, to networking, to saying "thank you," are divided into 20 sections. Each section begins with an introductory overview of that "type" of letter; the number of samples in each section varies.

Evaluation:

People love samples; so what could be better than 200 free letters for job hunters? This "site" is definitely worth a visit; not only is there a wide array of sample letters, the advice offered in "How To Write a GREAT Letter" is helpful, too. There are such seldom-seen inclusions as letters to "Prevent Firing," "Leave Gracefully," and "Negotiate a Pay Raise," as well as perennial favorites: i.e. "Cold Calls." Even entrepreneurs aren't forgotten: letters to "Promote Yourself in the Media" and "Become a Consultant" also appear. Unfortunately, the "site" is poorly formatted and difficult to navigate. From within one of the topic segments, i.e. "Writing to Strangers," users can move to the "next page," but not directly to the "How To . . ." main menu. Similarly, from within a letter section, users have to backtrack to access another section. Also, although there is a search engine for the site as a whole, there's no way to search through the letters. Despite its flaws, however, this is still a high-value resource.

Where To Find/Buy:

On the Internet at http://www.careerlab.com/letters/

Cover Letters

201 KILLER COVER LETTERS

★

Overall Rating
★
The book is basic; the disk
redundant

Design, Ease Of Use
★★
Plenty of samples (201) that
are clearly categorized

1–4 Stars

Author:
Sandra Podesta and Andrea
Paxton

Sandra Podesta is a principal in
the DeMartino Marketing Group
with 20 years experience as an
advertising copywriter. Andrea
Paxton is a recruiter with an
extensive background working
with Fortune 500 corporate
clients.

Publisher:
McGraw-Hill

Edition:
1996

Price:
$16.95

Pages:
258

ISBN:
0070504563

Media:
Book

Principal Subject:
Cover Letters

Description:

The authors believe that a killer cover letter is necessary to get a job in today's employment market, and their book is filled with sample cover letters. They emphatically maintain that a resume only conveys 20% of the information on which prospective employers base their hiring decision. The remaining 80% can—and should—be included in the cover letter. Chapter 1 "The Top Ten Rules for Writing Cover Letters" guides the reader through writing an appropriate letter (to a sample employment ad) using their ten rules. These rules advise letter writers to do such things as avoid standard openings and focus on the needs of the prospective employer. Both poor and good examples of letters are included in this chapter. Chapter two "How to Identify and Sell Your Strengths" contains two worksheets to help individuals pinpoint their assets. The remaining seven chapters mainly present sample letters by job category. Thank you and networking letters are also discussed.

Evaluation:

The authors stress the point that a great cover letter is the first chance, and often the only one, to get an interview. However, job hunters looking for lots of tips and strategies for writing that killer letter may be disappointed with this guide. This manual mainly consists of sample letters, great for folks who learn best by following examples, not so great for those looking for lots of advice and explanation; the letter-writing advice is often elementary. Also, some of the advice presented in this work contradicts what a large number of other cover letter manuals recommend. For example, in chapter four the authors suggest using a clever approach to attract attention, while many other career advisors discourage this kind of tactic. The sample cover letters and limited worksheets that make up the disk merely repeat the book. Many other cover letter books do a better job of explaining the cover letter writing process, and for samples alone, Internet users can find 200 free cover letters online at CareerLab. (See review.)

Where To Find/Buy:

Bookstores and libraries.

NETWORKING

The most important thing you need to know about networking is that it works. In my mind, it is the single most important aspect of your job search. There are lots of techniques for finding jobs, but what really works is talking to lots and lots of people and following up leads assertively.

Networking is connecting with people professionally for purposes of career advice, information, and mentorship. It is an essential strategy for entree into certain career fields, and is also an excellent way to unearth unadvertised job openings.

Keep your demands of the network contacts clear, simple, short and focused on getting more contacts. If the contact cannot help you ask them who they would recommend you talk to in your area of interest. Each company and career path has its own group of natural networkers. Finding one of these personable souls with a golden rolodex can be a real boost to your job hunt.

Arranging informational interviews with some of your contacts is a terrific idea. It shows initiative, motivation, and resourcefulness. To arrange an informational interview, it's a good idea to write first, letting the person know how you learned of them, and introducing yourself. Assure them that you understand their busy schedules, and ask for no more than a half-hour of their time. Follow up with a phone call to arrange a meeting.

Use this opportunity to seek general advice about entering the field, gaining related experience, or overall hiring outlook. Do not, however, ask directly for a job! You might ask about your contact's background and qualifications, how they rose to their current position, the best and worst aspects of their job, or what a typical day involves. Try to do some preliminary research so your questions reflect depth and organization. Should an appropriate opening arise in their organization, it's likely that your contact will inform you about it.

Your contact, moreover, will likely be a valuable source of referrals to colleagues or friends who may provide even more valuable information, advice, or specific job leads. Before ending an informational interview, it's a great idea to obtain the names of other professionals in your fields of interest. Ask permission to use their name in facilitating further introductions.

Finally, express your thanks to those who provide advice and information. Send thank you notes and keep in touch.

Five Tips For Successful Networking

- The vast majority of jobs are filled word of mouth. Don't neglect networking!

- Don't ask contacts specifically for a job. They are there to provide information and advice about their work.

- Prepare contacts ahead of time. Write first, then call or email to follow up.

- Make sure to obtain the names of others they know in the field, and ask whether you can use their name when contacting them.

- Make sure to follow up on appropriate leads, write a note of thanks, and stay in touch!

★★★

Overall Rating
★★★
Teaches non-networkers to network; focuses on overcoming "roadblocks"

Design, Ease Of Use
★★★★
Conversational tone; includes interactive worksheets and a few samples

1–4 Stars

Author:
Clyde C. Lowstuter and David P. Robertson

Mr. Lowstuter and Mr. Robertson are the authors of *In Search of the Perfect Job* and the founders of Robertson Lowstuter Inc., an executive career coaching and development consulting firm.

Publisher:
McGraw-Hill

Edition:
1995

Price:
$14.95

Pages:
229

ISBN:
0070388830

Media:
Book

Principal Subject:
Networking

Of Interest To:
Returning To The Workplace

Networking

NETWORK YOUR WAY TO YOUR NEXT JOB . . . FAST

 Recommended For:
Networking

Description:

Networking is one of the best—if not the best—ways to find a job. Yet networking doesn't come naturally to everyone. Helping readers overcome their networking objections is one of the goals of this guide; the other is to teach readers how to use networking in their job search. After Part 1's introduction to the topic, the authors reveal the 10 "secrets" to successful networking in Part 2. Secrets include understanding the "myths and realities" of networking, becoming comfortable with telephone networking, and writing "powerful" letters. "Mastering the 4 Avenues of Networking" (executive retainer search firms, target organizations, employment opportunities, and personal contacts) is another secret. There are also personal secrets, techniques for "managing your beliefs and behavior," focusing on the outcome to get results, and "beating" rejection. The final part, "The Next Steps," details the 61 "proven" strategies for networking. Interactive worksheets and samples appear throughout.

Evaluation:

In many ways this guide could be deemed "networking for non-networkers." Unlike other authors, Lowstuter and Robertson spend quite a bit of time building the reader's confidence. They don't simply say "do this, do that" without acknowledging that "just doing it" isn't an effective approach for everyone. In this book, "fears" of networking are taken seriously. For example, in the chapter "Manage Your Beliefs and Behavior," there are several exercises designed to help you identify and conquer such "roadblocks" as "I am too old," "I don't have much experience," and "I am embarrassed." If there are any similar roadblocks in your life, if you've been downsized or fired, or are returning to the work force, this is the networking guide for you! Other networking guides tend to ignore, downplay or dismiss hurdles, or are written for the experienced and confident. This one is for novices. Its tone is that of a tough, sympathetic teacher who understands your (perceived) limitations yet is determined to push you beyond them.

Where To Find/Buy:

Bookstores and libraries.

Networking

POWER NETWORKING

 Recommended For:
Networking

Description:

If you think you don't know enough people—or the right kind of people—to effectively network, you're wrong. You can be a "power networker," and Kramer's 10-chapter guide aims to show you how. To begin, Chapter 1 introduces the "10 Keys to Being a Great Networker," such as "never start a conversation talking about yourself," and "never sit with a friend at an event." In Chapter 2, Kramer explains how his career developed via networking, and how to use networking to find the right job for you. Topics include where to meet people and find leads (the Internet, business associations), and "what to say" to make contacts. Networking to increase sales and to raise money is described in Chapters 3–4. Chapter 5 offers tips and samples for writing introductory and follow-up letters. Chapters 6–7 detail "maintaining relationships" and networking at different corporate levels. "Good Networking Organizations," starting your own organization, and networking online comprise Chapters 8–10.

Evaluation:

In addition to text, Kramer provides sample introductory letters, information cover letters, and investor letters, as well as the names of "good networking organizations." He also includes lots of personal anecdotes and mock dialogues to illustrate networking scenarios. His advice is practical, if somewhat conservative; he often implies that conservative behavior/dress is a must for networking (e.g. never offend anyone). Kramer's own experience lends credence to his techniques; they worked well for him! It's hard to believe these tactics, if properly implemented, could fail to work. After all, if you resolved to meet at least 5 people an hour at every event you attended and followed up "within 2 business days," you'd make a lot of contacts! Kramer makes networking seem easy, which it won't be for everyone. (If networking makes you uncomfortable, try "Network Your Way To Your Next Job . . . Fast" for more personal guidance. See review.) Overall, this is a reliable resource on continuous networking.

Where To Find/Buy:

Bookstores and libraries.

★★★

Overall Rating
★★★
Practical, reliable tips for continuous networking

Design, Ease Of Use
★★★★
Easy to read; includes samples and mock dialogues

1–4 Stars

Author:
Marc Kramer
Mr. Kramer has been honored with nearly a dozen state and national entrepreneurial and business awards.

Publisher:
VGM Horizons

Edition:
1998

Price:
$12.95

Pages:
152

ISBN:
0844244945

Media:
Book

Principal Subject:
Networking

★★★

Overall Rating
★★★
Guidelines for "novice" networkers; not for seasoned professionals

Design, Ease Of Use
★★★
Inexpensive, quick reading

1–4 Stars

Author:
Meg Heenehan, MEd

Ms. Heenehan is both a career counselor in private practice and the Assistant Director of Career Education at Columbia University's School of International and Public Affairs. She is a co-author of *Job Smart*, and holds a M.Ed. in Counselor Education.

Publisher:
The Princeton Review

Edition:
1997

Price:
$4.95

Pages:
85

ISBN:
0679778772

Media:
Book

Principal Subject:
Networking

Networking

JOB NOTES: NETWORKING

Description:

Ms. Heenehan introduces readers to her chosen topic by describing 10 ways in which networking can be beneficial. For example, networking can garner valuable job search advice, as well as uncover "hidden" job openings. These benefits are undisputed, but the prospect of forming a "network" can be daunting. To allay such fears, a list of "first tier" resources, i.e. family, friends, alumni/ae, is provided and discussed. In "The Essentials of Effective Networking," the first step is to "know thyself." To that end, there is a "skills checklist," and an assortment of fill-in-the-blank exercises for self-assessment. Another "essential" element is research conducted prior to making contact. Written materials, informational organizations, pertinent websites, and other resources are cited. Various strategies for initiating contact are examined, such as phone tactics, elements of the "actual conversation," and letters of inquiry. Interviews, follow-up, and alternative approaches (i.e. internships) are also explored.

Evaluation:

Although all four of the Princeton Review's "Job Notes" books were designed primarily for first-time job seekers, the other three titles, "Cover Letters," "Resumes," and "Interviewing," easily traverse the age/experience gap: they are helpful to job seekers of any situation. (See reviews.) The same cannot be said for Ms. Heenehan's contribution. While novice "networkers" will benefit from this guide—particularly the sections on establishing contact, "informational interviews," and follow-up techniques—anyone who has been working for more than a few years will find this advice rudimentary. That said, however, this may be a good choice for people who have lost either confidence or contacts via a prolonged absence from the workplace. Ms. Heenehan's list of potential contacts (friends, family, etc.) serves to remind readers that no one is without resources, and "networking" can occur anywhere: PTA meetings, book clubs, volunteering, etc. For reassurance and good, "beginners" advice, this is a fine choice.

Where To Find/Buy:

Bookstores and libraries, or direct from the publisher at 800-793-2665.

Networking

NETWORKING

Description:

Under the auspices of "National Business Employment Weekly," "Networking" details strategies for "tapping the hidden market." It begins by introducing the concept of networking, mentioning that despite its current abuse, it has "proven to be the most productive technique for getting job market exposure." The author's aim is to give readers a solid understanding of what networking is (and isn't), along with specific tips for handling all aspects of the process. First chapters focus on defining networking and yourself as a "product," as well as figuring out who to tap in your own personal network. Chapter 4 takes us "Into the Fray," with advice about how to ask for meetings and how to survive being "screened." The next two chapters tell you what goes on in a networking meeting, what questions to ask, and how to keep a "good vibe" going. Chapter 7 gives examples of both successful and unsuccessful meetings. Other chapters focus on following up, overall planning, and other approaches such as long-distance networking.

Evaluation:

Mr. Richardson's guide is a thorough introduction to the concept of networking. Because it has so often been used as a "ploy" by job-hunters to get in the door, it has often been misunderstood and misused. The author gives you a solid understanding of this oldest and best job-hunting skill, laying out both the broad overview of the process as well as such specifics as how to walk away with the information you're looking for without turning off your contact in the process. The emphasis here is on honesty, forthrightness, and manners: these are the qualities that win people over in a networking situation, and not pushiness, being mechanical or lethargic. Readers will find plenty of canny advice; the author is no business neophyte, and the level of sophistication herein will appeal to the most hard-boiled job seeker. Particularly helpful are the "real-life" scenes and snippets from meetings that worked and those that didn't; these don't feel at all "canned," and are really quite enlightening.

Where To Find/Buy:

Bookstores and libraries.

Overall Rating

★★★

An excellent guide to networking with highly specific advice about how to "do it right"

Design, Ease Of Use

★★★

Lively, down-to-earth writing style; funny cartoons

1–4 Stars

Author:
Douglas B. Richardson

The author is president of Richardson & Co., "a career counseling and management development consulting firm in Bala Cynwyd, Pa." He has been a *National Business Employment Weekly* columnist since 1984.

Publisher:
Wiley

Edition:
1994

Price:
$10.95

ISBN:
0471310271

Media:
Book

Principal Subject:
Networking

INTERVIEWING

Successfully negotiating a job interview is certainly one of life's more anxiety-producing situations. The resources we review prepare you for this challenge, helping you to interview with insight, confidence, and positive results.

Focus, enthusiasm and language are the keys to a successful interview. You must be focused and able to tell the potential employer what you want to do for them and where you think you can fit in and contribute. Your focus must be sincere and thought out or they will catch your lack of clarity. Enthusiasm is going to come across if you are applying for jobs you really want to pursue. Let them know how seriously you are pursuing your goals. Let them know how long you have wanted to do this type of work and how you have prepared. Share that you are excited to be interviewing for a job so well suited to your goals.

Speak their language. Use the buzzwords and acronyms of the business. Talk as if you are one of them, rather than an outsider who wants to be in their shoes. To learn the lingo, browse their website, read trade journals or interview experts in the field.

We'll briefly summarize the various stages of the interview process below. Keep in mind that while an organization is interviewing you, you can also use the opportunity to size them up. How comfortable would you feel contributing to their organizational mission and becoming an integral member of their team?

Before the Interview: There's no substitute for in-depth preparation. Do your homework about the organization. Know their products or services. Read the company literature and annual reports. Has the company recently been in the news? The Internet can make much of your research easy, for you can often find such information on-line.

Bring a portfolio or briefcase with extra copies of your resume, a list of references with contact information, a notepad and a few thoughtful questions jotted down to ask at the end of the interview. Know the names and titles of those who will be interviewing you.

Finally, arrive in plenty of time. Allow twice as much time as you think you'll need. If possible, rehearse the route beforehand and take into account the realities of rush-hour travel. If you're flying in or driving a long ways, consider staying over the night before. You want to arrive physically and mentally rested and prepared.

During the Interview: Your task is to assure the recruiter that you're solid, personable, articulate, and someone they'd like to have on board. Greet the interviewer by name, with a firm handshake and a smile. Stay positive and keep the interview focused. They want to see if you're professional and a potentially good fit for the company. Be sure to communicate your enthusiasm and interest. In a behaviorally-focused interview, you may be asked to recount past experiences of leadership, success, or conflict, and how you handled them. If you sense that you've been thrown a curve ball, keep in mind that the recruiter may be assessing how well you handle unexpected stress, or your critical thinking or communication skills.

It's OK to ask the interviewer to rephrase a question, or to try to clarify if don't understand. Know your rights and what constitutes legal or illegal questions. Avoid asking about salary or benefits on a first interview; this is best left for the second interview, which tends to be longer and more in-depth, and during which you meet a greater number of potential colleagues and supervisors.

After the Interview: Write a thank you note immediately after the interview to all those who interviewed you. Reiterate your qualifications and why you think you're a good fit. You should ideally hear about their level of interest and whether they wish to conduct second interviews shortly thereafter. If you don't hear within two weeks, it's appropriate to politely call and follow up.

Five Tips For Successful Interviews

- Be prepared! Know the industry, clients, competitors, and recent developments.

- Always be ready to answer the question, "tell me about yourself" with a good, solid, one-minute sound bite.

- Bring extra copies of your resume, a typed list of references, questions for the employer and a notepad to jot down a few items.

- Keep it focused! They want to see if you're genuine, enthusiastic, and professional.

- Write a thank you note immediately after the interview. Reiterate your qualifications and why you think you're a good fit.

★★★★

Overall Rating
★★★★
A great tool for inexperienced job seekers, packed with helpful advice and strategies

Design, Ease Of Use
★★★★
To-the-point; charts are included for clarification

1–4 Stars

Author:
Marci Taub, M.A.

Ms. Taub holds an M.A. in counseling from Montclair State University and a Certificate in Adult Career Planning and Development from NYU. Currently in private practice, she specializes in job search coaching and career counseling. She is also co-author of *Job Smart*.

Publisher:
The Princeton Review

Edition:
1997

Price:
$4.95

Pages:
82

ISBN:
0679778756

Media:
Book

Principal Subject:
Interviewing

Interviewing

JOB NOTES: INTERVIEWS

 **Recommended For:**
Interviewing

Description:
There are several basic strategies involved in preparation for an interview. First, Ms. Taub addresses issues of scheduling, such as scheduling an interview while working full-time. She then explains the benefits of doing "homework." Readers are encouraged to research their prospective employers (a list of resources is provided) and are taught to assemble an interview "cheat sheet." Defining skills is another important preliminary step. Checklists for "I Am" and "I Can" skills allow readers to form an articulate repertoire of "selling points," to be used during the conversation. Developing this repertoire via illustrations and examples is discussed, as are details like appropriate dress. Techniques to be incorporated during the actual event comprise strategies common to all types of interviews and strategies for specific situations, i.e. the group interview. There are steps for "managing" the interview, practice "theme questions," and tips for handling illegalities. "FAQs" (Q&A) are scattered throughout.

Evaluation:
Although the techniques described in this guide are of value to all job seekers, they will be most beneficial to people with little interview experience. One of Ms. Taub's greatest strengths lies in her ability to create a clear picture of the entire process, which gives readers the confidence generated by knowing what to expect. There are other strengths, too, such as the section on preparation, notable for the helpful advice on "developing a repertoire." The "FAQs" (Frequently Asked Questions) are always pertinent and useful, and Ms. Taub tackles many contingencies job seekers may not have previously considered. For example, there is a chart for distinguishing between illegal and legal questions. As is her habit, Ms. Taub does not allow these "facts" to speak for themselves. Rather, she addresses them "head-on," offering realistic (not saintly) advice on how to deal with illegal questions, should they arise. Readers will find a similarly "in-depth" approach taken throughout this high-value resource.

Where To Find/Buy:
Bookstores and libraries, or direct from the publisher at 800-793-2665.

Interviewing

SWEATY PALMS
The Neglected Art Of Being Interviewed

 Recommended For:
Interviewing

Description:
Fourteen chapters address a variety of topics related to the art of being interviewed. Each chapter covers its topic, giving specific advice and discussing relevant anecdotes, and sums up points covered in a checklist at the end. Chapters 1–3 introduce the basics about interviews, preparation, and the different types of interviews out there (the screening interview, the selection interview) and interview styles (directed, non directive, stress, group, board, telephone). Middle chapters address such issues as the importance of attitude, handling the nuances of the question-and-answer format, avoiding assumptions, honesty, confidence, and dress. Chapter 10 focuses exclusively on "silence and power"; how to handle an interviewer's silence as well as using your own effectively. The final four chapters cover other issues: sex, salary, discrimination, and decisions. Appendices include lists of commonly asked questions, evaluation factors, questions asked during reference checks, and questions to ask of an interviewer.

Evaluation:
A well-known classic first published in 1978, and most recently revised in 1993, "Sweaty Palms" remains a timely, pertinent resource. As everyone knows, the art of getting a job is inextricably linked to the art of interviewing; it is often the stage that makes or breaks a potential applicant. As communication skills have become an indispensable in many fields, the "neglected art of being interviewed" has become ever more important. Too often, books that address this subject focus on how to give correct, canned answers to interview questions, or how to dress appropriately. This book sets itself apart by its focus on enthusiasm, spirit, and "being yourself" as the elements of a successful interview. The author's psychologically astute advice zeros in on the interview's unspoken but essential aspects: how to listen, how to relax by suspending judgment, how to use silence effectively, and how to "treat the interview as an experience" that you can grow and learn from. Highly recommended for seasoned and novice interviewees alike.

Where To Find/Buy:
Bookstores and libraries, or directly from the publisher at (800) 841-BOOK.

★★★★

Overall Rating
★★★★
A classic work on interviewing with invaluable, practical advice

Design, Ease Of Use
★★★★
Well written, concise, and humane

1–4 Stars

Author:
H. Anthony Medley
H. Anthony Medley is an author and attorney, who "pioneered the videotaped job interview for prospective employers."

Publisher:
Ten Speed Press

Edition:
1993

Price:
$8.95

ISBN:
0898154030

Media:
Book

Principal Subject:
Interviewing

V. How To Land
The Job You Want

★★★

Overall Rating
★★★
A quality "quick" guide; straightforward tips on "the basics"

Design, Ease Of Use
★★★★
Easy-to-use; the "10 minute" lessons keep text concise and direct

1–4 Stars

Author:
Dana Morgan

Ms. Morgan is a career consultant based in Columbia, Maryland; she offers seminars and workshops on all aspects of the hiring process. She is also co-author of ARCO's *Federal Jobs: The Ultimate Guide* and *Federal Jobs for College Graduates*.

Publisher:
Arco

Edition:
1998

Price:
$10.95

ISBN:
0028621360

Media:
Book

Principal Subject:
Interviewing

Interviewing

10 MINUTE GUIDE TO JOB INTERVIEWS

Description:
Each aspect of the interview process is presented and examined in a "10 minute lesson." There are 19 lessons in all, encompassing preparation, duration, and follow-up. For preparation, topics addressed include "evaluating your skills," "the two-minute bio," types of interviews and "alternative" formats (i.e. over the telephone, panel interviews), and "projecting success." For use during the interview, there are lessons on interviewing strategies, "interviewing hazards and how to overcome them," answering/asking questions, and illegal questions. "Thank you notes," salary negotiations and "evaluating the job offer" are also discussed. Each lesson begins with a brief statement of intent, explaining the technique/lesson's purpose, and ends with a summary. "Timesaver tips," "plain English" tips (e.g. definitions of new terms), and "panic buttons" (potential problem areas) are identified by icons and interspersed throughout the guide. Appendices provide lists of print and online resources for research.

Evaluation:
The advantages to Ms. Morgan's "10 minute" lessons are clear: readers can learn "the basics" quickly and (almost) effortlessly. The disadvantages, too, are obvious: "the basics" are general guidelines, and much of the information is dolled out in lists or bullet points. Whether or not the positive attributes outweigh the negative ones depends on the reader. A reader who will take the time to complete the suggested exercises will benefit the most from this guide; "the basics" do provide building blocks, but only if built upon. Readers who are less inclined toward written work may prefer a guide with more specifics, or one with fill-in-the-blank exercises. Also, readers should be aware that this is a very traditional guide book. The advice on dress, image, conversation techniques, etc., is quite conservative; it may not be best for all situations, i.e. a "cutting-edge" design firm or an alternative online magazine. Overall, this is a quality "quick" guide; there are occasional insights, but the brevity prohibits depth.

Where To Find/Buy:
Bookstores and libraries.

Interviewing

101 DYNAMITE QUESTIONS TO ASK AT YOUR JOB INTERVIEW

★★★

Description:

What do the questions a job seeker asks tell an employer? In a survey of 1,000 employers (conducted by Mr. Fein), over half said that a candidate's questions are a means of evaluating his/her fitness for the position; they are just as important as the answers an interviewer illicits. Hence, Mr. Fein's two-prong agenda: to help readers decide which questions to ask (by providing samples) and to keep them from "asking it badly." There are general guidelines for the type of questions one should ask, i.e. "the answer isn't obvious" or "you care about the topic," and advice on tone, manner, etc. There are also 101 sample questions about "the job," "the company," and "the industry/profession." Questions address a variety of topics, including "qualities for success," promotion opportunities, the company's structure/hierarchy, technological change, and "how to ask for the job." Interactive exercises help readers gage potential responses, and there are examples of "bad" questions for comparison. "Quick research" tips are discussed.

Evaluation:

Most books on interviewing prepare job seekers for every question but one: "Do you have any questions?" Many candidates dismiss this portion of the interview as unimportant, or at least less important, in comparison to the interviewer's previous questions. Yet part of excelling at interviews requires "selling yourself" at every opportunity. As Mr. Fein explains, asking "dynamite" questions is another way of "standing out." Asking the right questions can also help job seekers evaluate the job, company, offer, etc. The best thing about this guide is that provides both concrete examples (the sample questions), which give readers clues to appropriate language, tone, etc., and "categories" of topics, which give readers ideas for composing their own questions. Readers familiar with job searching techniques, i.e. researching, may find some suggestions "common sense," but this guide will be a great help to the interview novice or to those who are returning to the workplace after a long absence.

Where To Find/Buy:

Bookstores and libraries, or directly from the publisher at Impact Publications, 9104-N Manassas Drive, Manassas Park, VA 22111-5211 Tel. (703)361-7300

Overall Rating
★★★
Insightful, practical advice on "asking dynamite questions;" concrete, useful examples

Design, Ease Of Use
★★★
Clear language, well-formatted; easy to read or browse

1–4 Stars

Author:
Richard Fein

Mr. Fein is the Director of Placement at the University of Massachusetts (Amherst) School of Management. He is also the author of *Cover Letters, Cover Letters, Cover Letters* (Career Press) and *First Job* (Wiley).

Publisher:
Impact Publications

Edition:
1996

Price:
$14.95

ISBN:
1570230536

Media:
Book

Principal Subject:
Interviewing

V. How To Land The Job You Want

★★

Overall Rating
★★
Sound interview questions
and answers for many jobs;
Q&A format is limited

Design, Ease Of Use
★★★
Interviews helpfully arranged
by industry

1–4 Stars

Author:
Peter Veruki

The author is Director of Career
Planning and Placement at the
Owen Graduate School of
Management at Vanderbilt
University.

Publisher:
Adams Media Corporation

Edition:
1997

Price:
$19.95

Pages:
822

ISBN:
1558507094

Media:
Book + CD-ROM

Principal Subject:
Interviewing

Interviewing

JOB INTERVIEW ALMANAC & CD-ROM

Description:

This "almanac" of job interviews begins with three sections focusing on
general advice about interviewing. Part I discusses what to do before the
job interview (researching, preparing). Part II concentrates on the job
interview itself: how to make a good impression, how to field common
questions, and how to handle "zingers" (i.e. "Why should I hire you?").
Part II discusses what to do after the interview—writing follow-up letters
and negotiating the offer. Part IV, which comprises almost 700 pages,
is the heart of the book: included here are over 100 sample interviews
for various jobs in the following industries: accounting and finance;
administration; art and design; communications; computers and
engineering; education; executive and management; health and
medicine; legal and protective services; marketing and sales; science;
service; social and human services; and technical occupations. The
accompanying CD-ROM includes interview simulations, samples of
full-length interviews, and workshops.

Evaluation:

The first three parts of the book, concentrating on general advice
about interviews, is fairly useful but nothing to knock your socks off.
The real stuff, and the book's distinctiveness, lie in the 100+ sample
job interviews, which cover commonly-asked questions from various
industries. The scripted "answers" are sensible, thorough, but err
on the side of cautiousness—they tend to smack of "political
correctness" rather than insightfulness or creativity. Any "spin"
on these answers is, supposedly, up to you. Whether or not such a
book of questions-and-answers would be useful is also up to you: it
does give typical questions and good advice for various jobs within
certain industries, but your interviewer will certainly ask many other
questions as well. It does give sound sample answers, but a book that
lays out the principles and techniques of interviewing might be more
helpful to those who wish to take their own chances, or who already
have a feel for the type of questions they're likely to be asked.

Where To Find/Buy:

Bookstores and libraries.

Interviewing

101 GREAT ANSWERS TO THE TOUGHEST INTERVIEW QUESTIONS

★★

Description:
Two audiotapes of approximately an hour and a half each cover the basics of the interview process, giving strategies and advice for 101 interview questions. Following a brief introduction to the importance of the interview today, tape 1 continues with advice on how to gather information about your own life, using the enclosed data-gathering pamphlet. It continues to detail the types and levels of interviews: screening, telephone, stress, situational, and team, and the reasons employers use them. General questions and answers follow pertaining to your skills, accomplishments, and weaknesses. Tape 2 continues with "grilling" questions ("do you have trouble getting along with certain people?"), personal questions ("how do you handle conflict?"), hypothetical or situational questions, and questions college grads or novice interviewees can use to highlight their abilities. Finally, closing questions are included with "wrapping up" advice, as well as tips for after-interview etiquette.

Evaluation:
The author is, thankfully, possessed of a pleasant and lively voice, making it easier to follow along for the 3-hour duration. Hidden subtexts of interview questions are revealed and answering strategies explored in a clear, straightforward fashion; the author has arranged questions to reflect the likely progression of an actual interview. Samples of successful answers are highlighted along the way, and the author is quick to point out common pitfalls that await the interviewee in the most innocent of questions. All this is helpful. The most obvious advantages and the drawbacks here are both linked to the audio taped format—some people may find it easier to listen to information than to read it, but others are sure to find listening to all 101 questions and their answers a mind-boggling experience. That aside, the advice given here slides close to the innocuous—sample answers are nearly clichéd, though certainly "safe." Readers may be advised to skip this one in favor of a more in-depth treatment of the topic.

Where To Find/Buy:
Bookstores and libraries.

Overall Rating
★★
Thorough, though conventional, treatment of answering strategies

Design, Ease Of Use
★★
Taped format makes it hard to locate and retain specific information

1–4 Stars

Author:
Ron Fry

Ron Fry is the author of *Your First Interview* and *Your First Resume*, and has written or edited over 30 books.

Publisher:
HighBridge

Edition:
3rd (1996)

Price:
$16.95

ISBN:
1565111451

Media:
Audiotape

Principal Subject:
Interviewing

V. How To Land The Job You Want

★★

Overall Rating
★★
Sound, safe, but conservative approach to the interview process

Design, Ease Of Use
★★
Easy to work through; helpful preparation worksheets

1–4 Stars

Author:
Matthew J. DeLuca

The author is president of the Management Resource Group, Inc. in New York City, a Human Resources consulting firm. He has also written other books related to employment and the job search.

Publisher:
McGraw-Hill

Edition:
1997

Price:
$10.95

ISBN:
007016357X

Media:
Book

Principal Subject:
Interviewing

Interviewing

BEST ANSWERS TO THE 201 MOST FREQUENTLY ASKED INTERVIEW QUESTIONS

Description:

After introductory sections (Chapters 1 and 2) about the interview process and communication, the book launches into its 201 commonly-asked interview questions, grouped into chapters according to type. Chapter 3 contains questions related to disclosure issues. Chapter 4 discusses how to get to know the job, your interviewer, and the organization, with an explanation of the different types of interviews. Chapters 5–8 cover questions related to "small talk," personal issues, education, and experience. The next three chapters cover psychologically trying questions, such as "behavior questions" (e.g. "tell me about a difficult situation when you pulled the team together"), "stress questions" ("how do you think the interview is going?"), and open-ended and close-ended questions. Chapters 12 and 13 discuss illegal questions and questions you should raise in the interview, and the last chapter discusses follow-up activities such as the thank-you letter.

Evaluation:

Some parts of this guide are genuinely useful, such as the worksheets, while other parts are oddly irrelevant, such as the beginning section which discusses the cost and difficulty of the hiring process for employers. The meat of the book really lies in its plethora of common questions asked during the interview, with advice about how to field such questions and sample answers. A helpful feature is the "star" placed next to those most likely to be asked, for the applicant with little time to prepare. The advice given for these questions is sensible but conservative—some readers may find the advice a little on the dictatorial side (e.g. "Try to include the terms 'respect' and 'loyalty' when speaking in an organizational context"). This is a book for readers who like to stay on the safe side of interview questions, or who need a briefing into the hidden agendas of interview questions. This book might be most useful for inexperienced interviewees, but others won't find much in the way of innovative advice here.

Where To Find/Buy:

Bookstores and libraries.

Interviewing

101 DYNAMITE ANSWERS TO INTERVIEW QUESTIONS
Sell Your Strengths!

Description:

"101 Dynamite Answers to Interview Questions" actually contains a lot more than just questions. Several chapters at the beginning of the book are devoted to discussing interview types and techniques, "45 effective interview principles," and preparing for the interview. The next 2 chapters cover the "verbal" component of the interview with questions, strategies for answering, and sample answers, and the "nonverbal" component, such as image, composure, and dynamism. Chapter 7 contains "dynamite questions you should ask" of your interviewer, and chapter 8 discusses follow-ups such as writing the post-interview thank you letter, job rejection follow-up letter, and job offer acceptance letter. Finally, chapter 9 contains a summary of the 101 most commonly-asked questions, running the gamut from "why should we hire you?" to "how old are you?" to "what is the most important thing you've learned from the jobs you've held?"

Evaluation:

As the authors put it in the first chapter, "Interviews don't just count—they count the most." The focus here is most certainly on the importance of the job interview and communication skills. The stance towards being yourself and not trying to "memorize canned answers to interview questions" is a good thing, and the writing is clear and straightforward. However, the bulk of the advice here is overly general, and some of the responses to typical questions are themselves typical (e.g. "What are your weaknesses?" "I'm somewhat of a workaholic . . ."). Sometimes the authors make statements without giving real advice, such as "engage in positive nonverbal cues." On the other hand, there is some good advice about how to let nervousness work for you as opposed to against you, and a decent section on common questions and effective answers. This book provides an introduction to the interview, but readers should look elsewhere for more in-depth exploration of the topic.

Where To Find/Buy:

Bookstores and libraries, or directly from the publisher at (703) 361-7300, fax (703) 335-9486, Internet http://www.impactpublications.com, or by mail: 9104-N Manassas Drive, Manassas Park, VA 20111-2366.

Overall Rating
★
A thorough introduction to the interview, but advice is superficial and overly general

Design, Ease Of Use
★★
Clear writing, easy to read

1–4 Stars

Author:
Caryl Rae Krannich and Ronald L. Krannich, Ph.D.s

The Dr.s Krannich have published many other books and CD-ROMS related to the job search and careers.

Publisher:
Impact Publications

Edition:
1997

Price:
$12.95

ISBN:
1570230781

Media:
Book

Principal Subject:
Interviewing

V. How To Land
The Job You Want

SALARY NEGOTIATIONS

Start negotiating only after they offer a job.

Should you receive an offer, keep in mind there may be little room for negotiation. Learn industry averages for the position, allowing for cost of living differences for different cities and regions. Be realistic and, if you believe there is room for negotiation, know the salary range before you request a figure.

Do not argue; just ask for changes as desired. The best negotiation I know is to say "Oh" when they offer a low salary and be quiet. Often that will get you bumped up one notch.

The point is not to say or imply that you deserve it, or that you are better than others. The issue is simply that you would like them to make a better offer due to your needs, last salary, etc. Remember that a salary is just a point of reference and if you personalize it too much you will lose.

If it is a new job always say (if the initial offer is acceptable) that you would like to have the position reviewed in six months in fairness to everyone. That is, it is a new job and the real job description will depend on you and how you do the job. If you contribute well and persuade them to reassess the job you might get a mid-year review and upgrade plus your annual salary review. And, in reality, most new jobs are under rated at first and then grow.

While the paycheck is essential, also consider factors such as level of responsibility, potential for growth, ability to build skills, or autonomy.

Five Tips For Successful Salary Negotiations

- Don't talk about money until they raise the issue, and then always make it secondary until you have an offer to negotiate.

- Don't be passive. It is acceptable to ask what men are being paid for the same position. This lets them know you want equal pay for equal work.

- Be educated about the range of what is competitive.

- Don't be afraid of silent pauses. They can communicate your patience and places the pressure back on them.

- Understand the value of all the elements which may be part of your compensation package, such as stock options and benefits.

★★★★

GET MORE MONEY ON YOUR NEXT JOB

 Recommended For:
Salary Negotiations

Description:

How do you get the best deal from your new employer? In his guide, Miller, an employment law expert and practiced negotiator, presents the "25 Proven Strategies" for "getting more money, better benefits, and greater job security" at a new job. First, he introduces the "10 commandments" of negotiations, including "be prepared," "understand the dynamics," and "use uncertainty to your advantage," and examines how salaries are set, through "market rate," and other techniques. The 25 strategies, accompanied by explanations and advice, follow. Strategies include "making the most of your current salary," "negotiate the position, not the salary," "using follow-up memos as negotiating tools," and "how to win by conceding." There are also strategies for such situations as asking for equity and timing your start date to increase the value of your stock options. Final chapters address ensuring job security, gender differences in negotiations, negotiating with your current employer, and gaining "leverage" if you're unemployed.

Evaluation:

What makes this guide an effective tool for learning to negotiate is its dynamism. Rather than providing a rigid set of guidelines to follow in every negotiating scenario, Miller's strategies can be combined, used separately, dissected and reconfigured, and otherwise tailored to meet both your needs and the needs of the situation. By adding these strategies to your repertoire, you'll be prepared to negotiate any money matter with anyone. Though he expresses his tactics with fluid prose, this guide isn't just theory. There are anecdotes, case histories, and mock dialogues to support and illustrate the strategies in action, as well as instruction. Also of note is the chapter on job security, a rare inclusion, which offers advice on such issues as getting the terms of employment in writing in case of mergers, acquisitions or downsizing. This a superb resource for learning how to negotiate with confidence. (Women may want to use this book in tandem with *The Smart Woman's Guide to Interviews and Salary Negotiations*—see review.)

Where To Find/Buy:

Bookstores and libraries.

Overall Rating
★★★★
Confident, dynamic guide to negotiating; an effective tool

Design, Ease Of Use
★★★★
Engaging; makes good use of case histories and anecdotes

1–4 Stars

Author:
Lee E. Miller

Mr. Miller is a consultant for Advanced Human Resources Group, Inc., an Adjunct Professor at the Seton Hall University's Stillman School of Business, and a graduate of Harvard Law School.

Publisher:
McGraw-Hill

Edition:
1998

Price:
$14.95

Pages:
182

ISBN:
0070431469

Media:
Book

Principal Subject:
Salary Negotiations

★★★★

Overall Rating
★★★★
Advice on interviewing/
negotiating for women;
informative and enlightening

Design, Ease Of Use
★★★★
Well written, easy to use; an
index of topics is included

1–4 Stars

Author:
Julie Adair King

Publisher:
Career Press

Edition:
2nd (1995)

Price:
$12.99

ISBN:
156414206X

Media:
Book

Principal Subject:
Salary Negotiations

Secondary Subject:
Interviewing

Of Interest To:
Women

THE SMART WOMAN'S GUIDE TO INTERVIEWING AND SALARY NEGOTIATION

 **Recommended For:**
Salary Negotiations

Description:
Despite the progress made in the last few decades, women are still at a disadvantage when it comes to achieving career success. This disadvantage is particularly evident in interviews and salary negotiations. In Chapters 1 and 2, Ms. King explains that for a woman to be successful in these venues, she must combat discrimination (conscious or unconscious) and modify her behavior. Traditional female qualities like modesty and using qualifiers when speaking just won't cut it; yet (double standard) women shouldn't be perceived as "too hard," either. To help women "ace" the interview, Chapters 3–16 offer advice on such topics as interviewing "styles and trends," conducting preliminary research, and fielding gender-biased questions. How to "create chemistry," make a good first impression, and "sell yourself with confidence" is also discussed. Chapters 17–19 are designed to teach women how to negotiate for salaries and raises with "power and finesse." Resources for additional aid and information are detailed in Chapter 20.

Evaluation:
Despite hard-earned progress, gender discrimination, like minority discrimination, is alive and well in corporate America. Women are asked different questions in interviews, they receive less pay for similar work (72 cents to a man's dollar) and they can sabotage themselves in negotiations by being too "ladylike." What's the solution? Know what you're up against and know how to adapt. That's the premise of this informative, insightful resource. In it, Ms. King combines "tried and true" interview/negotiating techniques with advice specifically geared toward women. Much of the discussion is aimed at heightening women's awareness of the little "mistakes" they make. For example, in interviews, many women talk about why they want a job, whereas men emphasis how they can contribute to the company's profits. Adapting to corporate culture is much like adapting to any foreign culture: you have to learn the language and customs. Ms. King is here to guide you and she does it very well! This is "must" for any woman!

Where To Find/Buy:
Bookstores and libraries, or direct from the publisher at 1-800-CAREER-1 (NJ and Canada: 201-848-0310).

V. How To Land
The Job You Want

Salary Negotiations

DYNAMITE SALARY NEGOTIATIONS
Know What You're Worth And Get It!

★★★

Description:

It's a basic fact of life: how much you earn impacts not only your standard of living but your self-image as well. As the authors point out, salary helps "keep score" and brings "value" to one's work. Salaries are important, and so are salary negotiations. In this guide to successful salary negotiations, the authors expose the "30 deadly salary mistakes," dispel 16 negotiation "myths," analyze 30 "compensation trends," and enumerate 30 "rules for success." The text is divided into 12 chapters, 3 of which are aimed at job seekers. These chapters confront such issues as job searching, "dealing with salary history" on applications, and "communicating your value in job interviews." For employees, there is a chapter on "Salary Increases, Raises, and Promotions." Other chapters offer advice on calculating "your worth," "the going rate," and "your salary range" (salary charts are included), and there are techniques and tips for actual negotiations, renegotiations, and for "finalizing the offer."

Evaluation:

There are some nice touches in the Krannich doctors' guide: charts of selected salary ranges, "6 steps for calculating your worth," lists of resources for researching salaries and salary trends, and sound, non-salary-related interview tips. The author's emphasis on individual performance as the crux of any negotiation, rather than ephemeral "clever tactics," is also commendable. One of the side benefits to this book is that it's bound to inspire a sense of greater self-esteem. (An interactive exercise whereby the reader rates her/his achievements is a factor in "calculating your worth.") Still, to put most of the Kranniches' techniques to work requires a certain business savvy and familiarity, which the authors assume their audience already possesses; this is no "beginner's" guide. (Women would be wise to use this resource in tandem with "The Smart Woman's Guide to Interviewing and Salary Negotiation," which addresses issues specific to them. See review.) For serious, "hard core" tactics, look here.

Where To Find/Buy:

Bookstores and libraries.

Overall Rating
★★★
Hard-core advice on salary negotiating

Design, Ease Of Use
★★★
Generally well formatted; includes interactive exercises and salary charts

1–4 Stars

Author:
Caryl Rae Krannich and Ronald L. Krannich, PhDs

Dr.s. Caryl and Ronald Krannich are the authors of several career and travel books. The two former university professors currently operate Development Concepts Incorporated, a training, consulting, and publishing firm.

Publisher:
Impact Publications

Edition:
3rd (1998)

Price:
$15.95

ISBN:
157023079X

Media:
Book

Principal Subject:
Salary Negotiations

V. How To Land
The Job You Want

GOING SOLO

INTRODUCTION

At the dawn of the 21st century Americans find themselves in the midst of a dramatically changing labor market. Technological advances have eliminated some jobs through automation or computer-based implementation. Recession and other macro-economic forces have influenced many corporations to streamline their organizations and "downsize" or "rightsize" the number of full-time workers they employ, especially middle managers. A global economy has lead to some jobs being "outsourced" outside the country, to locales with a cheaper cost of labor. Contingency work, including temporary, contract and part-time work is on the rise. These trends have all contributed to a weakening of the traditional model of lifetime employment with a single company.

The infamous "downsizing" of America, as the process has come to be known, has received the majority of the country's attention. Dire statistics and ominous forecasts have created an aura of fear; job security, in the classical sense, is fast disappearing. Downsizing has received so much negative press that many people are aware only of its victims: the displaced factory workers and surplus executives we hear from on the news.

But the downside of downsizing is only half the story. There are hidden benefits to the reshaping of the traditional employment model. The 9-to-5, work-at-one-company-until-you-retire world whose decline we lament, is the very world many Americans enjoy resenting. Exhibit A: The immense popularity of the cubicle-dwelling, management-spamming Dilbert.

Responding to the perceived or real loss of job-security, many workers have begun to more actively manage their career. The mantra of career coaches in today's job market is: think of yourself as being self-employed no matter where you work. Be loyal to yourself. Consider yourself your own business and invest in research and development. Continually develop new skills, especially technological know-how. Embrace career transitions rather than fear them. Learn how to be a "project junkie," jobs columnist Carol Kleiman's term for workers who go from job to job, employer to employer, using their specific skills.

Others have seized on the moment to fulfill a long held desire to be their own boss. They literally become self-employed. The flexibility of the self-employment option has spawned a thousand variations. Some choose to do the same work but as a consultant rather than an employee. Others with an entrepreneur's zest for adventure and stomach for risk start a new business. Some parents are choosing to work part-time, flex-time, seasonally or telecommute, options rarely available in traditional professional work. In its many flavors, the ranks of the self-employed have swelled in recent years.

We are a nation of capitalists and individualists. We don't like to be told what to do, we want to spend time on the things we like, we want a balance of family and work, we want freedom and autonomy. The American spirit is the entrepreneurial spirit, the do-it-yourself spirit, and technological advances are creating a society that not only allows that spirit to flourish but demands its resurgence. "Generation X" was once lambasted for such traits as lack of company loyalty and the refusal to work "traditional" hours; today, more and more mid-careers feel the same way. Why work for someone else when you can work for yourself? Especially now, when personal computers, fax machines, the Internet, video conferencing and other innovations make it easy to stay connected from a home office.

In this chapter, we review a variety of resources designed to help you "go solo." Going solo is an umbrella term for all types of self-employment, covering freelancing, consulting, temping, and starting your own business. The reviews are divided into three sections, General Self-Employment, Freelance & Consulting, and Entrepreneurship. In General Self-Employment, you'll find resources that discuss a wide range of solo options. Many of these resources explore personal assessment and planning: Am I cut out for this? and What would this adventure entail?

The Freelance & Consulting chapter includes resources for creative freelancing, taking your executive skills "on the road," contract and contingency work, and professional temping. The Entrepreneurship chapter concentrates on resources for starting a small business or a home based business. Because certain aspects of freelancing, consulting, and operating a home based business are common to all solo ventures, looking through the reviews in all three sections will garner the best results.

GENERAL SELF-EMPLOYMENT

By the end of 2001, it's estimated that more than 36.5 million individuals will be self-employed. Perhaps you'd like to join their ranks, but you're not sure how to turn your talents and skills into a profitable business. In this section, we review a variety of resources designed to help you explore your options and decide if self-employment is right for you. Some guides, "Working Solo" and "Going Indie," for example, detail the variety of self-employment paths available, while others concentrate on the personal side of going solo: restructuring your lifestyle, self-discovery, and using self-employment as a way to balance family, work, and personal fulfillment.

One of the gripes of the self-employed is the isolation of working alone. Websites can be a source of information and camaraderie. Some specialize their attention. WAHM.com, for example, offers ideas, inspiration, and support for moms who want to work at home. We review several websites that incorporate bulletin boards, listservs, chat rooms and other tools for communicating with fellow soloists. The sites can be excellent venues for networking and support.

This chapter also contains reviews of general reference resources that apply to an array of solo enterprises, such as Fast Company Online, the Idea Cafe, and AboutDomains.com, a website that provides information about domain names.

FAST COMPANY ONLINE

Recommended For:
General Self-Employment

Description:

This is a huge site with lots of departments, including "FCToday" (daily topics, polls, an online column), "Community" (discussion forums, book clubs), the magazine's archive of articles, and a "Career Center." The home page doubles as an explicit table of contents from which visitors can navigate the site. Whether users are looking for "at work" advice or advice on "going solo" (there's a featured article on "How to Create a Killer Business Plan") the "Career Center" is a good place to start. The "Center" has six sections: "Find Your Calling" (i.e. career choices, self-assessment), "Search for a Job," "Make a Choice" (i.e. job offers), "Build Brand You" (i.e. improving skills, get promoted), "Go Free Agent," and "Move On" (i.e. relocating). Each section has links to and descriptions of pertinent "FC" articles, outside articles, and other online resources as well as book lists for additional research. (Menu bars appear at the top and bottom of each page for ease of movement.)

Evaluation:

The print version of "FC" gains acclaim everyday with its cutting edge philosophy and style, and its online version is just as fresh, informative, and exciting! Whether you're looking for advice on career decisions, getting ahead within your current company, or going solo, this is the place the go. You could spend hours and hours at this site, with pleasure; there's so much here! Aside from the magazine's articles, polls, "behind the scenes" tidbits, interviews, interactive forums, etc., the "Career Center" alone is a virtual library of valuable resources. For instance, in "Go Free Agent," you can read about other entrepreneurs, learn about the "talent market," get tips on a "killer" business plan, use the links to check out related sites like SBA Online and the Idea Cafe (see reviews), and peruse book reviews. If "hours and hours" sounds ominous, don't worry! This site is so well organized, you can find particulars as quickly as it takes to read the succinct descriptions beneath the headings. The final verdict? Don't miss this site!

Where To Find/Buy:

On the Internet at http://www.fastcompany.com

Overall Rating
★★★★
Whatever your business needs, visit this site!

Design, Ease Of Use
★★★★
Well organized, exciting design, easy to navigate

1–4 Stars

Author:
Fast Company Online is the online product of Fast Company, Inc., the publishers of the print magazine of the same name.

Publisher:
Fast Company Inc.

Edition:
1998

Media:
Internet

Principal Subject:
General Self-Employment

VI. Going Solo

★★★★

Overall Rating
★★★★

A fun "hangout" for entrepreneurs; a great place for financial advice and networking

Design, Ease Of Use
★★★

Engaging design, but navigating can be a slight problem

1–4 Stars

Author:
Francie Marks Ward

Ms. Ward is a veteran business owner who has started and run a variety of small businesses.

Publisher:
Idea Cafe

Edition:
1998

Media:
Internet

Principal Subject:
General Self-Employment

General Self-Employment

IDEA CAFE
The Small Business Channel

 Recommended For:
General Self-Employment

Description:
The Idea Cafe serves up a variety of dishes for current and potential entrepreneurs. The home page provides access to the site's main areas, such as the "Coffee Talk with Experts" "Q&A" forum, the "Biz Comm Zone's" articles, tech reviews, and the "Financing Your Business" "menu." The "Financing" menu includes articles on "women getting money," "minorities getting money," "cleaning up your credit," and sources of money, i.e. borrowing money, getting investors, and "creative financing." There are also "self-exams" for determining the "right financing for you" and "getting ready emotionally," and an "All-In-One Budget Calculator" for finding out how much money you need. For "cyberschmoozing" with other small business owners, there are two chatrooms: one on financing and one on starting, running and managing your business. The site has a variety of "fun" features, too, i.e. horoscopes, "Dilbert" comics, contests, etc. Links to other online resources are organized into the Cafe's web guide, the "Business Directory."

Evaluation:
The Idea Cafe is one of the more famous sites on the Net for current and budding entrepreneurs. Since it's a relatively high-traffic site, it's definitely worth checking out the "cyberschmooz" chatrooms for informational networking. There are lots of other terrific features, too. The section on "Financing Your Business" is particularly well done, with a extensive "menu" of options for figuring out your personal financial needs and getting the money. Of special note is the "creative financing" segment, which explores such possibilities as "strategic partners," "convertible debt," and borrowing from friends and family. The site is basically well-formatted, though there isn't a site map and the constant metaphorical language (the food/Cafe allusions are used throughout, i.e. the "Idea Cafe Fridge") can make navigating slightly difficult. (The "Idea Cafe Fridge" seems to be a mini-map of the "Biz Comm Zone's" contents.) Still, whether you want coffee chat or a hearty advice stew, the Cafe is certainly worth a visit!

Where To Find/Buy:
On the Internet at http://www.ideacafe.com

General Self-Employment

CREATING A LIFE WORTH LIVING

★★★

Description:

In Ms. Lloyd's experience, many artistic and innovative people feel frustrated by the traditional approaches to career planning. In response to that frustration, she created workshops which apply the creative process to career building. Since this book grew out of those workshops, it is designed to be read and practiced in weekly segments. Part 1, "The Dive," begins by "strengthening your relationship to your dreams" via a series of daily tasks, i.e. "ecstatic tasks" like dancing or meditation, and "idea-generating" exercises. In Part 2, "The Dig," the reader uses memories to resurrect "forgotten career paths," clarifies their non-artistic needs, and explores their "creative type." The reader's ideas are given concrete form in Part 3, "The Design," wherein exercises combat indecisiveness, confront competing interests, and "map out" goals. Part 4, "The Doing," takes the reader from conceptualization to action through specific techniques for reinventing "your workday," forming support networks, and "balancing your life."

Evaluation:

An artist and innovator herself, Ms. Lloyd speaks to her audience as an equal who's "been there, done that." She is not a traditional career counselor, which is perfect for anyone disdainful of "the system." Rather than encouraging readers to find their niche, as so many career guides do, she urges them to create their place in the world based on their own agendas, and no one else's. Her approach relies heavily on self-analysis and self-discovery, but she also employs daily exercises, planning methods, and motivational techniques. This is not "all talk, no action." There are also lots of interviews with successful people who have self-styled careers. These interviews provide both examples and valuable insight; each person offers advice, discusses the creative process, and shares personal struggles. For readers who are committed to realizing their dreams, this is smart, inspiring alternative to run-of-the-mill career guides. For square pegs longing to escape their round holes, this is the resource!

Where To Find/Buy:

Bookstores and libraries.

Overall Rating
★★★
A new approach to career planning; inspiring, insightful, creative

Design, Ease Of Use
★★★
Engaging; involves time commitment (approximately 12 weeks)

1–4 Stars

Author:
Carol Lloyd
Ms. Lloyd is a writer, performer, and entrepreneur. She is the founder of The Writing Parlor, a San Francisco literary arts center, and has led Life Worth Living workshops for over seven years.

Publisher:
HarperPerennial

Edition:
1997

Price:
$14.00

Pages:
309

ISBN:
0060952431

Media:
Book

Principal Subject:
General Self-Employment

Secondary Subject:
Aptitude and Interest Analysis

VI. Going Solo

GOING INDIE
Self-Employment, Freelance & Temping Opportunities

★★★

Overall Rating
★★★
Sensible and inspirational guide to self-employment; coverage is broad, not deep

Design, Ease Of Use
★★★
Easy to read and work through; chapters arranged from exploration to practice

1–4 Stars

Author:
Kathi Elster and Katherine Crowley

Kathi Elster is an adjunct professor at Baruch College and the New School in New York City, where she runs The Business Strategy Seminar, a business support program. Katherine Crowley is a partner in The Business Strategy Seminar.

Publisher:
Kaplan (Simon & Schuster)

Edition:
1997

Price:
$15.00

ISBN:
0684837560

Media:
Book

Principal Subject:
General Self-Employment

Description:

After an introductory chapter entitled "Welcome to the Indie Revolution" in which the possibilities of self-employment are explored, Kaplan's guide continues with a section on how to choose the right business by discovering your talents, skills, and passions. Exercises, checklists, and focus questions are given. Individual chapters follow to tell you how to find out about business trends and opportunities, how to "put it all together" and test out your ideas. Anecdotes of other self-employed folks are included along the way. Section 3, "Essential Skills," includes chapters on self-management, decision-making, and risk-taking, along with practical matters such as marketing, sales, and financial planning. The final chapter gives advice, interview-style, from "real indies"—a graphic designer, a hat designer, and an owner of a computer information systems business. A list of resources for self-employment entrepreneurs rounds out the book.

Evaluation:

"Going indie" is believed to be one of the smartest ways to tackle the modern job market, in which corporate downsizing and out sourcing have led to a decrease in traditional 9–5 jobs and a corresponding increase in self-employment opportunities. Here, Kaplan throws its hat into the ring with a book dedicated to exploring the ins and outs of succeeding "on your own." Kaplan's guide distinguishes itself from other books on this subject through its equal emphasis on the "intangibles" of self-employment, such as figuring out your marketable talents, and the "tangibles," such as marketing and sales. In self-employment, as in any business, one needs a dose of both vision and practicality. At times, the book wanders into vagueness, as in the exercises focused on pinpointing your talents and skills, but this seems to be a danger related to the field itself, which is highly variable. Overall, readers will find this to be a generally useful guide to both the potentials and practicalities of the indie lifestyle.

Where To Find/Buy:
Bookstores and libraries.

General Self-Employment

WAHM: WORK AT HOME MOMS

Description:

Despite styling itself as an "online magazine" (substantiated only by Ms. Demas' weekly editorial column), WAHM is more accurately described as an online networking "hub" for work at home moms and potential work at home moms. There is "advice and FAQs" on general home-business issues, and the site features an online bookstore, classifieds, and links to related resources. However, the primary focus is on networking. There are three ways to network with other WAHMs (work at home moms): you can search for a "WAHM Near You" by state, you can search by "WAHM Businesses" type, i.e. "Home Decorating," "Writer," etc., or you can browse in "Business Opportunities." In any case, the results of your search will either be a personal or business home page or an e-mail address for the work at home mom you chose. Since all of the work at home moms accessible through WAHM are willing to discuss their businesses, you can write to them for advice, query, ideas, information, etc.

Evaluation:

The last couple of years have seen the emergence of a new breed of website: those dedicated to women's business networks. WAHM is a perfect example of these female-oriented networking "hubs." If a home-based business is your bread-and-butter, or your dream, this site is a must visit! Valuable advice can be gleaned from those who have "been there, done that," and such mentoring is the paramount attraction at WAHM: it's a virtual network of work at home experts! The contacts available via WAHM have a wide range of careers; they are freelance writers, children's clothiers, desktop publishers, etc. Perhaps you'll find a work at home mom in your area to confer with and exchange ideas. Or perhaps this is a site where you can offer a advice or encouragement. The down sides: the original content is skimpy and there isn't much practical "how-to" advice. (A word of caution: be aware that folks use this and similar sites to troll for recruits for their multi-level marketing businesses.)

Where To Find/Buy:

On the Internet at http://www.wahm.com

★★★

Overall Rating
★★★
The content is skimpy, but the networking possibilities are endless!

Design, Ease Of Use
★★★
Simple format and search mechanisms; easy to navigate

1–4 Stars

Author:
Cheryl Demas

Ms. Demas is a work at home mom with two daughters. She began WAHM when she started working from home in 1994.

Publisher:
Miracle Communications

Edition:
1998

Media:
Internet

Principal Subject:
General Self-Employment

Of Interest To:
Women

VI. Going Solo

★★★

Overall Rating
★★★
A solid introduction to going solo with excellent tips on "the details"

Design, Ease Of Use
★★★
Explicit chapter headings and straightforward language; dense

1–4 Stars

Author:
Terri Lonier

Ms. Lonier is president of Working Solo, Inc. She advises such clients as Microsoft, Hewlett-Packard, and Claris on how best to access and communicate with the small business and SOHO (Small Office Home Office) market.

Publisher:
John Wiley & Sons

Edition:
2nd (1998)

Price:
$14.95

Pages:
354

ISBN:
0471247138

Media:
Book

Principal Subject:
General Self-Employment

General Self-Employment

WORKING SOLO

Description:

So you want to go solo? It can be an intimidating—yet exciting—prospect. In this 4 part guide, Ms. Lonier offers potential entrepreneurs advice on the entire process, from choosing a business to "celebrating success." The first step, understanding the benefits of going solo and choosing the "right" business, is discussed in Part 1, "The Dream." (To help readers generate business ideas, Ms. Lonier provides a "Solo Business Directory," a list of over 1,000 "hot" prospects.) Part 2, "The Decision" addresses the basics of getting started: drafting a business plan, finding support (moral and financial), choosing your business structure (i.e. "Should I Incorporate?"), legal issues, and attracting clients/customers through marketing. Part 3 looks at "The Details:" making the most of technology and the Internet, bookkeeping, taxes, and insurance, time management, using goals, associates and employees, etc. Finally, Part 4 celebrates "The Delights" with tips for growth and expansion. A list of "Solo Resources" appears in the appendix.

Evaluation:

There a lot to think about if you want to start your own business! In most respects, Ms. Lonier does a good job of simplifying the process. She presents the basics (i.e. taxes, business structures) in everyday language that even a novice businessperson can understand. Actually, her book is at its best when dealing with "The Details;" Part 4, which discusses technology, money management, insurance, etc., is the most in-depth and helpful section. The first 2 parts, however, are not as well done. Most of Ms. Lonier's advice on choosing the "right" business, which involves pages and pages of self-assessment-style questions, can be summed up in one sentence: do what you like. (On the whole, this is a better resource for readers who already have a business in mind.) And, though she offers some insightful "dos and don'ts" for writing a business plan, there aren't any step-by-step instructions or samples. Still, as a solid introduction to starting a business, and an excellent source for defining terms, this is a valuable book.

Where To Find/Buy:
Bookstores and libraries.

General Self-Employment

WORKING SOLO SOURCEBOOK

★★★

Description:

Where do you go to find the information you need for starting and/or managing your own business? How do you make contacts or take advantage of Internet resources? Ms. Lonier's "sourcebook" for going solo provides over 1,200 listings for all types of entrepreneurial-related help: magazines, books, websites, professional associations, support groups, etc. The listings are arranged in chapters by category. Categories/chapters include "Business Planning," "Choosing a Business," "Computers and Technology," "Consulting," "Legal Information," "Taxes," and "Women-Owned Businesses." Each chapter has an introductory paragraph followed by the listings. Listings detail pertinent information (i.e. book titles are followed by price, ISBN number, etc., organizations contain contact addresses, etc.) and are accompanied by descriptions and easy-reference icons. For example, a spider-web icon appears beside a website listing, a book icon beside a book, etc. An alphabetized index of resources can be found in the back.

Evaluation:

If you feel overwhelmed by the plethora of resources available to entrepreneurs, Ms. Lonier's "sourcebook" may be for you. It's a concise, straightforward, well-organized grouping of the most popular, well-respected, and generally well thought of resources "out there." And it covers them all, from print to Internet sites to professional associations. By dividing the listings into categories, such as "Starting a Business," the author makes it easy to browse or to search the text for specifics. (Familiarize yourself with the table of contents first, though, to make sure you're in the right category.) The icons are helpful, too; you can see what you're getting without having to read the whole description. If you want a "yellow pages" for going solo, this is the one to choose. (Keep in mind that similar material can be found online at Ms. Lonier's "Working Solo" website. It has an even better search engine, of course, plus it's free.) (See review.)

Where To Find/Buy:

Bookstores and libraries.

Overall Rating
★★★
1,200 resources for going solo; a good "one stop" reference book

Design, Ease Of Use
★★★
Well organized; uses icons for ease of reference

1–4 Stars

Author:
Terri Lonier

Ms. Lonier is president of Working Solo, Inc. She advises such clients as Microsoft, Hewlett-Packard, and Claris on how best to access and communicate with the small business and SOHO (Small Office Home Office) market.

Publisher:
John Wiley & Sons, Inc.

Edition:
2nd (1998)

Price:
$14.95

Pages:
315

ISBN:
0471247146

Media:
Book

Principal Subject:
General Self-Employment

VI. Going Solo

★★

Overall Rating
★★
Upbeat and inspiring; better for brainstorming than specific ideas

Design, Ease Of Use
★★★
Well-formatted; includes checklists, graphics, cartoons

1–4 Stars

Author:
Carol Eikleberry, Ph.D.

Dr. Eikleberry is a career counselor at the University of Pittsburgh Counseling Center.

Publisher:
Ten Speed Press

Edition:
1995

Price:
$11.95

Pages:
198

ISBN:
0898157579

Media:
Book

Principal Subject:
General Self-Employment

Secondary Subject:
Career/Job Descriptions

General Self-Employment

THE CAREER GUIDE FOR CREATIVE AND UNCONVENTIONAL PEOPLE

Description:

Dr. Eikleberry defines Part 1 of her book as the "what's going on part." In it, she examines personality types, provides self-evaluative checklists, and takes an "inside look at the creative personality." Topics discussed include esthetic sensitivity, "divergent thinking," and nonconforming behavior. Part 2 investigates career possibilities. Skills and ideas for jobs are discussed, as are options for "composing your own career," i.e. freelance work, small businesses, grants. Part 3 explores ways to "take action." There are strategies for motivation, thinking constructively, time management, and forming a support network. For an "intuitive approach" to setting goals, there is a "guided imagery/focusing exercise." To help readers find inspiration from within, Dr. Eikleberry leads readers on a metaphorical "journey" through their creative development, past, present, and future. "Real-life success stories" and quotes are scattered throughout; the appendix contains descriptions of 216 "creative" careers.

Evaluation:

For many "creative and unconventional people," support and encouragement may be just what they need to jump start a new career. In that case, this book is fine choice: it's a warm bear hug and a touchy-feely "you're OK" comforter. Dr. Eikleberry provides insights into the psychology of the "creative personality," such as how "your unique sensitivity" can be translated into useful skills. She also acts as the reader's greatest advocate and most sympathetic counselor; for example, segments include "Our World Needs Your Work" and "It Takes Courage To Be Yourself." However, this is not an effective "career guide." There are "ideas" for various career "trails," i.e. the "idea trail" (writers, performers) or the "ideas and people trail" (instructors, negotiators), but the suggestions offer little more than categories for further thought. The career descriptions are too brief to be helpful, either. This is a resource for boosting morale and brainstorming, not for career investigation or practical guidance.

Where To Find/Buy:

Bookstores and libraries.

General Self-Employment

SECRETS OF SELF-EMPLOYMENT

★ ★

Description:

Going solo means just that: going "out there" alone. For the Edwards, the psychology of being self-employed is just as important as the "how to." In their guide, which is divided into 8 chapters, they focus primarily on the personal side of being your own boss, though they do address such practicalities as organizing your office, cutting costs, and marketing. Stories, examples, and interactive exercises are used throughout the book to explore topics. Chapters 1 and 2 introduce the "new breed" of entrepreneur and discuss "making the mental shift to independence." Time management and "getting the business to run itself" (i.e. using technology effectively, etc.) are examined in Chapters 3 and 4. Self-motivation is the subject of Chapter 5, which includes such questionnaires as "What Motivates You?" and "Are You Ready For Success?" "Riding the Emotional Roller Coaster," i.e. handling depression, is treated in Chapter 6, while Chapters 7 and 8 focus on "Staying Up" and "Overcoming Obstacles."

Evaluation:

With the exception of Chapter 4, which offers tips for using technology to help run your business and some general marketing theory, this guide isn't concerned with the practicalities of being self-employed. (This isn't the resource for writing a business plan, financing, or learning about taxes.) Whenever "how to" guidelines pop up, they seem out of place with the rest of the content, which is far more concerned with the mental health of the entrepreneur than the viability of his/her business. The vast majority of this book is made up of self-esteem boosters, i.e. when you make a mistake, the authors say "Compliment yourself for your courage and ingenuity in trying what you did. . . . Don't berate yourself." Other advice samples: "Get plenty of exercise," "Become an optimist," "Remind yourself of your own capabilities." If you're starting a business and it's moral and mental support you desire, this is the place to go. It's certainly upbeat! Look elsewhere for practical tips and how-to advice.

Where To Find/Buy:

Bookstores and libraries.

Overall Rating
★★
An interactive mental health workbook for the self employed; not "how to"

Design, Ease Of Use
★★★
Engaging, easy to read; conversational style with lots of stories and exercises

1–4 Stars

Author:
Sarah and Paul Edwards
Sarah and Paul Edwards are authors of the best-selling "Working From Home" book series. They are columnists for "Home Office Computing" magazine and speak frequently on radio, television, and online.

Publisher:
G.P. Putnam's Sons

Edition:
2nd (1996)

Price:
$13.95

Pages:
381

ISBN:
0874778379

Media:
Book

Principal Subject:
General Self-Employment

VI. Going Solo

★★

Overall Rating
★★
An interesting but overly vague look at self-employment opportunities

Design, Ease Of Use
★★
Too many pages devoted to "exploration"; not enough practical suggestions

1–4 Stars

Author:
Paul and Sarah Edwards

Paul and Sarah Edwards are the creators of books, radio and television shows, and columns devoted to information and advice about self-employment.

Publisher:
Jeremy P. Tarcher (Putnam)

Edition:
1996

Price:
$16.95

Pages:
465

ISBN:
087477795X

Media:
Book

Principal Subject:
General Self-Employment

Secondary Subject:
Aptitude/Interest Analysis

VI. Going Solo

General Self-Employment

FINDING YOUR PERFECT WORK
The New Career Guide To Making A Living, Creating A Life

Description:

Paul and Sarah Edwards are the authors of another book on self-employment, as well as the creators of radio and TV shows, online resources, and a magazine column, all focused on the same subject. Here, they compile a number of anecdotes and exercises designed to help the reader find his or her "perfect work." Part I discusses the possibilities in self-employment, and how the changing nature of "the job" is creating more independent workers through out sourcing, small business services, and growing niche markets. Part II includes exercises for self-reflection to help you discover talents you can "harvest," along with profiles of others who have successfully used their gifts. How to connect your abilities to the needs of consumers is the focus of Part III, including six ways to spot opportunities. An epilogue includes a "personal style survey" designed to help you determine what type of work comes naturally to you, and a directory of self-employment careers which is also broken down by "personal styles."

Evaluation:

The title, "Finding Your Perfect Work," is slightly misleading. The advice is devoted to exploring careers, but solely in the realm of self-employment. For many, self-employment may not be their vision of "perfect work," but for those longing for independence, this may be the road to travel. The authors build up an argument for the benefits of breaking away from the traditional job and "finding your own way." One would hope that such a book would go on to discuss the practicalities involved with self-employment (e.g. starting up one's own business), but it mostly focuses on the preliminaries of exploring what type of work would suit your profile. Do we really need 465 pages for that? The attendant "exercises" border on the vapid, and chapters tend to be long-winded. However, the bountiful anecdotes of others who have successfully paved their way to self-employment are interesting, and a helpful index lists hundreds of possible self-employment careers. These are almost—but not quite—worth the price of the book.

Where To Find/Buy:

Bookstores and libraries.

General Self-Employment

ABOUTDOMAINS. COM

Non-Rated Resource

Description:
Just as the name suggests, this site is all about domain names: how to find out if a name is available, how to "park," "reserve," and "register," how to secure a domain name that's on "hold," etc. There's also information on InterNIC, proposed extensions (i.e. arts.), and selling domain names, as well as a list of domain-related service providers.

Publisher:
AboutDomains.com

Media:
Internet

Principal Subject:
General Self-Employment

Where To Find/Buy:
On the Internet using the URL: http://www.aboutdomains.com

BIZY MOMS

Non-Rated Resource

Description:
In addition to information about books and resources for work-at-home moms, Folger's site offers women an assortment of features for starting a home business. There's are 180+ business ideas, "FAQs," message boards, tips from successful "bizy moms," and a list of "scams" to avoid. Folger also offers phone consultations and her own advice column.

Author:
Liz Folger

Ms. Folger is a freelance writer, author and stay at home mom. She is the author of "The Stay At-Home-Mom's Guide to Making Money."

Media:
Internet

Principal Subject:
General Self-Employment

Of Interest To:
Women

Where To Find/Buy:
On the Internet using the URL: http://www.bizymoms.com

WORKING SOLO ONLINE

Non-Rated Resource

Description:
Entrepreneurs, consultants, free agents, e-lancers, and any other self-employed persons will find over 1,000 listings for publications, audio and video products, professional associations, tech help, and online resources at this advice site from entrepreneur and author Terri Lonier. The site is searchable by keyword and also includes such features as "FAQs" about small businesses, news and events, and a free newsletter.

Author:
Terri Lonier

Ms. Lonier is an author and president of Working Solo, Inc. She advises such clients as Microsoft, Hewlett-Packard, and Claris on how best to access and communicate with the small business and SOHO (Small Office Home Office) market.

Publisher:
Working Solo, Inc.

Media:
Internet

Principal Subject:
General Self-Employment

Where To Find/Buy:
On the Internet at http://www.workingsolo.com

VI. Going Solo

FREELANCE AND CONSULTING

The difference between an entrepreneurial business owner and a consultant or freelancer, is the difference between owning a business and being a business. Owning a business conveys an image of a store, a few employees or at least an inventory. When you are the business, your work is portable and your skills are your product.

The thought of going solo as a freelancer or consultant (broad terms that can be used to describe any number of solo ventures) is initially frightening to many people. It may seem like a roller coaster, without dependable income or any type of security. Ironically, in the coming decades, freelancing, consulting, contingency, temporary or other types of contract employment will be some of the more dependable, secure, and prolific types of work available.

As companies and corporations continue to cut back on full time employees, the demand for "portable executives" and other contingency workers will increase substantially. Small businesses, the nation's fastest growing employers, will need contract and temporary workers, too. If you always thought of freelancing as the realm of writers and artists, think again; by 2005, it's estimated that over half a million self-employed workers will be managers, administrators, and executives.

If you want to take advantage of the evolving workplace—the trend away from full-time workers to part-time, contingency, and contract workers—this section will help you choose the best resources for your specific needs. There are guides to becoming a "Portable Executive" and for "Creating You & Co.," websites for creative freelancers, and resources for professional temping. Although temping through a temporary service agency isn't self-employment in the conventional sense (you are paid by the agency), it is a way to remain adaptable, independent, and consistently employed, on your own terms and in the manner that best suits your lifestyle. There are also resources in General Self-Employment and Entrepreneurship that will be beneficial to you, so be sure to read through those sections as well. You will find resources on the nuts-and-bolts issues of running a business, such as taxes, marketing and billing clients, in all the Going Solo chapters.

VI. Going Solo

THE PORTABLE EXECUTIVE

Recommended For:

Freelance/Consulting

Description:

The economy is doing great, so why are so many executives facing downsizing and "no-fault termination," or being asked to accept early retirement? The fact is, the work world is changing; it's outsourcing, hiring more contractors and fewer full-time employees. To flourish in this new job market, and to discover the satisfaction and freedom of self-employment, many executives are taking their skills on the road. They're becoming "portable executives," and in this guide, entrepreneur John Thompson shows readers how to join their ranks. Preliminary chapters explore the "new reality" of business, profile the "portable executive," and discuss breaking the corporate "habit." Readers then assess their portable skills, "invent" their business, learn to network, and form an "action plan." (Interactive exercise are included.) "Maintaining your skills," marketing and sales, setting up a business, and pricing are addressed next, while the final chapter takes an in-depth look at 5 individuals who are "Portable, and Loving It!"

Evaluation:

While there are lots of books on freelancing, consulting, and contract-work, few are as insightful and thoughtful as this one. Mr. Thompson was a corporate executive before he began his own business and knows first hand the advantages and disadvantages of both positions. In his book, Thompson cleverly interweaves quotes and stories from "portable" executives, creating a hopeful, inspirational tone. Such feel-good optimism is balanced by practical, "you can do this" exercises and directions. This is a terrific resource for executives and managers who are leaving or who want to leave corporate America. In many respects, this is a book that all executives should read, even if you're not "planning" to leave. "Job security" is becoming an oxymoron, and this guide provides the tools, confidence, and "how to" for surviving and blossoming in the new work world. Turn a seeming defeat, i.e. downsizing, job loss, or early retirement, into a victory: read this book.

Where To Find/Buy:

Bookstores and libraries.

★★★★

Overall Rating

★★★★

A real find for executives who want to go solo! Inspiring and realistic

Design, Ease Of Use

★★★★

Well written and engaging; includes interviews and interactive exercises

1–4 Stars

Author:

John A. Thompson and Catharine A. Henningsen

Mr. Thompson is the founder of IMCOR, the nation's first interim management firm. Ms. Henningsen is a writer and consultant whose articles have appeared in "The Atlantic" and "The New York Times."

Publisher:

Fireside

Edition:

1997

Price:

$12.00

Pages:

267

ISBN:

0684818914

Media:

Book

Principal Subject:

Freelance/Consulting

VI. Going Solo

★★★

Overall Rating
★★★
Irreverent but insightful;
temping as a "lifestyle choice"

Design, Ease Of Use
★★★★
Straightforward format, very
well written; full of humor
and anecdotes

1–4 Stars

Author:
Brian Hassett

Mr. Hassett lives in the highest-
income ZIP code in the U.S.—
10021, in New York City—and he
hasn't held a real job in fifteen
years.

Publisher:
Carol Publishing Group

Edition:
1997

Price:
$11.95

Pages:
211

ISBN:
080651843x

Media:
Book

Principal Subject:
Freelance/Consulting

Freelance And Consulting

THE TEMP SURVIVAL GUIDE
How To Prosper As An Economic Nomad Of The Nineties

Description:
Mr. Hassett has made a lucrative career (implied) out of temping, and, says in his book—if you can type, you can too. Using lots of humor, anecdotes, and pop-culture references, Mr. Hassett explains the advantages of "A Temping Life," "The Way the Business Works," and the "ins & outs" of getting started: the necessary skills, choosing an agent, "acing" the interview, etc. He then prepares you for "Your First Day" with advice on arriving prepared, tackling "massive complicated documents" (and bosses), and adjusting to office "culture;" he also details the "philosophy of temping" and the "Radar O'Reilly Temporary Hall of Fame." There are strategies for "Making the A-Team" (i.e. "collecting rave reviews," "getting yourself booked back") and "Survival Techniques" for avoided such temp pitfalls as feeling subservient, patronized, etc. Other chapters include tips on raises, taxes, new agencies, "Milking the Cows," and "Going Permanent." The "Temp Commandments" and appendices of resources are provided.

Evaluation:
From page one of this engaging guide, it's clear that this isn't an average career resource. (Among the reasons cited in favor of "A Temping Life" is the temp's opportunity to appraise the "singles scene" at various businesses; the sub-chapter is called "Sex and Where to Get It.") Mr. Hassett is the denizen of a temp underworld, a world in which creative, insouciant, dynamic individuals like himself use temping to flit into the "real world of work," "milk the cows," and escape unscathed (a.k.a. take the money and run and never get your hands dirty). The underlying theme of this guide? If you want to work as little as possible and you have the smarts/ personality to make everyone else think you really care, temp. Sure, it sounds great; with his irreverent humor and terrific writing, Hassett makes it sound even better. But is it realistic? Most people who possess the skills needed to get the high-paying temp jobs would just as soon get a "real" job. For talented "nomads" who resent even the concept of a "real job," this is the book!

Where To Find/Buy:
Bookstores and libraries.

Freelance And Consulting

CREATING YOU AND CO.
Learn To Think Like The CEO Of Your Own Career

Description:
This is not a career guide based on the idea of finding a job. Rather, it is dedicated to helping you discover what skills/interests you can exploit in the "new" workplace. The basic idea is that technological advances are "dejobbing" America; many companies are moving away from the idea of traditional jobs. Dr. Bridges believes that by changing your career game plan, you can learn to thrive in this "new" job market. His book is divided into three sections. Part 1, "Why You Need You & Co.," explains his premise and the evolving work force. To help you evaluate your resources for dealing with these transitions, Bridges introduces the concept of determining your Desire, Abilities, Temperament, and Assets (D.A.T.A.). In Part 2, "Mining your D.A.T.A.," you explore these concepts using introspective questions and worksheets. The final part, "Turning Your D.A.T.A. Into A Product," focuses on reinventing careers and formulating a plan for career development based on your self-analysis.

Evaluation:
The Information Age, with its technological advances, is fast overwhelming the Industrial Age; "jobs" as we know them, so says Dr. Bridges, are an endangered species. The idea of facing the "instability" implied in a mobile work force of freelancers, temps, consultants, etc., can be frightening to those who are unprepared and who don't understand what's happening. (To put it simply: Bridges thinks you should "go solo.") The best thing about this book is that it goes a long way in increasing optimism and confidence. Not only will it inspire a "hey, I can do this!" response, it also emphasizes the "positives" of "going solo," i.e. greater satisfaction, control, etc., over the perceived negatives. The only problem is that Dr. Bridges is (deliberately) short on specifics. This is, despite its title, not about the daily grind of freelancing or the "how to." It's a self-assessment book designed to inspire creative career ideas. For that reason, this is a better choice for inspiration than for pragmatic problem solving.

Where To Find/Buy:
Bookstores and libraries.

★★★

Overall Rating
★★★
Self-analysis for "transitioning" to freelance, consulting or temporary work

Design, Ease Of Use
★★★
Easy-to-read, clear topic headings

1–4 Stars

Author:
William Bridges

William Bridges, Ph.D. is a consultant on work transitions. He travels widely to speak, lead workshops and consult with corporations. He is also the author of "Job Shift" and "Transitions."

Publisher:
Addison-Wesley

Edition:
1997

Price:
$22.00

Pages:
184

ISBN:
0201419874

Media:
Book

Principal Subject:
Freelance/Consulting

VI. Going Solo

★★★

Overall Rating
★★★
A good place to get a feel for freelancing and freelancing opportunities

Design, Ease Of Use
★★★
Simple, straightforward format; easy to use

1–4 Stars

Author:
Freelance Online is a professional online service for freelancers in the publishing and advertising fields. It serves as a directory for employers and as a resource and information center for freelancers.

Publisher:
Freelance Online

Edition:
1998

Media:
Internet

Principal Subject:
Freelance/Consulting

Secondary Subject:
Job/Resume Online Database

VI. Going Solo

Freelance And Consulting

FREELANCE ONLINE

Description:

Created to help freelancers make "matches" with employers in the publishing and advertising industries, this self-titled "Resource Center" features its own database of jobs and a "Directory" of freelancers' profiles/biographies. There's a member-fee of $15 (per annum) to post a profile, but non-members and "newbies" can use the rest of the site, including the job bank, free for six months. (Before the job listings are made available, users will be asked for their member number/code; as a non-member, don't enter anything, just click on "submit." The listings then appear for free.) Job listings are arranged by type, i.e. "art-related," "editorial-related," etc. Each listing contains contact information and a description of the position. Information for new freelancers can be found in "FAQs," covering topics such as necessary equipment, finding work, and what to charge. The site also offers messageboards for networking and links to additional resources, i.e. related sites, professional organizations, newsletters, etc.

Evaluation:

While there are other "matchmaker" sites out there for freelancers, most are much more expensive than this one. (The member fee is $15.) Thankfully, the operators of this site are kind enough to let non-members explore for free (for six months), which is just what you should do if you're interested in art/editorial-related freelancing. It's not an expansive, enormous site; the job bank is comparatively small and there aren't many participants in the networking forums. But that's not the point. If the idea of freelancing is appealing to you but you're not sure how to proceed, this is the perfect introduction. The "FAQs" are brief but educational (there are links in the text for further information), especially for writers, proofreaders and editors, and browsing the job listings is a terrific way to get a feel for "what's out there." You can see what other freelancers are up to by taking a look at the "Directory," and the "Resources" list of links is worth bookmarking. This is a site worth visiting.

Where To Find/Buy:

On the Internet at http://www.freelancersonline.com/index2.html

Freelance And Consulting

TEMPING: THE INSIDER'S GUIDE
Find The Career That's Right For You

★★★

Description:

Mr. Rogers' "Insider's Guide" to temping has two primary concerns: to explain the growing role and function of temporary employment in America's "changing workscape" and to explore the benefits of temping for today's job seeker. To accomplish the first of these tasks, Mr. Rogers dedicates a third of his guide (Chapters 1–4) to answering such questions as "Temping—What is It?" and "Who Does It and Why?" Once "The Role of the Temporary Help Service" (Chapter 4) is understood, readers learn how to choose the "right" temp service/agency, how to "sign up" (i.e. testing, the interview), and how the employee-agency relationship works (i.e. responsibilities, dos and don'ts). Going "on assignment" is next discussed, i.e. how to dress, how to negotiate for money, "ice breakers," etc. The final third of the guide examines the "pluses and minuses" of "career temping," "Temping Your Way to Full-Time Employment," and "High-End Temping." Insights from temping professionals are incorporated throughout the text.

Evaluation:

This is a straightforward guide to temporary employment, a virtual "how to" manual that explains simply and succinctly how temping works, why it may (or may not) be right for the job seeker, and how to go about "getting started." It provides all the "need to know basics" and a few insights (though most of the advice is common sense); altogether, it's a fine resource for anyone contemplating temp work. Readers will learn what to expect upon entering a temp service, what the possibilities are for continued employment (either full-time or as "career temps"), and exactly how the relationship between temp-agency-client really works, both practically and legally. Although the benefits of the "nouveau" "temp lifestyle" are discussed, this book is more "mainstream" than its counterpart, "The Temp Survival Guide" (see review). Mr. Rogers' guide is a more appropriate choice for those interested in using temp work in the "traditional" ways: as a "steppingstone" in one's career path, as an expedient way to make money, etc.

Where To Find/Buy:

Bookstores and libraries.

Overall Rating
★★★
A straightforward guide to the "need to know" basics of temping

Design, Ease Of Use
★★★
Simple, direct language, easy to use

1–4 Stars

Author:
Richard Rogers

Publisher:
Arco

Edition:
1996

Price:
$14.95

Pages:
202

ISBN:
0028610601

Media:
Book

Principal Subject:
Freelance/Consulting

VI. Going Solo

Freelance And Consulting

CREATIVE FREELANCERS ONLINE

Non-Rated Resource

Description:
Creative Freelancers Online is in the business of connecting freelance talent with the people who hire freelancers. Although there is a $300 annual fee to post your portfolio, non-members can view job listings for free and take a peek at other people's portfolios, for information and/or research. (Or just to check out the competition.) Users can search for job postings by category, i.e. writer, and/or post a brief resume.

Publisher:
Creative Freelancers

For 20 years, Creative Freelancers has provided freelance talent to advertising agencies, publishers, major corporations and small businesses.

Media:
Internet

Principal Subject:
Freelance/Consulting

Where To Find/Buy:
On the Internet at http://www.freelancers.com

NATIONAL ASSOCIATION OF TEMPORARY AND STAFFING SERVICES

Non-Rated Resource

Description:
The NATSS site offers visitors interested in temporary and staffing services an online directory of member agencies. (There are more than 1,600 members.) To find a staffing company, users can search by location (city and state), company name, country (for international listings), or by service/skill segment (i.e. health care). Search results frequently contain a link to the company's website as well as contact information.

Publisher:
NATSS

NATSS, the National Association of Temporary and Staffing Services, represents more than 1,600 staffing companies that operate approximately 13,000 offices throughout the U.S.

Media:
Internet

Principal Subject:
Freelance/Consulting

Where To Find/Buy:
On the Internet at http://www.natss.com

ENTREPRENEURSHIP

The approximately 23 million small businesses currently operating in the U.S. employ more than half of the private workforce and generate more than half of the nation's gross domestic product. They are the primary source of new jobs in the country. With the advent of high technology, especially Internet technology, starting and operating a business is easier today than ever before. Of the 1.25 million businesses started in 1997, over half began in the garage, spare bedroom, or at the kitchen table.

Owning your own business is the quintessential American dream. We envision the freedom, the personal satisfaction, the success, the independence, the glory—all of the benefits and rewards of not only being the boss, but of being the instigator, the creator, the entrepreneur.

Although the entrepreneurial streak is common among Americans, it isn't the right path for everyone. Starting a business is very, very hard work. For the first few years (at least), as a new business owner, you'll work long hours and multiple jobs, you'll be constantly "on call," you're finances will be tied to your business finances, and you may not see a profit. You'll be responsible for daily operations, hirings and firings, taxes, employee benefits, and all those other day-to-day realities that don't appear in your fantasy. And that's after you're up and running.

Before you can run a business, you must start a business, and the start-up requires a great deal of research, planning and know-how. Tasks such as creating a business plan, finding financing, conducting market research, and buying office equipment are only the tip of the iceberg.

Still interested? The resources reviewed in this section will assist you through the rigorous obstacle course of starting a business. Some provide advice on all facets of starting a business, such as SBA Online (the Small Business Administration's website) and Entrepreneurial Edge Online. Others, like CCH Business Owner's Toolkit, provide free tools: shareware, model documents, financial spreadsheet templates. The SCORE website offers free, 24-hour e-mail counseling. There are also resources for inspiration, networking, chatting with other entrepreneurs, marketing, and choosing business ideas. (Be sure to look through "General Self Employment" for additional help.)

The more prepared you are before you start your business the better your chances of success. Take advantage of these resources, educate yourself, assess your situation, and get advice from the experts. The entrepreneur's task is one of the most difficult, but, as we all know, the more difficult the task, the greater the rewards.

★★★★

Overall Rating
★★★★
Interactive, informative, in-depth resource for budding entrepreneurs!

Design, Ease Of Use
★★★★
Simple, elegant design; easy to navigate and use

1–4 Stars

Author:
Jill Bond, an entrepreneur, founded "Entrepreneurial Edge" in 1990 to help small business owners. In 1995, "Edge" was acquired by the Edward Lowe Foundation, a non-profit organization founded by the creator of Kitty Litter and Tidy Cat.

Publisher:
Edward Lowe Foundation

Edition:
1998

Media:
Internet

Principal Subject:
Entrepreneurship

ENTREPRENEURIAL EDGE ONLINE

 Recommended For:
Entrepreneurship

Description:

The online version of "Edge" magazine offers new entrepreneurs more than its archives; there's a "Business Toolbox," "Business Resources," and a "Virtual Network." In the "Toolbox," users will find a variety of free tools for starting and growing a small business. There are fill-in-the-blank, self-calculating financial management/assessment tools, i.e. a profit and loss statement, a cash budget, etc., and a series of "training modules." The "modules" are interactive, educational worksheets that walk users step-by-step through such procedures as marketing, financing, managing, and promoting a business. The section for "Business Resources" includes links to related sites, news and trends, and access to "smallbizNet," "Edge's" sister site, a database of 5,000 documents on small business issues. For networking, the "Virtual Network" has two features: a "brainstorming boardroom" and an "interactive forum." The site's archives contain hundreds of articles on entrepreneurism, i.e. business planning, using technology, etc.

Evaluation:

When you arrive at this site, don't be deceived by the blank space that takes up a large amount of the screen. Move the cursor to one of the section headings, i.e. "Business Resources," and the blank space is filled by a description of that section. And that's only the first pleasant surprise awaiting visitors. There are tons of delicious gems at this quiet, unassuming site, and they aren't hard to find. Everywhere you go has something valuable to offer, from the networking possibilities of the "Virtual Network" to the one-click-away "smallbizNet," with its enormous database of informational documents. The best surprise, however, is how easy it is to use the "Toolbox." To use one of the financial tools, i.e. the balance sheet, just plug in your numbers and hit "calculate." The "training modules" are fantastic, too: interactive, self-paced, educational, and readily available—you don't have to download anything! "Edge" is owned by a non-profit organization, and the true love of helping shines through in every screen.

Where To Find/Buy:

On the Internet at http://www.edgeonline.com

Entrepreneurship

SBA ONLINE
Starting Your Business

 Recommended For:
Entrepreneurship

Description:

The SBA's site offers a wide range of informational resources for small business owners, including sections on regulations, financing, expanding, and "Starting Your Business." The "Starting" section has its own "main page" and its own menu, whereby visitors can access such pages as "FAQs" (Frequently Asked Questions), "Do Your Research," "Training," "Counseling Help," "Special Assistance," "Patents & Trademarks," and "Outside Resources." There's a "Success" page, with links to articles and tips from "winning" small business owners, and a "Startup Kit." The "Startup Kit" examines all aspects of starting: i.e. types of business organizations, marketing, finding the money you need, government regulations, SBA assistance and financial programs, etc. For creating a business plan, users can download the SBA's "tutorial" or view the business plan outline, which explicitly defines each element of the plan, i.e. "description of the business." Business-related shareware, i.e. "files for starting your business," is also available.

Evaluation:

The government is notorious for creating "no frills" sites and the SBA site is no different. Still, what it lacks in glamour it more than makes up for in content. If you're starting your own business or thinking about starting, this is the place to begin. It's all here: resources for starting, financing, expanding, etc., plus all the necessary information on government regulations and SBA financial assistance. For beginners, the "Starting Your Business" section is just what you need: straight, explicit talk about the "nuts and bolts" of becoming an entrepreneur. The "Business Plan" "tutorial" is easy to follow and understand, and the "Startup Kit" is a mini-reference library of essays defining and discussing such particulars as sole proprietorship, partnerships, corporations, borrowing money, how your loan request will be reviewed, etc. This isn't the place for creative inspiration, but when you're done dreaming about your business and are ready to get down to the nitty gritty, the genuine "how to," visit this site.

Where To Find/Buy:

On the Internet at http://www.sbaonline.sba.gov/starting

Overall Rating
★★★★
One of the best sites for starting a business; everything you need

Design, Ease Of Use
★★★
Simple, no frills layout; easy to use and quick download (for tutorials)

1–4 Stars

Author:
The U.S. Small Business Administration, established in 1953, provides financial, technical and management assistance to help Americans start, run, and grow their businesses. SBA is the nation's largest single financial backer of small businesses.

Publisher:
U.S. Small Business Administration

Edition:
1998

Media:
Internet

Principal Subject:
Entrepreneurship

VI. Going Solo

★★★★

Overall Rating
★★★★

Free e-mail counseling, informative workshops, a great web guide, plus lots more!

Design, Ease Of Use
★★★

User friendly and well organized; use the site map for initial navigating

1–4 Stars

Author:
The SCORE association (Service Corps of Retired Executives) is a resource partner with the U.S. Small Business Administration. It is a non-profit organization dedicated to the formation, growth, and success of small businesses nationwide.

Publisher:
SCORE Association

Edition:
1998

Media:
Internet

Principal Subject:
Entrepreneurship

Entrepreneurship

SCORE: SERVICE CORPS OF RETIRED EXECUTIVES
Counselor's to America's Small Business

 Recommended For:
Entrepreneurship

Description:
SCORE is a non-profit organization comprised of more than 12,000 volunteer business executives. Affiliated with the SBA, SCORE is dedicated to helping entrepreneurs and small business owners. Their site (which can best be navigated via the site map) offers free e-mail counseling (to all U.S. citizens), whereby users can pose questions of the volunteer "experts." Counseling is available 24 hours a day, 7 days a week, and users choose the counselor. SCORE's other online features include archives of "success stories" and informational "workshops." The "success stories" are profiles of successful small businesses and represent a wide array of types, i.e. ANAgraph, Inc. and Better Baskets by Cindy. The "workshops" are "how to" articles that cover such topics as starting and planning a business and "Technology for Small Business." For additional research, SCORE provides a "Business Resource Index," with links for specific issues, i.e. domain naming, and an annotated web guide titled "Business Hotlinks."

Evaluation:
There is absolutely no reason not to take advantage of the free counseling offered by SCORE's army of volunteer business executives. Not only is it free "expert" advice, it couldn't be more convenient or user-friendly. The service is available all the time, it's confidential, you initiate contact, and you pick the counselor (from a wide range of choices). (You must be a U.S. citizen to be eligible.) You could visit every entrepreneur site on the Net and you won't find a better offer than that! Of course, though the counseling is the best reason to drop by this site, there are other good reasons to visit. The "workshops" are informative, the "success stories" are inspirational, and the web guide is absolutely a "must" for browsing or bookmarking. The site is well-organized, so it's easy to find particulars. There's a constant side-bar "menu," but familiarize yourself with the contents, via the site map, first. The site map is explicit and includes everything, i.e. all the archived workshops, etc.; the home page is a bit ambiguous.

Where To Find/Buy:
On the Internet at http://www.score.org

Entrepreneurship

CCH BUSINESS OWNER'S TOOLKIT

★★★

Description:

From the CCH home page, small business owners (and potential entrepreneurs) can access the main sections of the site: the "SOHO Guidebook," "Power Tools," "Business Tools," and "News and Advice." Each of these main sections has its own table of contents for navigating. Within the "Guidebook," users will find tips and articles on such "essentials" as "starting and planning your business," "getting financing," "marketing your product," and "controlling your taxes." "Power Tools" include business/credit reports, trademark and patent searches, and industry information. "Business Tools," for such categories as "Business Finance," "Marketing," and "Starting Your Business," comprise the basic "toolkit." There are step-by-step checklists (i.e. a Start-Up Checklist), model business documents (i.e. Loan Application Bank Review Form), and fill-in-the-blank financial spreadsheet templates. The site also features access to "SCORE's" free e-mail counseling and an archive of news items and "Ask Alice" advice columns.

Evaluation:

There are (primarily) two types of websites for budding entrepreneurs: the glamorous, inspirational, networking ones (like Idea Cafe or Fast Company, see reviews) and the practical, "nuts and bolts" sites, like this one. Used in tandem with the SBA's site (see review), CCH's "Toolkit" will help you get started on the practical side of starting your business: the money, the documents, the basics. In "Business Tools," the number one reason to check out this site, there are all sorts of quick and effective tools (checklists, model documents, financial spreadsheet templates) for getting organized. For example, the tools for "Starting Your Business" include a "Family Monthly Budget Form" as well as checklists for "Start-up," "Business Selection," and "Cost Assessment." While some of the tools are a little simplistic, they admirably fulfill their chief function: to get you ready for action. Plus, CCH is partnered with "SCORE" (see review), so there's access to free e-mail counseling. This truly is a "Business Owner's Toolkit!"

Where To Find/Buy:

On the Internet at http://www.toolkit.cch.com

Overall Rating
★★★
Lots of free tools and model documents for starting your own business

Design, Ease Of Use
★★★★
Easy to use, well formatted and well designed

1–4 Stars

Author:
CCH Incorporated is a provider of business, legal, and tax information and software to the business community.

Publisher:
CCH Inc.

Edition:
1998

Media:
Internet

Principal Subject:
Entrepreneurship

VI. Going Solo

★★★

Overall Rating
★★★
Entertaining and insightful stories and advice from successful entrepreneurs; inspiring

Design, Ease Of Use
★★★★
Simple format, engaging design, easy to navigate

1–4 Stars

Author:
The Benlore Company offers technology and business planning strategies to both emerging and established businesses. Its product, "The Entrepreneur's Mind," is sponsored by Arthur Anderson Consulting.

Publisher:
Benlore Company

Edition:
1998

Media:
Internet

Principal Subject:
Entrepreneurship

VI. Going Solo

Entrepreneurship

THE ENTREPRENEUR'S MIND

Description:
Unlike resources that focus on the business plan, financing, or other nuts and bolts aspects of entrepreneurship, EM (the Entrepreneur's Mind) answers the question "how does one start a business" by presenting the personal stories and first-hand accounts of successful entrepreneurs. In addition to the selected "Keynote Entrepreneur" and the "Launch Pad" business that are featured on the home page, visitors can browse archives of previously featured people/businesses. Each entrepreneur/business profile has its own "table of contents," for moving within the document, and examines such issues as "industry direction," "concept development," "marketing," and "product launch." Background on the company and its founders is also provided. (Archive profiles include HandsOnToys, Inc., Nantucket Nectars, and ID Software.) Besides the "real-life" profiles, there are articles on international business concerns (in "Global Perspective") and advice from "industry experts" and the site's sponsor, Arthur Anderson.

Evaluation:
OK, so this isn't a "how to start a business" site, though there are some valuable articles in the "Expert's Corner" on creating an effective business plan, etc. It is an entertaining, enlightening, insightful look into the real-life experiences of some of today's great (and often unlikely) success stories. Here, for budding entrepreneurs of any sort, is proof-positive that the American Dream can, and does, happen. The profiles cover a variety of businesses, and (for those technophobes), there are plenty that are not computer-based. There's the story of Nantucket Nectars, a multi-million dollar "new age" beverage company which began in a "dockside shanty," and the tale of HandsOnToys, Inc., a toy maker. Of course, there's also ID Software, Secure Technologies, and MecklerMedia. The stories aren't all "smiles and sunshine," they discuss the problems and difficulties, too, and are educational as well as engaging. Best of all, this "advice" is from the "real" experts: the entrepreneurs themselves.

Where To Find/Buy:
On the Internet at http://www.benlore.com/index2.html

Entrepreneurship

SMALL TIME OPERATOR

★★★

Description:
Operating your own business is a lot of work; so is starting one. To help readers through the entire process, from choosing a location to understanding taxation, Mr. Kamoroff has creating a combination explanatory guide and workbook. There are six sections: "Getting Started," "Bookkeeping," "Growing Up," "Taxes," "Appendix," and "Ledgers." "Getting Started" explores such issues as financing, business location, legal structure, licenses and permits, and insurance. Business bank accountants, credit sales, recording expenditures, and profit and loss analysis are among the subjects examined in "Bookkeeping." Hiring help, partnerships, incorporation and L.L.C. are primary topics in "Growing Up," while "Taxes" provides an in-depth look at various tax issues, i.e. self employment tax, retirement deductions, state and local tax, etc. The "Appendix" covers a potpourri of subjects, such as husband and wife businesses, computers, freelancing, and consulting. Eight fill-in-the-blank ledgers comprise the final section.

Evaluation:
Many budding entrepreneurs blanche at the thought of daily ledgers and retirement deductions encroaching on their happy dreams of freedom and riches. Not surprisingly, most guides aimed at entrepreneurs deal at length with topics such as business ideas and marketing strategies. However, the author's background as a CPA is evident in this book's focus on taxes and other financial aspects of operating your own business. Though perhaps less inspiring than a series of vignettes about successful entrepreneurs, chapters on bookkeeping, taxes, licenses and other financial issues are quite necessary. For tackling these "drudge" elements of owning a business, this is the book to choose. It's not a fun read, but it is helpful, informative, and realistic. Mr. Kamoroff is excellent at defining terms and explaining important topics such as excise taxes, self-employment tax, IRS regulations, etc. Plus, the included ledgers are truly useful. This isn't a resource for choosing a business or writing a business plan, but for $17, it's a great paperback CPA.

Where To Find/Buy:
Bookstores and libraries.

Overall Rating
★★★
A good choice for small business money matters: taxes, accounting, bookkeeping, etc.

Design, Ease Of Use
★★★
Well crafted and well written; includes a series of fill-in-the-blank ledgers

1–4 Stars

Author:
Bernard B. Kamoroff, CPA
Mr. Kamoroff is a business consultant, Certified Public Accountant, university instructor, author, columnist, and small business operator; he started and operated two of his own small businesses.

Publisher:
Bell Springs

Edition:
23rd (1998)

Price:
$16.95

Pages:
180

ISBN:
0197510143

Media:
Book

Principal Subject:
Entrepreneurship

VI. Going Solo

Overall Rating
★★
Provides a quick overview of the start-up process and what to expect; lacks detail

Design, Ease Of Use
★
Easy to watch, but you'll have to pause, rewind, etc. to take notes

1–4 Stars

Author:
The Richard Diercks Company

Publisher:
Richard Diercks

Edition:
1992

Media:
Videotape

Principal Subject:
Entrepreneurship

VI. Going Solo

Entrepreneurship

HOW TO START AND OPERATE YOUR OWN BUSINESS

Description:

Small businesses are popping up with greater frequency than ever, but few survive beyond infancy. Although no one can guarantee a long life span for your business, thorough planning and research at the start can make the difference in the end. In this video, this type of "initial preparation" is the primary focus. The video is a combination of dramatic vignettes and "how to" commentary from a host. The vignettes follow a fictional couple who have an idea for a start-up. Scenes of the couple are interspersed with scenes of the host, who explains the action to the viewers and provides explanations and advice. "Preparation" begins with defining your business by identifying objectives and pinpointing your "distinct advantage," the thing that makes your business unique. The next step is conducting market research and "building a team," i.e. bringing in "experts" to compensate for "weaknesses." For example, the video couple brings in a third partner for finance know-how. Assessing your financial needs is also discussed. Tips on creating a comprehensive business plan, getting financing, and daily operations, i.e. choosing a computer system, follow. A bonus video on sales, "Everyone in Your Company is a Salesperson," is included.

Evaluation:

If you think you can learn to start and operate a business in 45 minutes, you have at least one of the entrepreneur qualities this video exhorts: optimism. However, you also have one of the "warning signs" of failure: unrealistic expectations. While the 25 minute segment on "initial preparation" is a useful look at what planning a business entails, the video compresses its treatment of such important subjects as business plans, getting financing, and daily operations into 20 minutes of "highlights." These "highlights" comprise little more than buzzwords and tips. For example, the segment on "getting financing" briefly lists the types of loans available and then tells viewers to contact the SBA or SCORE. (See the SBA Online and SCORE reviews.) Viewers are also told to "customize" their approach to each lender, but no explanation of how to do so is provided. Similarly, the segment on daily operations offers this advice on choosing a computer system: choose the software that will do what you need first, then choose the hardware. Period. And don't expect any guidance on creating a business plan; you have to buy another video for that. For a look at the entire start-up process (without a lot of detail), this resource may be a good choice; at least it's quick. For real "how to," look elsewhere.

Where To Find/Buy:

Bookstores and libraries?

Entrepreneurship

AMERICAN INDIVIDUAL MAGAZINE AND COFFEEHOUSE

Non-Rated Resource

Description:
In addition to message boards, chat "houses," and a "library" of print resources, this site offers a descriptive web guide for entrepreneurs and potential entrepreneurs. From the home page, under "Places to Go," visitors can find links for such topics as "Starting A Business," "Working From Home," and "Career Information." Just click on a topic for a alphabetical list of relevant websites.

Publisher:
Kasia Communications

Media:
Internet

Principal Subject:
Entrepreneurship

Where To Find/Buy:
On the Internet at http://www.aimc.com/aimc

EPA SMALL BUSINESS GATEWAY

Non-Rated Resource

Description:
If you're a prospective small business owner with environmental concerns, the EPA offers an informational "gateway" just for you. In addition to "FAQs" and general guidelines, the site features segments on "Environmental Regulations and Laws," "Environmental Assistance and Technical Help," and contacting environmental experts.

Publisher:
EPA

The mission of the U.S. Environmental Protection Agency (EPA) is to protect human health and safeguard the natural environment.

Media:
Internet

Principal Subject:
Entrepreneurship

Where To Find/Buy:
On the Internet using the URL: http://www.epa.gov/smallbusiness

WEB MARKETING INFORMATION CENTER

Non-Rated Resource

Description:
Mr. Wilson's site is overflowing with resources for entrepreneurs/home-based business owners interested in doing business on the Web. There are links to hundreds of articles on subjects ranging from "Banner Ads" to "E-Mail Marketing." There's also an "E-Commerce Research Room" with hundreds of links for researching online sales, including links to information on web store design, online transactions, and international exporting.

Author:
Ralph F. Wilson

Dr. Wilson is Director of Wilson Internet Services, which offers services in website design and consulting.

Publisher:
Wilson Internet Services

Media:
Internet

Principal Subject:
Entrepreneurship

Where To Find/Buy:
On the Internet at http://www.wilsonweb.com/webmarket/

VI. Going Solo

RESOURCES OF INTEREST TO SPECIFIC GROUPS OF JOB SEEKERS

RACIAL AND ETHNIC MINORITIES

Minorities have a greater presence in the American work world today than ever before, and their ranks are growing. By 2005, African-Americans, Latinos, Asians and other ethnic groups will represent 27% of the U.S. labor force. Between 1990 and 2005, these groups will also account for 35% of entrants to the labor force. Yet, despite the increasing diversity, minorities still face unique challenges in the workplace. Job discrimination and racial bias still occur, as do cultural misunderstandings and misperceptions.

For the most part, as a member of a minority group, your career and job searching needs are the needs of every worker and job searcher. Almost all of the resources we review are for general audiences; techniques for writing cover letters, using the Internet, networking, and career exploration cross cultural, ethnic, and gender lines. That said, there are aspects of career management that are specific to minorities. These issues may be discussed in a section of an "all-inclusive" resource, or they may be the raison d'être for an entire resource.

For example, you may want to find the top employers for minorities. You may want advice on assuming a leadership role and/or coping with being "the only" in a white-dominated environment. Or you may simply want a resource that presumes you are its audience, and so tailors its entire content to meet your interests.

In this section, we highlight resources created for and by minorities. These resources are not intended to replace resources geared to a general audience. Rather, they make effective and positive supplements. Some of the resources address all minority groups, such as The Minority Career Book and the Minorities Job Bank, while others target specific ethnicities, such as Latino Web and Saludos Web. The job banks include postings from employers who are actively recruiting minorities and postings for Spanish-English bilinguals. There are also websites, like Black Collegian Online, that offer information on anti-discrimination laws and resources. To learn more about these resources, be sure to read the full-page review.

Finding the right type of assistance and support is a must for any individual; it is doubly important for those who find themselves in the minority. As you probably know, Corporate America isn't always a level playing field for minorities, so the more players you have on your team, the better. These resources are on your team; they are your cheerleaders, your coaches, your fans. They have only one goal in mind: to help you win. Take advantage!

Racial And Ethnic Minorities

Title:	**The Minority Career Book**
Author:	Miquela Rivera, Ph.D.
Overall Rating:	★★★
Media Type:	Book
Short Description:	For many minority professionals, apt career guidance can be hard to come by; their concerns and experiences are frequently ignored by "mainstream" resources. Not so in this guide. Designed to prepare minorities for "the winner's circle," Dr. Rivera addresses such topics as career planning, "being the 'only'," managing office politics, and assuming leadership. Changing careers and the "basics of job winning" (i.e. interviewing) are also discussed.

■ **Read The Full Review Of This Resource On Page 74.**

Title:	**The Black Collegian Online**
Subtitle:	The Career Site For Students And Professionals Of Color
Overall Rating:	★★★
Media Type:	Internet
Short Description:	The Black Collegian Online "rides the fence" between college and post-collegiate enterprise. Although it offers special features for students, it also contains features applicable to all job seekers: African-American career advice, a database of job listings, a resume bank, a list of "Top 100 Employers," and articles from "The Black Collegian" archives. Articles include resume writing tips and "reports" on selected industries/careers.

■ **Read The Full Review Of This Resource On Page 114.**

Title:	**Saludos Web**
Subtitle	Careers, Employment, Culture
Overall Rating:	★★★
Media Type:	Internet
Short Description:	Saludos Web is one of the first career websites specifically designed for an Hispanic audience. It provides a database of job listings and a resume bank for bilingual job seekers, an "Hispanic Resource Center" with links to Hispanic-related sites, and a "Career Center." The "Career Center" features articles, resume writing tips, internship listings, profiles of 12 "career fields" (i.e. "law and order"), and "mentor profiles" of successful Hispanics.

■ **Read The Full Review Of This Resource On Page 117.**

Title:	**Minorities' Job Bank**
Subtitle	Career & Lifestyle Site For People Of Color
Overall Rating:	★★
Media Type:	Internet
Short Description:	The Minorities' Job Bank is dedicated to assisting African-Americans, Asian Americans, Hispanic Americans and Native Americans with their job search needs. In addition to job and resume banks, the site offers employer profiles, career-related articles, news commentary, and career development advice. There are also "virtual villages" for each ethnic group which contain ethno-specific articles, features, lifestyle segments, etc.

■ **Read The Full Review Of This Resource On Page 119.**

Racial And Ethnic Minorities

Title:	**LatinoWeb**
Subtitle:	A Latino Virtual Community
Overall Rating:	N/R
Media Type:	Internet
Short Description:	LatinoWeb is a gateway site dedicated to serving the needs of the Latino/Hispanic community. It provides annotated lists of direct links to Internet resources, including resources on business, government (i.e. federal jobs), education, publications, and nonprofits. The site also offers a chat room, free software (i.e. web browsers), and a database of jobs from companies specifically interested in hiring Latino/Hispanic employees.

■ **Read The Full Review Of This Resource On Page 104.**

Despite the fact that there are as many women entrants to the labor force in the 1990s as there are men and despite the fact that women are projected to constitute half of the labor force by 2005, women still encounter subtle and not-so-subtle discrimination at work. Women still make 72 cents to the man's dollar. Women still face a different work reality than men do.

In the U.S., gender bias in the professional workplace is generally assumed to be a rarity. While attention is paid to the "glass ceiling" said to frustrate the attempts of women to reach the executive ranks, the existence of gender bias in the daily business world is less accepted. The truth is, it's difficult to quantify "how much" gender bias exists. In many instances, bias on the part of an employer, co-worker, or interviewer, may be unconscious. That is to say, they may not realize that they are treating women differently from men. Sexism isn't always intentional and it isn't always perceived. That doesn't mean it doesn't exist. Bias is often subtle, as when an interviewer asks a woman (illegally) if she plans to have children in the near future.

Aside from outright discrimination, many women encounter another obstacle in the workplace: the workplace itself. In order to be considered "serious about their career," women have had to adopt a workaholic, family-second job-first set of priorities. The notion of balancing work and family has only recently been adopted as an acceptable concern for those in the upper echelons of management.

Corporate culture in America has been, traditionally, the culture of men. The hierarchical male culture of business is changing; over the last two decades, a new emphasis has been placed on business models that promote "female" paradigms: cooperation, communication, decision-making through consensus. These changes reflect both women's greater involvement in business and the evolution of business practices themselves. Still, the corporate world has a way to go before the numbers of women in business transform business politics, language, and culture.

In addition to being aware of gender discrimination, women must also be aware of the ways in which their own culture—their upbringings and perceptions—can clash with corporate culture. Women's culture has historically impressed upon women the virtues of being "ladylike," being likable, and putting themselves second rather than first. Those are virtues indeed, in certain circumstances; in business, such traits can be self-sabotaging. For example, women typically ask for less money in salary negotiations than men do because they undervalue their monetary worth. Women are more modest about their accomplishments, too. In interviews, women frequently emphasize the personal importance of the job, making statements that begin with "I think it would be good for me to . . . ," where as men emphasize what they can do for the company.

WOMEN

These examples do not imply that women cannot excel in all facets of business, be it negotiating, interviewing, or getting promoted. Nor do they describe every woman or suggest that women should be like men. Traits such as self-confidence, assertiveness, and guilt-free self-interest are androgynous, not male. Rather, they convey a need for awareness: an awareness of the environment in which you work, an awareness of where possible obstacles lie.

In this section, we highlight a variety of resources that address the workplace concerns of women. Some of the resources focus on issues of discrimination, such as illegal interview questions (and how to field them) and discriminatory firings. Some are selected because they pay attention to the different ways men and women typically approach a task such as salary negotiations or networking, and coach women to overcome self-defeating thoughts and behaviors.

There are also general resources for all women, like the website Women's Wire, which offers an array of advice and support tools. For moms who want to work and stay at home, there are websites like WAHM.com and Bizy Moms, which provide both networking opportunities and self-employment information. (If a description interests you, be sure to read the full-page review.)

In the work world, it shouldn't matter which gender you are; usually, it doesn't. But if an occasion arises when it does matter, these resources can help.

Women

Title:	**The Smart Woman's Guide To Interviewing And Salary Negotiation**
Author:	Julie Adair King
Overall Rating:	★★★★
Media Type:	Book
Short Description:	Women face two major obstacles to career success: discrimination (conscious and unconscious) and their own conditioned behavior (i.e. to be unassuming, modest, etc.). Nowhere are these obstacles more evident than in interviews and salary negotiations. To help women succeed in these situations, Ms. King offers advice and techniques for "playing the salary game," "selling yourself with confidence," handling difficult questions, and negotiating a raise.

■ **Read The Full Review Of This Resource On Page 190.**

Title:	**Getting Fired**
Subtitle:	What To Do If You're Fired, Downsized, Laid Off, Restructured, Discharged, Terminated, Or Forced To Resign
Author:	Steven Sack
Overall Rating:	★★★★
Media Type:	Book
Short Description:	Sack guides readers on what to do to protect themselves if they sense they might be fired or have already received the dreaded pink slip. Major sections include: Determining When You Are Being Treated Illegally Or Unfairly, Negotiating The Best Severance Package After You Are Fired and Fighting Back.

■ **Read The Full Review Of This Resource On Page 80.**

Title:	**Women's Wire: Work**
Overall Rating:	★★★
Media Type:	Internet
Short Description:	Women's Wire is promoted as an online resource for "busy women." In its "Work" portion, visitors will find tools, tips, and "talk" on a variety of career issues, from child care to management strategies. There are quizzes, articles, chat rooms, message boards, and a Q&A forum, as well as a job database and resume builder. Profiles of "Hot Careers" are also provided; the profiles include segments on "what it's like" and "stuff to know."

■ **Read The Full Review Of This Resource On Page 133.**

Title:	**WAHM: Work At Home Moms**
Author:	Cheryl Demas
Overall Rating:	★★★
Media Type:	Internet
Short Description:	Created by a work at home mom, WA HM offers a variety of networking and support resources for women who currently work or wish to work in the home. Ms. Demas offers advice, book selections, a weekly column, and links to related websites. The site's primary focus is on networking. Readers can find/contact "WAHMs Near You" and/or learn about "WAHM businesses" from their female founders.

■ **Read The Full Review Of This Resource On Page 201.**

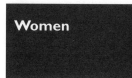
Women

Title:	**Career Change**
Author:	David P. Helfand, Ph.D.
Overall Rating:	★★★
Media Type:	Book
Short Description:	Dr. Helfand's guide addresses both the universal issues involved in changing careers, i.e. job searching, and the issues faced by particular groups, i.e. women, minorities, people over 50. Topics discussed include "adult development," "conquering fears," self-assessment, and "time and money." There are also chapters on layoffs, firings, etc., and for people with disabilities and ex-military personnel. Profiles of 10 career changers provide examples.
■ **Read The Full Review Of This Resource On Page 62.**	

Title:	**It's Only Too Late If You Don't Start Now**
Subtitle:	How To Create Your Second Life After 40
Author:	Barbara Sher
Overall Rating:	★★
Media Type:	Book
Short Description:	Sher postulates that "Your first life belongs to nature. Your second life (which begins at forty or whenever you experience a mid-life crisis) belongs to you." Part I focuses on "Nature and Instinct" the governing forces of your first life. Part II, Reclaiming Your Original Self: Your Second Life, inspires readers on the endless possibilities of life after forty.
■ **Read The Full Review Of This Resource On Page 66.**	

Title:	**Advancing Women**
Author:	Gretchen Glasscock
Overall Rating:	★★
Media Type:	Internet
Short Description:	Ms. Glasscock has assembled a variety of resources for women who want to "get ahead" at their current job or find a better one. There are articles on "overcoming barriers," balancing work and family, and using the Internet to advance "your self and your career." Strategies for advancing your career in the workplace are presented, and there are chat rooms and message boards for networking/mentoring. Links to related sites/articles are included.
■ **Read The Full Review Of This Resource On Page 77.**	

Title:	**How To Get That Job!**
Subtitle:	Tools, Techniques, and Strategies "Borrowed" From Successful Job Applicants
Author:	Ruby N. Gorter
Overall Rating:	★
Media Type:	Book
Short Description:	The author discusses the steps of the job search process with the first-time or returning applicant in mind. A portion of the advice is tailored to women returning to the work force after time away, and how to highlight their skills and accomplishments. Chapters range from how to research potential employers to setting up information interviews, writing a resume/ cover letter, and dealing successfully with the employment interview.
■ **Read The Full Review Of This Resource On Page 138.**	

Women

Title:	**Beatrice's Web Guide For Women And Careers**
Overall Rating:	N/R
Media Type:	Internet
Short Description:	Beatrice's Web Guide is a directory of women-related websites on a wide variety of subjects, including "Fab Finds" for online career information. On the "Careers" page, visitors can choose from such topics as "Aptitude Tests," "Fired," "Maternity Leave," "Starting a Business," and "Starting a Job Hunt Working." Click on a topic for direct links to and descriptions of relevant websites. The site also offers online chat and message boards.

■ **Read The Full Review Of This Resource On Page 102.**

Title:	**The Feminist Majority Foundation Online**
Subtitle:	Directory of Women's Organizations
Overall Rating:	N/R
Media Type:	Internet
Short Description:	Professional associations are both important sources of career information and great venues for networking. To help women take advantage, this site offers lists of women's business, legal, and medical organizations. In "Business," entries range from "American Association of Black Women Entrepreneurs" to "American Society of Women Accountants." Each entry contains contact information and a direct link to the association's website (where possible).

■ **Read The Full Review Of This Resource On Page 104.**

Title:	**Bizy Moms**
Author:	Liz Folger
Overall Rating:	N/R
Media Type:	Internet
Short Description:	In addition to information about books and resources for work-at-home moms, Folger's site offers women an assortment of features for starting a home business. There's are 180+ business ideas, "FAQs," message boards, tips from successful "bizy moms," and a list of "scams" to avoid. Folger also offers phone consultations and her own advice column.

■ **Read The Full Review Of This Resource On Page 207.**

THE
DISABLED

There are 49 million people with disabilities in the U.S., constituting the country's largest minority. With the advent of the Americans with Disabilities Act (ADA) and other similar legislation, employment opportunities for this diverse group are growing every year. Companies and agencies that receive government funding, as well as large companies and corporations, are among the forerunners in offering accommodations and employment to the disabled. Unfortunately, that trend is only beginning to trickle down to smaller businesses, the nation's primary source of new jobs.

Depending on your disability, most of the resources we review will be applicable to your job search and career management needs, but it's important to supplement those "mainstream" guides with resources created specifically for your situation. You should familiarize yourself with both the ADA and other pertinent legislation; the resources we highlight in this section will help you do that. They will also help you keep abreast of new adaptive technology, your greatest ally.

The development of high technology and adaptive technology heralds a new era in career possibilities for the disabled. Today, there is voice-activated software that will allow you to enter data into word-processing, spreadsheet, database, and other applications by speaking, rather than typing; there are even voice-activated telephones that place calls. Other software systems magnify data, text, cursors and scrollbars, while others translate print documents to Braille. E-mail and Internet technology can assist individuals who are communication-impaired.

Resources in highlighted here can help you learn what different types of technological tools can do and how to obtain them, either privately or through your employer. Our list of special resources on these topics is short, so be sure to read the full reviews and to keep an eye out for other resources that touch on similar issues. Yahoo!, for example, though not listed here, includes a selection of links on its employment page for disabled persons. We also suggest you check out the chapter on "Going Solo"; you may find that a home based or Internet business is an ideal option.

Whatever your career ambitions are, they needn't be affected by being differently-abled. You have within you the ability to realize your full potential; education and adaptive technology can help. Capitalize on these resources, find support, and go for it!

The Disabled

Title:	**Career Success For People With Physical Disabilities**
Author:	Sharon F. Kissane, Ph.D.
Overall Rating:	★★
Media Type:	Book
Short Description:	People with physical disabilities need not curtail their ambitions. Rather, they can reach the
■ **Read The Full Review Of This Resource On Page 136.**	highest levels in the profession of their choice. This guide is designed to help readers prepare for career success, regardless of the physical challenges. Dr. Kissane offers advice on identifying personal talents/needs, choosing a career, and job searching (i.e. resumes, networking, etc.). The benefits of assistive devices and new technology are also discussed.

Title:	**Careers On-Line**
Overall Rating:	N/R
Media Type:	Internet
Short Description:	Careers On-Line is designed to provide career-related assistance to people with disabilities.
■ **Read The Full Review Of This Resource On Page 140.**	There are job and internship postings, a database of "Adaptive Technology Products & Resources" (currently under construction), and a "Job Accommodation Handbook." The "Handbook" includes a review of the Americans with Disabilities Act, employer "profiles," and resources for additional information.

ACADEMICS AND PHDs

Job searching in the academic world is not the same as job searching in the business world; it shares the same basic requirements of networking, cover letters, and interviewing, but additional knowledge, preparation, and skills are a must for success. Academia is a breed apart from other industries, a hybrid of profit and not-for-profit businesses that has its own hiring practices and agendas. In many ways, it is an insular world that few "outsiders" can understand. Doctoral candidates, PhDs, post-docs, academics and others interested in scholarly work must supplement the usual career resources with those resources designed specifically to meet their needs.

Today's PhDs face a job market that differs considerably from that of their predecessors. Positions at universities and four-year colleges are fiercely competitive. There are several factors contributing to the competitiveness, not the least of which is that there are more PhDs than ever before. The "tenure track," which is still the dominate structure in academic hiring and promotion practices, is another contributor. Now that institutions are prohibited from requiring faculty members to retire at a certain age, many tenured professors are continuing to teach past the time of traditional retirement, greatly reducing the turnover rate. Factors such as cutbacks in government funding and the trend toward market-driven hiring practices—institutions competing for candidates in "hot" fields—are also responsible for the surplus of qualified job seekers, particularly for the surplus of candidates in the humanities.

The "tenure track" is being supplanted in many institutions by more cost-effective "temporary" positions: instructorships, lectureships, visiting and research assistant/associate professorships. That's both good and bad news for academics. Although these "temporary" positions may be (relatively) easier to come by and may be held by the same individual year after year, they do not necessarily represent a "first step" toward permanent employment. It's frequently the case that when a tenured professor does retire, his or her position is converted into one of these "temporary" positions; thus, retirement doesn't always lead to an opening on the tenure track. When a tenure track position does become available, a nation-wide (or even larger scale) search is conducted.

A highly competitive job market, combined with industry-specific practices (such as using a C.V. versus a resume), that make academic job searching and career management unique. In this section, we offer a selection of resources written for PhDs by fellow PhDs and academic career counselors. These guides provide "insider" information on job searching and career management, offer first-hand accounts from "the trenches," and include advice on transferring from academia to the professional work world. Be sure to read the full-page reviews for an in-depth look at each guide.

The academic job search is an arduous one, so you should capitalize on every available resource. Talk with people in your department, network, use the career planning services at both your institution of employment and/or at your alma mater, conduct research and employ the strategies espoused in "mainstream" career resources. Keep in mind, too, that there are always other employment options, such as two-year community colleges, government agencies, and non-profit organizations, as well as opportunities in business.

By obtaining a PhD, you've demonstrated a passion and commitment to pursuing your interests; apply that same passion and commitment to achieving your career goals and you will succeed.

Academics And PhDs

Title:	**The MLA Guide To The Job Search**
Subtitle:	A Handbook For Departments And For Ph.D.s and Ph.D. Candidates In English And Foreign Languages
Author:	English Showalter, Howard Figler, Lori G. Kletzer, Jack H. Schuster, and Seth R. Katz
Overall Rating:	★★★★
Media Type:	Book
Short Description:	The MLA put this guide together to aid Ph.D.s and Ph.D. Candidates in English and Foreign Languages in the academic and nonacademic job hunt. It includes essays by 5 different writers (professors and a career consultant) on specific job hunting techniques for both academic and nonacademic positions, as well as on the general outlook for humanists in the professional labor market. Employment/salary statistics are also included.

■ **Read The Full Review Of This Resource On Page 126.**

Title:	**On The Market**
Subtitle:	Surviving The Academic Job Search
Author:	Christina Boufis and Victoria C. Olsen
Overall Rating:	★★★
Media Type:	Book
Short Description:	The authors, two English Ph.D.s, conceived this as "an emotional guidebook to the academic job search by the candidates themselves," feeling there was a niche for the "human side" of the job hunt. They group essays on a range of topics and experiences, from "First Words: The Application Process" and "Cattle Call: The Academic Conference and Interview," to "Identities and Politics" and "Alternative Careers."

■ **Read The Full Review Of This Resource On Page 132.**

Title:	**The Academic Job Search Handbook**
Author:	Mary Morris Heiberger and Julia Miller Vick
Overall Rating:	★★★
Media Type:	Book
Short Description:	Finding positions in any discipline, or changing positions, can be a bewildering task for new Ph.D.s. This handbook is designed to guide readers through the academic job search process. There is advice on "positioning yourself in the market," locating job listings, participating in conferences, and negotiating offers. Preparing vitas, cover letters, and abstracts is also discussed; samples are included, as is a timetable and appendix of scholarly associations.

■ **Read The Full Review Of This Resource On Page 128.**

INTERESTED IN NON-PROFIT SECTOR

Career experts note a trend toward seeking personally enriching, meaningful work. There is an undeniable appeal to working in the non-profit sector. Non-profit jobs offer both competitive wages and the personal satisfaction of "doing good," a combination which, for many people, makes them the ideal job. As an individual interested in working for a non-profit, most aspects of your job search will be the same as if you were looking for any other type of work. You will need to network, write cover letters and resumes, and interview. Your primary job search resources will be those aimed at a general audience that constitute the majority of our reviews.

To optimize the results of your job search and career management, we suggest you use the resources presented in this section as supplements. These resources deal specifically with non-profits; they provide information on thousands of organizations, as well as advice and online job postings.

As you browse these short descriptions, pay particular attention to the websites. Some of these websites are fantastic avenues for research, offering direct links to non-profits' home pages and publications. Others detail upcoming events, volunteer and networking opportunities, and relevant news stories. One site, the Internet Nonprofit Center, has a "mapblast" feature that displays the locations of every tax-exempt organization in the U.S.! To learn more about these and the print resources, be sure to read the full-page reviews.

Before you begin your non-profit job search, you should be aware that you are entering a relatively tight job market. Jobs at the more famous organizations, such as Amnesty International or the American Red Cross, will be more competitive, not only because these organizations are better known but also because they attract a larger number of volunteers. Don't focus your pursuit on the "big names" only; make sure you are equally familiar with the opportunities available at smaller, local organizations. Also, since non-profits often rely on volunteers for the low- to mid-level jobs, some may reserve their paid positions for mid- and high-level administrators, executives, and persons with special skills and/or higher degrees, such as PhDs, MDs, RNs, and JDs.

One of the best ways to find a non-profit job is to volunteer. By volunteering, not only will you become acquainted with the organization—which will enable you to better "sell yourself" as the best candidate when the time comes—they will become acquainted with you, too. Non-profits frequently fill paid positions "from within" by hiring volunteers. Plus, volunteering is great way to help others and yourself at the same time.

**Interested In
Non-Profit Sector**

Title:	**Idealist**
Subtitle:	15,000 Organizations Under One Roof
Overall Rating:	★★★★
Media Type:	Internet
Short Description:	The Idealist is designed to help you help others by offering information on thousands of nonprofit organizations worldwide. Visitors to the site can search for jobs, internships, or volunteer positions, locate a specific organization by name, location, or "area of focus," and find particular services and programs. Other features include a database of "upcoming events" (i.e. fundraisers, workshops) and lists of nonprofit publications and materials.

■ **Read The Full Review Of This Resource On Page 108.**

Title:	**100 Best Nonprofits To Work For**
Subtitle:	Find Your Dream Job—And Launch A Rewarding Career Doing Good!
Author:	Leslie Hamilton and Robert Tragert
Overall Rating:	★★★
Media Type:	Book
Short Description:	Many people dream of having a job that combines "doing well" financially with the personal fulfillment of "doing good." For such people, working for a nonprofit organization can make that dream a reality. In this guide, the authors profile 100 nonprofits which offer the "likeliest" chances for career potential. Each profile includes contact information, an overview of operations, staff and budgeting data, and advice on finding work.

■ **Read The Full Review Of This Resource On Page 46.**

Title:	**Internet Nonprofit Center**
Overall Rating:	★★★
Media Type:	Internet
Short Description:	Created to provide information to "volunteers and donors," the Internet Nonprofit Center also serves as a tool for job seekers conducting research on nonprofit organizations. The site includes a "Library" of resources, i.e. bibliographies, a list of "Top 40 Charities" (23 of which are profiled), a "Gallery" of links, and a "Parlor" for live chat. Locations/addresses for over 1 million organizations can be found via the site's "Nonprofit Locator."

■ **Read The Full Review Of This Resource On Page 49.**

Title:	**Good Works**
Subtitle:	A Guide To Careers In Social Change
Author:	Donna Colvin
Overall Rating:	★★
Media Type:	Book
Short Description:	Public interest employment may not be as financially rewarding as jobs in the private business sector, but for many people, the psychological rewards are just compensation. In this guide, job seekers can find information on over 1,000 organizations dedicated to social change, including the organization's aims and projects, names and addresses for contact, staff sizes and salaries. Search indexes are provided, as are lists of additional resources.

■ **Read The Full Review Of This Resource On Page 50.**

Interested In Non-Profit Sector

Title:	**Philanthropy Journal Online: Nonprofit Jobs**
Overall Rating:	N/R
Media Type:	Internet
Short Description:	The Philanthropy Journal Online is an industry journal for nonprofit foundations and organizations; it's job page includes a database of nonprofit job openings. Users can search the database by U.S. region (i.e. northeast, southwest, etc.) and/or by job category. A resume bank is also provided, as are lists of annotated links to career resources.

■ **Read The Full Review Of This Resource On Page 120.**

Title:	**Good Works Online**
Overall Rating:	N/R
Media Type:	Internet
Short Description:	Looking for a job with a nonprofit organization? From the producers of the print resource "Good Works" (see review), this site provides a database of job posting from nonprofits. Users can search for openings by state, then click on the job title of interest for a short description of the position.

■ **Read The Full Review Of This Resource On Page 120.**

RETURNING TO THE WORKPLACE

When Kathy Staples received an unexpected inheritance, she thought about investing the money for retirement. After looking over their family finances and discussing Kathy's burn-out in her work as an accountant, they decided instead to use the money to provide a two year "sabbatical" for Kathy. She used her time to volunteer for organizations she supports and to enjoy hobbies like reading and gardening she had neglected for years. After her relaxing respite, she faced re-entering the workplace at fifty. Feeling her job search skills were a bit rusty, she needed a resource designed for professionals with work experience.

Amy McCallum retired from the Air Force to spend a year at home with her new baby. A highly skilled engineer with a graduate degree from Harvard, there were no shortage of options for Amy when she decided to return to the workplace. However having never held a job outside of the military, she needed help with the basics of the job search and wanted to know if others felt as disoriented as she did in the transition from work to home and back again.

Stories like these illustrate the special questions, issues and needs of workers returning to the workplace. Although none of the resources listed here is written expressly for this group, they each contain a section or two which addresses their concerns. If you are returning to the workplace after a season, or lifetime, apart, these resources may help smooth the transition.

Returning To The Workplace

Title:	**Using The Internet And The World Wide Web In Your Job Search**
Subtitle:	The Complete Guide To Online Job Seeking And Career Information
Author:	Fred E. Jandt & Mary B. Nemnich
Overall Rating:	★★★★
Media Type:	Book
Short Description:	Readers will find guidance on accessing and using the Internet for the job hunt, along with explicit instructions for creating and submitting an electronic resume, conducting online interviews, and understanding electronic etiquette. Interspersed throughout are graphics of actual Internet screens, newsgroup postings, and sample resumes. Though tailored to be "user-friendly" for new users of the Net, experienced users will also find useful information.

■ **Read The Full Review Of This Resource On Page 95.**

Title:	**Network Your Way To Your Next Job . . . Fast**
Author:	Clyde C. Lowstuter and David P. Robertson
Overall Rating:	★★★
Media Type:	Book
Short Description:	There are no "natural" networkers; networking is a skill anyone can develop. In this guide, authors Lowstuter and Robertson teach the "secrets of networking" and how to use them to find a new job. Chapters address such topics as focusing mind and energy to produce results, telephone networking, writing "powerful" letters, beating rejection, and the "myths and realities" of networking. Interactive worksheets and samples are included.

■ **Read The Full Review Of This Resource On Page 174.**

Title:	**Change Your Career**
Author:	Kent Banning and Ardelle Friday
Overall Rating:	★★★
Media Type:	Book
Short Description:	Whether you want to change career paths or are reentering the workplace after time away, this combination guide/workbook is designed to help you through the process of finding a "second" (or third) career. Chapters address such issues as self-assessment, preparation, job search, resumes, letters, and interviews. Interactive exercises are used throughout.

■ **Read The Full Review Of This Resource On Page 61.**

Title:	**The Résumé Doctor**
Subtitle:	How To Transform A Troublesome Work History Into A Winning Résumé
Author:	John J. Marcus
Overall Rating:	★★★
Media Type:	Book
Short Description:	The author shows you how to use the functional format to "fix up" your resume. Common problem areas and their solutions are explained, with examples, for such common problems as having a history of unrelated positions, job-hopping, periods of unemployment, and lack of experience or approaching retirement age. Other chapters address special situations, cover letters, and whether or not to use the "resume-letter."

■ **Read The Full Review Of This Resource On Page 153.**

Returning To The Workplace

Title:	**Super Job Search**
Subtitle:	The Complete Manual For Job-Seekers & Career-Changers
Author:	Peter K. Studner
Overall Rating:	★★★
Media Type:	Book
Short Description:	Designed to assist both "midcareer" job changers and people who are re-entering the work force, this 7-day program covers all aspects of job searching, from evaluating "what you want" to negotiating the salary. Topics discussed include networking, writing a "winning Performance Resume," getting interviews by telephone, and "controlling" interviews. Places to find jobs are detailed, and there are tips for using the Internet.
■ **Read The Full Review Of This Resource On Page 134.**	

Title:	**Transitions**
Subtitle:	Making Sense Of Life's Changes
Author:	William Bridges, Ph.D.
Overall Rating:	★★
Media Type:	Book
Short Description:	A classic in the field of psychological development, Dr. Bridges' guide establish a framework for understanding unexpected life transitions. He identifies three stages: Endings, The Neutral Zone and New Beginnings. Using anecdotes and narratives, the author weaves an optimistic guide to embracing life changes.
■ **Read The Full Review Of This Resource On Page 69.**	

Title:	**It's Never Too Late**
Subtitle:	150 Men And Women Who Changed Their Careers
Author:	Robert K. Otterbourg
Overall Rating:	★
Media Type:	Book
Short Description:	Written for career changers in their early thirties to mid-fifties, Mr. Otterbourg's book has a twofold purpose: to investigate the "trends and dynamics" affecting career changers and to tell the stories of 150 individuals "who changed their careers." The book's first half explores such topics as "Why Change Careers?" "The Pink Slip Arrives," and "Planning a Career Change," while the second half offers career descriptions and personal profiles.
■ **Read The Full Review Of This Resource On Page 15.**	

INDICES

TITLE INDEX

AUTHOR INDEX

PUBLISHER INDEX

MEDIA INDEX

Book

Book + CD-ROM

Book + Software

Software

Videotape

Audiotape

SUBJECT INDEX
1–4 Stars (4 = Best)

Going Solo

ABOUT THE EDITOR

David Goodenough is a career and management consultant with over two decades of experience in helping individuals and corporations with career transitions. He presently provides career and mental health counseling, and business development and training, through The Goodenough Company, a Seattle-based career counseling firm he founded in 1983. He holds a Masters degree from the University of Oregon in Interdisciplinary Studies/Counseling and BA degrees in both Sociology and Education. As a Certified Mental Health counselor, he is qualified to administer and interpret psychological and vocational tests. Prior to his work as a career consultant, he held administrative positions with a variety of social service programs and helped found and manage three separate non-profit companies.

GUIDEBOOKS FOR LIFE'S BIG DECISIONS

For every important issue we face, there are resources available that offer suggestions and help. Unfortunately, we don't always know much about the issue we've enountered. Thus, we don't know:

- Where to find these sources of information

- Much about their quality, value, or relevance

Resource Pathways guidebooks help those facing an important decision or challenging life-event, by directing them to the information they need to understand the issues they face and make decisions with confidence. Every Resource Pathways guidebook includes these important values:

- We **describe and evaluate virtually all quality resources** available in any media (books, the Internet, CD-ROMs, videotape, audiotape, and more).

- We **explain the issues** that are typically encountered in dealing with each subject, and **classify each resource** we review according to its primary focus.

- We **make a reasoned judgment** about the quality of each resource, give it a **rating**, and decide whether or not a resource should be **recommended**. We select only the best as "Recommended" (roughly 1 in 4).

- We **provide information on where to buy or how to access** each resource, including ISBN numbers for books and URL "addresses" for Internet websites.

- We **publish a new edition of each guidebook frequently**, with updated reviews and recommendations.

Those who turn to Resource Pathways guidebooks will be able to locate the resource they need, saving time, money, and frustration as they begin their research and learning process.

LIFECYCLES SERIES

■ *". . . a calm and hope-filled guide . . ."*

Anxiety & Depression:
The Best Resources To Help You Cope

Editor: Rich Wemhoff, PhD
ISBN: 1-892148-09-9 (2nd Ed)
256 Pages (Available July, 1999)

■ *". . . an invaluable guide that will save time,*
emotional energy, and money . . ."

Divorce: The Best Resources To Help You Survive

Editor: Rich Wemhoff, PhD
ISBN: 1-892148-00-5 (2nd Ed)
324 Pages

■ *". . . valuable and remarkable directory . . ."*

Marriage: The Best Resources To Help Yours Thrive

Editor: Rich Wemhoff, PhD
ISBN: 1-892148-05-6
256 Pages (Available April, 1999)

PARENTING SERIES

■ *". . . an incredible resource guide . . ."*

Raising Teenagers:
The Best Resources To Help Yours Succeed

Editor: John Ganz, MC, EdD
ISBN: 1-892148-04-8
268 Pages

■ *". . . an easy-to-use, succinct, yet thorough*
resource book . . ."

Having Children: The Best Resources To Help You Prepare

Editor: Anne Montgomery, MD
ISBN: 1-892148-06-4 (2nd Ed)
256 Pages (Available May, 1999)

■ *". . . exciting, comprehensive, and hands-on*
practical . . ."

Infants & Toddlers:
The Best Resources To Help You Parent

Editor: Julie Soto, MS
ISBN: 1-892148-10-2 (2nd Ed)
288 Pages (Available August, 1999)

HIGHER EDUCATION & CAREERS SERIES

■ *". . . quintessential guide to the guides . . ."*

College Choice & Admissions:
The Best Resources To Help You Get In

Editor: Dodge Johnson, PhD
ISBN: 0-9653424-9-2 (3rd Ed)
336 Pages

■ *". . . comprehensive . . . a real time and money saver . . ."*

College Financial Aid:
The Best Resources To Help You
Find The Money

Editor: David Hoy
ISBN: 1-892148-01-3 (3rd Ed)
278 Pages

■ *". . . thorough, honest, and complete . . ."*

Graduate School:
The Best Resources To Help You Choose, Get In, & Pay

Editor: Jane Finkle, MS
ISBN: 0-9653424-7-6
278 Pages

■ *Career Transitions:*
The Best Resources To Help You Advance

Editor: Resource Pathways Editors
ISBN: 1-892148-08-0
256 Pages (Available June, 1999)

■ *". . . a clear and concise roadmap . . ."*

Starting Your Career:
The Best Resources To Help You Find The Right Job

Editor: Laura Praglin, PhD
ISBN: 1-892148-03-X
248 Pages

Your favorite bookstore or library may order any of these guidebooks for you, or you can order direct, using the pre-paid postcards on the following pages.

ORDERING INFORMATION

Order by phone: 888-702-8882 (Toll-free 24/7)
Order by fax: 425-557-4366
Order by mail: Resource Pathways, Inc.
22525 SE 64th Place, Suite 253
Issaquah, WA 98027-5387

ORDER FORM

Order by phone: 888-702-8882 (Toll-free 24/7)
Order by fax: 425-557-4366

Order by mail: Resource Pathways, Inc.
22525 SE 64th Place, Suite 253
Issaquah, WA 98027-5387

☐ *Anxiety & Depression:*
The Best Resources To Help You Cope

☐ *Divorce:* The Best Resources To Help You Survive

☐ *Marriage:* The Best Resources To Help Yours Thrive

☐ *Raising Teenagers:*
The Best Resources To Help Yours Succeed

☐ *Having Children:* The Best Resources To Help You Prepare

☐ *Infants & Toddlers:* The Best Resources To Help You Parent

☐ *College Choice & Admissions:*
The Best Resources To Help You Get In

☐ *College Financial Aid:*
The Best Resources To Help You Find The Money

☐ *Graduate School:*
The Best Resources To Help You Choose, Get In, & Pay

☐ *Career Transitions:* The Best Resources To Help You Advance

☐ *Starting Your Career:*
The Best Resources To Help You Find The Right Job

_____ copies at $24.95 = _____

Shipping (USPS Priority Mail): $3.95 for first copy; $2.00/copy for additional copies

+ Shipping & Handling = _____

We will include an invoice with your shipment

Total = _____

Name (please print) _____

Organization _____ Title _____

Address _____

City _____ State _____ Zip _____

Phone _____ Email _____

ORDER FORM

Order by phone: 888-702-8882 (Toll-free 24/7)
Order by fax: 425-557-4366

Order by mail: Resource Pathways, Inc.
22525 SE 64th Place, Suite 253
Issaquah, WA 98027-5387

☐ *Anxiety & Depression:*
The Best Resources To Help You Cope

☐ *Divorce:* The Best Resources To Help You Survive

☐ *Marriage:* The Best Resources To Help Yours Thrive

☐ *Raising Teenagers:*
The Best Resources To Help Yours Succeed

☐ *Having Children:* The Best Resources To Help You Prepare

☐ *Infants & Toddlers:* The Best Resources To Help You Parent

☐ *College Choice & Admissions:*
The Best Resources To Help You Get In

☐ *College Financial Aid:*
The Best Resources To Help You Find The Money

☐ *Graduate School:*
The Best Resources To Help You Choose, Get In, & Pay

☐ *Career Transitions:* The Best Resources To Help You Advance

☐ *Starting Your Career:*
The Best Resources To Help You Find The Right Job

_____ copies at $24.95 = _____

Shipping (USPS Priority Mail): $3.95 for first copy; $2.00/copy for additional copies

+ Shipping & Handling = _____

We will include an invoice with your shipment

Total = _____

Name (please print) _____

Organization _____ Title _____

Address _____

City _____ State _____ Zip _____

Phone _____ Email _____

BUSINESS REPLY MAIL

FIRST-CLASS MAIL   PERMIT NO. 176   ISSAQUAH, WA

POSTAGE WILL BE PAID BY ADDRESSEE

RESOURCE PATHWAYS INC.

22525 SE 64TH PL STE 253

ISSAQUAH WA 98027-9939

BUSINESS REPLY MAIL

FIRST-CLASS MAIL   PERMIT NO. 176   ISSAQUAH, WA

POSTAGE WILL BE PAID BY ADDRESSEE

RESOURCE PATHWAYS INC.

22525 SE 64TH PL STE 253

ISSAQUAH WA 98027-9939

DISCOUNTS AND SUBSCRIPTIONS
FOR PROFESSIONALS

Do you provide professional services to couples or families experiencing these life-events?

If so, you should know that Resource Pathways offers very attractive discounts to professionals for subscriptions to current and new editions of any title.

To obtain additional information or place an order, complete and return this postcard, or call 425-557-4382 (8-6 PST), or 888-702-8882 (Toll-free 24/7).

Name (please print) _____

Organization _____ Title _____

Address _____

City _____ State _____ Zip _____

Phone _____ Email _____

DISCOUNTS AND STANDING ORDERS
FOR LIBRARIES

Resource Pathways' titles are distributed to libraries throughout North America by the National Book Network, through Ingram, Baker & Taylor, and many other regional wholesalers.

You can order any of our titles through your usual wholesaler or distributor, or direct from the National Book Network:

**National Book Network, Inc., 15200 NBN Way, Blue Ridge Summit, PA 17214
800-462-6420 / 800-338-4550 (fax)**

You can order directly from Resource Pathways at very attractive discounts, for both individual and standing orders.

To obtain additional information or place an order, complete and return this postcard, or call 425-557-4382 (8-6 PST), or 888-702-8882 (Toll-free 24/7).

Name (please print) _____

Organization _____ Title _____

Address _____

City _____ State _____ Zip _____

Phone _____ Email _____

```
IIIII
```

BUSINESS REPLY MAIL

FIRST-CLASS MAIL   PERMIT NO. 176   ISSAQUAH, WA

POSTAGE WILL BE PAID BY ADDRESSEE

RESOURCE PATHWAYS INC.

22525 SE 64TH PL STE 253

ISSAQUAH WA 98027-9811

```
IIIII
```

BUSINESS REPLY MAIL

FIRST-CLASS MAIL   PERMIT NO. 176   ISSAQUAH, WA

POSTAGE WILL BE PAID BY ADDRESSEE

RESOURCE PATHWAYS INC.

22525 SE 64TH PL STE 253

ISSAQUAH WA 98027-9811